DANTE
A Life in Works

ROBERT HOLLANDER

Yale University Press   New Haven and London

Library of Congress Cataloging-in-Publication Data
Hollander, Robert, 1933–
Dante : a life in works / Robert Hollander.
p.   cm.
An Italian version of this study was published by Editalia,
Rome, 2000; this English text is longer and differs in format.
Includes bibliographical references and index.
ISBN 0-300-08494-3 (alk. paper)
1. Dante Alighieri, 1265-1321.   2. Poets, Italian—
To 1500—Biography.   I. Title.
PQ4335 .H63   2001
851'.1—dc21
[B]   00-049539

Printed in the United States of America.

A catalogue record for this book is
available from the British Library.

The paper in this book meets the guidelines
for permanence and durability of the Committee
on Production Guidelines for Book Longevity of
the Council on Library Resources.

10 9 8 7 6 5 4 3 2 1

In memory of my teachers at Collegiate School,
especially Henry Adams, Emilio J. Calvacca,
Wilson Parkhill, and Reginald DeKoven Warner

7/01

CONTENTS

Preface

However we account for the emergence of the first verses of *The Divine Comedy* from its author's pen around 1306, however we align the magnificent poem, finished by 1321, in the history of human consciousness, we are understandably curious about its place in the only real biography that we do possess of Dante, what he left us of his life in words. No one would certify the notion that any of his other writings—individual poems, a collection of verse-with-commentary, several treatises—or even all these together could rival his *Comedy*. It is a supreme work of the imagination. How did Dante come to it? What were the steps in his development that at least begin to explain the extraordinary making of the poem in no more than fifteen years in the life of this Florentine exile? This book is an attempt to deal with these questions, to sketch out the lines of Dante's intellectual biography. It is intended for those who, having encountered the *Comedy* in a course or read it out of curiosity, want to know more about its author's other writings. For this reason *Dante* pays attention mostly to these other works, but in such a way as to suggest their relation to the great poem, which is at the center of things, as it should be. The assumption made is that the reader knows something about the *Comedy* and wants to know more about it and its author. Thus the reader will find, for example, in the treatment of the earliest extended work, the *Vita nuova,* a discussion of Dante's eventual theologically determined poetics in the *Comedy,* or analysis of the divergences in Dante's beliefs about certain subjects in his later masterwork from various arguments put forward in *Convivio* and *De vulgari Eloquentia*. Further, the treatment of Dante's epistles on various subjects is interspersed among various discussions of his works, in order better to reflect concerns encountered in them.

An Italian version of this study was published first (Rome: Editalia, 2000). This English text is longer and differs somewhat both in format and in some particulars. If it helps to bring readers back to the *Comedy* prepared to consider its remarkable range of interests with a spirit of inquiry and pleasure, its author will be satisfied.

CHRONOLOGY OF DANTE'S LIFE

This brief summary of the main events and activities of Dante's life is essentially based on the chronology supplied by Giorgio Petrocchi. Datings of individual works will be found in the discussions of those works. A parenthetical "?" indicates pɑ cularly questionable data.

Late May–early June 1265	Birth of Dante in the San Martino quarter of Florence
26 March 1266	Baptism in San Giovanni with the name Durante (?)
1270–75	Death of Dante's mother, Bella
1274	First meeting with Beatrice
9 January 1277	Marriage contract with Gemma Donati
1280	Death of relative Geri Del Bello in a brawl
1281–83	Death of Dante's father, Alighiero
1283	Second meeting with Beatrice
1285	Marriage to Gemma Donati
1287	Birth of Dante's first child, Giovanni (?)
1286–87	Brief stay at Bologna
1289	Dante present at battle of Campaldino and siege of Caprona
June 1290	Death of Beatrice
1291–94	Thirty months' study at "le scuole de li religiosi," probably with both Dominicans at Santa Maria Novella and Franciscans at Santa Croce
1294	Death of Brunetto Latini; Charles Martel in Florence; election and abdication of Pope Celestine V; accession of Pope Boniface VIII

by 1295	Dante's name inscribed in the Arte dei Medici e Speziali (guild of doctors and apothecaries)
1295	Beginning of political career among the Trentasei del Capitano, thirty-six representatives of the "populace"
1296	Post in the Council of One Hundred
1297	First evidence of continuing financial troubles
1299	Worsening political situation in Florence; exile of Corso Donati
1300	Jubilee Year proclaimed by Boniface
	7 May — Assignment as ambassador at San Gimignano
	13 June — Dante among the six elected priors of the city
	23 June — Yet another outbreak of hostilities between Florentine factions; fifteen Blacks and Whites (Cavalcanti among the latter) banished by priors
	July — Attempt on the life of papal legate Matteo d'Acquasparta; Blacks banished from city
	September — Dante's departure from office after end of his term as prior; new priors' revocation of banishment of the seven Whites, which offends Matteo—and Boniface
1301	Dante present at various meetings of the Council of One Hundred
	19 June — Dante alone on council in opposing papal invitation to furnish troops in the Maremma, the eventual cause of his later condemnations by the Blacks
	5 September — Charles of Valois with the pope at Anagni: thickening of plot against Florence

	October	Florentine embassy to Boniface, probably including Dante; Dante detained when the pope sends most of the group back home to Florence
	November	Sack of Florence by the Blacks; entrance of Charles of Valois
1302		
	27 January	Dante banished for two years; fine of 5,000 florins set in the event of his return
	February	Hostility of Boniface and Charles of Valois reawakened by meeting in Gargonza of exiled Whites and Ghibellines
	10 March	Dante's sentence, along with that of fourteen other exiles, increased to death by being burned alive, in the case of his eventual return to the city
	8 June	Meeting with other exiles at San Godenzo in the Mugello to plan war against the Blacks in the city; initial successes; alliance in military disarray by summer
	autumn	at Forlì
spring 1303		Continued defeats of the White-Ghibelline alliance in the Mugello
	May or June	First stay in Verona
	11 October	Death of Boniface
	22 October	Election of Pope Benedict XI
1304		
	17 March	Cardinal Niccolò da Prato sent by new pope to pacify Florence by reuniting the divided Guelphs—the motive for Dante's leaving Verona at once, as reflected in his epistle

		(*Ep.* I) to Niccolò, written in late March or early April
	May	Arrival at Arezzo
	June	Total failure of Niccolò's mission
	7 July	Sudden death of Pope Benedict
	20 July	Disaster for the White-Ghibelline alliance in the field at La Lastra; Dante, having broken with the alliance, still in Arezzo on this day of Petrarch's birth in that city
1304–6		Dante at Treviso, at court of Gherardo da Camino (?) or at Padua and Venice (?)
5 June 1305		Election of Pope Clement V
6 October 1306		Dante by now the guest of the Malaspina family in Lunigiana
1307–8		Stay in the Casentino (?)
1308–9		Stay at Lucca (?)
1309–10		Voyage to Paris (??)
1310–12		Visits to various places during the descent of Henry VII: Asti, Poppi, but mainly again in the Casentino
1312–18		Renewal of Dante's residence in Verona, now as guest of Cangrande
July–August 1315		Dante's rejection (*Ep.* XII) of the offer of the Florentines, under attack by the Ghibelline leader Uguccione della Faggiuola, that the exiles be allowed to return upon payment of a greatly reduced portion of the original fine
1318–21		Residence of Dante in Ravenna, as guest of Guido Novello da Polenta
August–September 1321		Dante's mission as ambassador to Venice; malarial fever on return; death during night of 13–14 September.

Dante

INTRODUCTION

This is an attempt to delineate the intellectual biography of the greatest narrative poet of the modern era, and perhaps of all time. The difficulty of such a task will be apparent to anyone who has begun to study the subject. Despite recent noteworthy efforts,[1] we know relatively little about the composition and dating of the works of Dante, a writer who left us no work in his own hand. Our ignorance reflects not only problems of interpretation, which is always subject to doubt and second-guessing, but also the lack of historical detail.

For his first readers, Dante was essentially, as he is for most of his public today, a "one-book author." Scholars are aware, as they read the *Comedy*, of its intimate (and sometimes puzzling) relations with Dante's other extended works — *Vita nuova* (the only one to receive significant attention from its earliest readers — among them Boccaccio), *Convivio*, *De vulgari Eloquentia*, *Monarchia*. As for the *Rime*, *Epistole*, *Egloghe*, and the *Questio*, they tend, with significant exceptions, to be studied less in relation to the *Comedy* than as things in themselves. The same may be said for *Il Fiore* and *Il Detto d'Amore*, the authenticity of which remains questionable.

It is a curious fact that all the greatest literary figures of the fourteenth century in Europe — Dante, Petrarch, Boccaccio, and Chaucer — eventually almost sacrificed the viability of their other writings by producing works nearly immediately recognized as masterpieces — the *Comedy*, the *Canzoniere*, the *Decameron*, and the *Canterbury Tales*, respectively. It is probably fair to say that, had Dante not written his *Comedy*, he would be known to scholars and to few others; it is the *Comedy* that directs our attention to all the rest. And yet, if we try to reconstruct

Dante's intellectual development, it is clear that when he undertook them, the other works were in his eyes not "minor" in any sense at all. All of them are marked by the signs of his considerable excitement at assuming a new role in the nascent history of Italian letters, whether as poet or as commentator, apologist or polemicist. And each of them begins either with an unblushing announcement of its importance (*Convivio, De vulgari Eloquentia, Monarchia*) or with an absorbed self-awareness that has a similar effect (*Vita nuova*). It is also clear that these works were never far from his mind as he wrote beyond them (the telling presence in *Inferno* I of phrases found in *Convivio* IV offering but one example).[2] And thus the central task of this study is to examine the course of this writer's development from work to work, while also considering each work on its own terms.

One of the striking aspects of almost all Dante's extended writings is their autobiographical character. *Vita nuova, Convivio,* and the *Comedy* are written as part of an unfolding autobiography in its changeful development. And as he moves forward, we continually witness his backward glances to review the paths taken and abandoned. There is so much objectivity in Dante's visionary gaze that we tend to forget the extraordinary amount and degree of subjectivity informing his texts. His obsessive telling and retelling of his own narrative is one clear indication of that subjectivity.

DANTE'S LIFE

One cannot overstate the importance of the fact that we have little certain knowledge of Dante's life, as is reflected in the numerous biographies that are such a significant feature in the study of his work, especially those written from the last third of the fourteenth century into the Renaissance (the main names are those of Giovanni Villani, Boccaccio, Filippo Villani, and

Leonardo Bruni[3]). For all the impact that Dante has had on literary history, he left few traces in actual history, and not a single autograph of any kind. We may want to keep in mind the clamorous difference, in this respect, between him and the other two "crowns" of Florence, Petrarch and Boccaccio, from whom we have so much precious autograph material.

The central figure in the second half of the twentieth century in two major aspects of Dante studies is Giorgio Petrocchi. It was he who single-handedly established the current standard text of the *Comedy*.[4] And while some, most notably Antonio Lanza,[5] now call for major revision of Petrocchi's criteria and results, it is clear that, until further work helps to establish still better criteria, Petrocchi's apparatus remains the best that we have ever had.[6] The same can be said with respect to Dante's biography. Petrocchi, whose *iter* in plotting Dante's *itinerarium* began in 1964,[7] spent much of the last quarter-century of his life on this task. His contribution remains the best available.[8] Nonetheless, like Heraclitus' river, Dante studies are always in motion—one can never step a second time into the same current. One day we may well know more than we do today, but that day, too, shall have to yield—as long as these studies continue.

The brief summary of the main events and activities of Dante's life in the chronological table at the beginning of the book is essentially based on the chronology supplied by Petrocchi. (Discussion of the dates of individual works will be found in the discussions of those works.) In broad outline, Dante's life followed a difficult path, his initial promising steps as poet and politician turning to a march through abandoned experiments and enforced exile, until that very exile, with its removal from the day-to-day concerns of Florentine reality, gave him the unwanted liberty to think on a grander scale.

Dante wrote his first poem around 1283 and spent most of the next ten years as a striving lyric poet. The first moment, one has a certain sense, in which he himself knew that the effort was worthwhile is reflected in the completion, possibly in 1293, of the carefully developed text of *Vita nuova*. The next ten years are less linear in their movement, marked by poetic experiment and involvement in the political life of Florence. As the financial and military center of Tuscany, the city was at that time one of the most important of European cities, swollen with new wealth and consequent political activity. In 1300, at a time when there were only six priors, Dante served the customary two-month term in the priorate, the highest political office in the city. By 1302, having inherited the wrong political identity, he lost practically everything when his party, the White Guelph faction, was outfoxed by the Black Guelphs, supported by the allied forces of Pope Boniface VIII and the French king. He was exiled in 1302 and never came home again. He then lived a mainly itinerant life in northern Italy, with two longish stays in Verona and a final one in Ravenna, where he died of malarial fever in September 1321 at the age of fifty-six.

The political situation of northern Italy during his lifetime was distinguished by factionalism. The emperors who were nominally supposed to govern all of Europe had, for centuries, mainly avoided their Italian responsibilities. The last of them to have ruled in Italy was Frederick II (we hear of him in *Inferno* X and XIII), and he, while one of the greatest figures in Europe, was not a leader to Dante's liking. Frederick, who died in 1250, was the last emperor to govern from Italy. Dante hoped for an imperial restoration of the proper kind, and, to everyone's amazement, including his own, found his hopes rewarded when the newly crowned Henry VII, a compromise candidate from Luxembourg (allowed to become emperor primarily because of the machinations of Pope Clement V), descended into the peninsula to rule Europe from Italy in 1310. When his military expedition eventually failed (it had not been following a propitious course, in any case) because of his death in 1313, Dante's imperial hopes were dealt a terrible blow, but not finally dashed. To the end of his days (and in the text of *Paradiso* XXVII and XXX) he insisted on believing that a new "Augustus" would fulfill God's design for Italy and Europe.

On the local level, late thirteenth-century northern Italy was in constant turmoil. (Milan, to the north, and Rome, to the south, are barely on Dante's personal political map; rather, we hear, in addition to Florence, of such cities as Genoa, Lucca, Pisa, Pistoia, and Siena.) The two main "parties" were the Guelphs (essentially allied with the papacy) and the Ghibellines (aligned with the emperor—when there was one to be aligned with—or at least with imperial hopes). But most politics were local, as they are in our own time. And there labels did not count so much as family. In Florence the Ghibellines had been defeated and banished in 1266, a year after Dante's birth, leaving the city entirely Guelph. But that hardly betokened an era of unity. The Guelphs themselves were already divided (as they were in many northern cities) into two factions, the "Blacks," led by the Donati family (into which Dante married), and the "Whites," led by the Cerchi. (It is probably correct to say that the Whites were more devoted to a republican notion of governance, while the Blacks were more authoritarian in their attitudes.) The first impetus toward political division in the city had occurred early in the century, when a young man, a member of the Ghibelline Buondelmonti family, broke off his engagement to a young woman of the Amidei family and married a Guelph Donati. The result was a bloody feud that divided the city into warring factions. Even after the Ghibellines were no longer around to play the antagonists, there was enough hostility among the Guelphs themselves to guarantee turmoil in the city. As a member of a White Guelph family, and even if he had married into a lesser branch of the most important Black family,

Dante was tied to the interests of the White faction. If he was a Guelph, how do we explain his patent allegiance, in the *Comedy*, to the imperial cause? In 1306 or so he seems, on rereading the Latin classics, to have reformulated his own political vision (as is first evident in the fourth and fifth chapters of the last treatise of the *Convivio*, before which there is not a clear imperialist sentiment to be found in his writing). And so, nominally a Guelph, Dante was far more in accord with Ghibelline ideas, except that, in practice, he found Ghibellines lacking in the religious vision that he personally saw as the foundation of any imperialist program. Nonetheless, politics are everywhere in the poem, which is far from being the purely religious text that some of its readers take it to be.

The first ten years of his exile, 1302–12, were marked by frequent movement, so much so that his biographers are often at a loss to account for his whereabouts, mainly around Tuscany, with the sure exception only of a stay in Verona, 1303–4. This is the period in which he somehow managed to write *Convivio, De vulgari Eloquentia,* and just about all of the first two *cantiche* of the *Commedia*. In short, it is the crucial period in Dante's intellectual development, and the one of which we know the least. The final period of his life, 1312–21, was perhaps the happiest. He enjoys his longest settled existence (1312–18) at the court of Cangrande della Scala at Verona and then in Ravenna, where, as the guest of Guido Novello da Polenta, he finished the *Commedia*.

Had Dante reached the three score and ten years that the Bible and the first verse of the poem predicate as normative, what would have become of him? Would Florence finally have welcomed back its prodigal son, now one of the most famous writers of his time? And whether or not the life had had the happy ending that the poem does, what would Dante have done with the rest of it? What does a poet write after he has finished what surely even he recognized as a miracle of human contriving? The English historian Gibbon, having finished his *Rise and Fall* and being surprised to find himself with some leftover life to fill, wrote a slender and graceful autobiography. What would Dante have done? Would he have turned to more poetic composition in Latin? (We tend to forget how much of the work that accompanied the writing of *Paradiso* is, in fact, in Latin— the subject of the last section of this study.) Would he have done another turn as self-exegete, as he had in his letter to Cangrande, by supplying the glosses to his entire poem? Would he have extended his skills as the greatest vernacular poet of his day (or any day?) to other subjects? Our speculations remain moot. It was perhaps a mosquito from a swamp between Venice and Ravenna that put the final punctuation mark to the works of that great spirit.

FIRST LYRICS

In certain respects, Dante's birth as a writer is proclaimed by the opening chapter of *Vita nuova,* but that was written at least ten years after the actual "birth," marked by the first lyrics. While we have a fairly good sense of which of the poems attributed to him should in fact be considered authentic,[9] we frequently have no sure sense of when Dante wrote them. The *Rime* include the thirty-one that he assembled in *Vita nuova* and number, in Barbi's edition, eighty-eight compositions in various forms. In subject and in treatment they seem conventional enough. Most are sonnets, almost all are expressions of love for the poet's lady, and most speak of the power of the god of love, a constant presence in the preceding lyric tradition, from the Provençal, Sicilian, and earlier northern Italian "schools" of poetry. As Dante himself points out in *Vita nuova* XXV, the tradition of the Provençal and Italian love lyric had begun only some 150 years before. It is obvious from his own poems that Dante desires somehow to set himself apart from his precursors and copractitioners. Such a desire is made still more manifest by the prose of the *Vita nuova*. Nonetheless, if we confine ourselves to the uncollected poems, some fifty-seven compositions if we do not include the *rime dubbie,* what surprises us is the relatively wide range of their subjects and their styles, given the central role allotted to love.[10] Had Dante not composed *Vita nuova,* which has understandably enough had the effect of relegating most of the earlier uncollected lyrics to secondary status, it would perhaps be more apparent how deeply he was already captivated by the demon of experiment.[11] This need to set off in new directions is most pointedly evident in the later poems, but we can sense it in some of the earliest as well.

We know little of Dante's early life, either as a writer or as a man. Two aspects of a single problem, one that has importance to any eventual view of Dante's intellectual development, illustrate the point: Did he ever visit France? Did he write *Il Fiore?* If he ever crossed the Alps, and even if he did so fairly late in his creative life (those who currently argue for such a journey suggest 1309–10 as its date), we might draw some further conclusions about his sense of French literary culture. But we cannot say with any certainty that he did, and the absence of anything like positive proof leaves the question unresolved. The question whether he wrote *Il Fiore* is probably more important and perhaps still more difficult, even if in recent years the efforts of Contini have convinced most *dantisti,* especially those in Italy, that Dante was its author.[12] If Dante wrote it, and if he wrote it early on, as Contini insists (around 1286, a date with which Petrocchi concurs[13]), we are left with a writer who possessed, at the beginning of his intellectual development, a close knowledge of surely the most important literary text produced in Old French, *The Romance of the Rose.* And if that is true, we would expect to find evidence of this awareness from the pages of *Vita nuova* onward. But we find very little before, at the earliest, *Purgatorio* XXV, despite Coglievina's claims for resonances in *Inferno* XIV,[14] and no certain resonances before *Paradiso* II (the moon spots).[15] In any case, whatever position one takes on this question (and this book adopts an agnostic view), it is clear that it and many other major issues in Dante studies may never be resolved without significant new discoveries.

The sonnet that became the first of the thirty-one poems gathered in *Vita nuova* is representative of one poetic form that engaged Dante in his first exercises. However, it is difficult to be sure about the dating of these compositions, even after the extensive labor of editors. In the 1280s and 1290s Dante managed to involve himself in several lyric traditions, each of which offered new challenges to a young poet who wished to set out on his own, to stamp himself as "different." Perhaps no other practitioner of the lyric of love offered a better model or a greater challenge than Guittone d'Arezzo (around 1230–94). His facility in perfecting the Italian sonnet, first practiced by Giacomo da Lentini around 1225,[16] made him and his followers (most notably Dante da Maiano) necessary precursors and rivals for Dante Alighieri in his own first efforts.[17] If there is a recognizably Guittonian style in Dante's early love lyrics, as many observe,[18] it nonetheless exists alongside still other Dantean styles.

Because Dante's own extensive commentary conferred extraordinary status on the poems collected in the *Vita nuova*, we understandably tend to think of them as being the central work of the early years. Yet their neighbors, the poems excluded from the *Vita nuova*, written with at times enormous skill, are often greatly different in spirit and reveal his inclination to experiment very early on. The series of poems he exchanged with Dante da Maiano (XXXIX–XLVII) shows him involved in casuistic analysis of love, as well as in the still less attractive rhetorical techniques of the flattery that he aimed at the older poet. Another group (V–VII, XLVIII–XLIX) shows him attempting the style of the provençalizing Sicilian school of love poets, describing grief at a lost love (V) or at the death of a lady (VI and VII), composing a sonnet (XLVIII) to flatter another poet, Lippo (Pasci dei Bardi?), which is offered as introduction to a sonnet on the familiar Provençal and Sicilian theme of love from afar (XLIX). Then there is Dante's first *canzone*, as he tackles a more difficult form, in which he is a "prisoner of love" (L), alongside an amusing sonnet (LI), a "sightseeing poem" in which he castigates his eyes for having been so fixed upon the Garisenda tower (see *Inf.* XXXI, 136) that they missed the sight of a lovely lady who was passing by. And then there is the famous sonnet to Guido Cavalcanti (LII) in which Dante wishes that he and Guido and Lapo (Gianni) were all off on a magical boatride, accompanied by the two other poets' ladies, Giovanna and Lagia, and his own, someone numbered "thirty" (and thus not Beatrice, always identified with the number nine); this is Dante's version of the Provençal *plazer*, a poem positing an impossible easeful happiness (of the kind described in the American hobo song, "The Big Rock Candy Mountain"). And there is the "hunting song" (LXI) modeled on the poems of Folgore di San Gimignano, who delighted in the portrayal of "scenes from daily life" in the Tuscan countryside; or the graceful short-lined *ballata* (LVI) in praise of a lady called Fioretta; or the threatening love song (LVIII) addressed to "Violetta," advised to yield her favors to her lover or suffer torment for not doing so — a sort of humorous precursor to the *rime petrose*, with their frank and frustrated sexual longing.

Dante is of unitary disposition only within the boundaries of whatever work involved him as he wrote. If this makes us think of Montaigne, who is open in admitting his mutability, it offers us an indication of how thoroughly writerly a writer Dante was, one far less interested than Montaigne, however, in proclaiming his different moods and modes. Dante simply followed these, as his instincts led him to experiment with forms and ideas, all different from one another, each absorbing for its particular possibilities.

One source of information about the way in which his efforts reflected this need to outdo, to stamp himself as special, can be found in his colleagues' response to them. For some thirty of such responses have been preserved. The largest share of these come from five other practitioners of the art of verse, Cino da Pistoia (eight poems), Dante da Maiano (six), Guido Cavalcanti (five), Cecco Angiolieri (three), and Forese Donati (three). One senses that at least some of his fellow poets were intent on keeping Dante in his place, particularly in such responses as those of Dante da Maiano to *Rime* I (all numeration of the *Rime* derives from Barbi's edition), with its coarse jests at Dante's expense (*Rime* IV). The elder Dante, suggesting that the sonnet revealed its author to be quite mad, claimed he would not be dissuaded from this opinion until his namesake, the youthful love poet, having washed his private parts in order to cleanse his wavering mind, had had his urine examined by a doctor. Or there is Cecco's playfully nasty discovery (*Rime* XXXVIII) of a supposed contradiction in the last poem ("Oltre la spera"—around 1291) included in *Vita nuova* (*Rime* XXXVII); or the often noted and much discussed example of Guido Cavalcanti's harsh attack on Dante's poetic and personal predilections (*Rime* XXIX), in which Cavalcanti upbraids Dante for the unpleasant company he now keeps; or Guido Orlandi's rather abrupt assault on Dante's pride as maker (*Rime* LXIV).

None of this takes into account the two extensive sets of *tenzoni,* poems deploying a playful but nonetheless painful attack and counterattack, those exchanged by Dante da Maiano and the younger Dante (we may wonder whether their shared name was part of the reason for the rivalry—*Rime* XLI–XLVII) and, later (1293–1296?), by Dante and Forese (*Rime* LXXIII–LXXVIII).[19] And there are also Cecco's harsh rebukes (*Rime* CVII, CVIII), to which we do not have Dantean responses, if such there were.[20] What we can sense in some of these displays of hostility, no matter how playful they may have been, is the difficulty any new poet had in making his way into the company of his older peers. With the major and significant exceptions of Guido Cavalcanti, a strong supporter at first,[21] and of Cino da Pistoia, loyal to Dante at least until late in his life,[22] Dante's fellow poets were far from welcoming. It is important that we, certain in our sense of Dante's worth, remember that at the outset his path to glory was not an easy one. That he was intent on finding such a path is clear. He wanted to storm the Olympus of Florentine lyric from the time he was a teen-ager, although he hoped at first merely to be accepted as one among a group of practitioners. He tells us in *Vita nuova* III that he sent "A ciascun'alma presa e gentil core" (To every captive soul and gentle heart), "a molti li quali erano famosi trovatori in quello tempo" (to many famous lyric writers of that time), thus revealing how keenly he felt the need to make his way in a world controlled by others. That need is readily apparent in all his work before the *Comedy*. Within the confines of the later work he seems, while hardly bashful or retiring, completely at his ease in nearly every move that he makes.

VITA NUOVA

The poems contained in *Vita nuova* are thirty-one in number. Their dates of composition, while uncertain, probably run from 1283 to 1292. It is useful to try to imagine what a very different awareness of Dante's work as lyric poet we would have had he not composed his celebrated *libello*, for *Vita nuova* teaches us something of importance about this writer: as commentator of his own work he is a markedly free spirit. Because he first assembled and then commented on his poetry, it is manifest that both the arrangement and the interpretation of this corpus reflect the writer's will rather than an obedient sense of "history." The poems may have meant or suggested one thing when they were written; their prose integuments put them to a service that may be quite different from that originally envisioned. As we shall see, the same thing may be said, with perhaps still greater force, of the prose expositions of the *canzoni* that served to launch *Convivio*.

Vita nuova is, in anyone's estimation, a difficult and puzzling work.[23] One of its students has well described it in the title of an essay, "Dante's *Vita nuova* as Riddle."[24] It is also the first reliable evidence we have of Dante's genius. First and foremost, it has no precise or certain model in Western literature. Some have drawn parallels between it and the *Consolatio philosophiae* of Boethius (whose work Dante at this point may have known only slightly, as the relevant passage of *Convivio* [II, xii, 2] seems to suggest). Indeed, Francesco Tateo claims that the initial canzone of *Convivio* is "the first proof of Dante's knowledge of Boethius" that we find.[25] Dating *Vita nuova* to late 1293 or perhaps early in 1294, he argues that the *Consolatio* had a general influence on the shaping of the prose of *Convivio*. One must acknowledge that no one has yet found clear citations of Boethius in the *libello*, whereas these do exist in *Convivio*. A possible understanding is that Dante knew of the text, had some awareness of it, but had not yet studied it closely. Dante's reference in *Convivio* II, xii, 2, to the "book of Boethius not known to many" ("quello non conosciuto da molti libro di Boezio") may or may not indicate his new acquaintance with Boethius after the death of Beatrice, or a rereading (however, he does not say "rileggere" but "leggere"; and his following reference to Cicero's *De amicitia* also seems to indicate a first reading). Yet if *Vita nuova* shares with the *Consolatio* the mixture of prose and verse and thus may join in the tradition of Menippean satire, it is difficult to say exactly how significantly Boethius' text inspired Dante's work. Others have argued for the influence of the anthologies of Provençal lyrics, with their prose lives of the poets (*vidas*), or the brief explanations of the poems (*razos*).[26] Although these are certainly examples of the mix of prose and verse that Dante would later employ, it remains true that we possess no earlier example in the history of Western literature of a writer who gathered *his own* poems into a collection and then wrote commentaries on them. That is a very long step from any previous poet's practice. The *Vita nuova* is, as one can rarely say with such certainty, unique. Nothing in the tradition of Dante's Romance predecessors, or indeed of any precursors, serves as a sufficient model. One can only imagine the concern, even trepidation, with which the young poet assumed the office of *lector* of his own literary production. The practice was literally unheard of.

Like his two subsequent (unfinished) works, *Vita nuova* did not have a wide diffusion, as is evident from the forty manuscripts studied by Barbi in his great edition of 1907, including that copied by Boccaccio, the autograph of which we possess. And it is most of all to Boccaccio that we owe an early sense of the work's importance, thanks to his defense of the historical reality of Beatrice and his citations of the text of *Vita nuova* in most of his own vernacular work. In fact, the early manuscript diffusion seems mainly limited to the area including Tuscany. As a printed book *Vita nuova* got a late start: not until 1576 did the famous edition of Bartolomeo Sermartelli appear, with its "reforms" of the text, including the excision of religious language and citations of Scripture. The date of its composition is still a matter of dispute, but the range of possibility is far more limited than once it was: no earlier than late in 1292, no later than 1295.

Greater precision is perhaps impossible, although an earlier date seems more in accord with the indications made within the work itself, perhaps reason enough to incline one to honor Barbi's unwavering defense of the earlier dating (1292-93).

It has become a commonplace in the later critical tradition, and rightly so, to insist on the primacy of the prose of *Vita nuova*.[27] Reading the poems, one is not often led to the conclusions drawn about them by their author, now at a distance of some ten years from the writing. Of these compositions he knits a new fabric. And one can only imagine the reasons for the inclusion of some of his earlier lyrics and, more puzzling perhaps, the exclusion of still others. For instance, the canzone "Lo doloroso amor" ("The sorrowful love" — *Rime* LXVIII), the only other lyric to mention Beatrice's name ("Per quella moro c'ha nome Beatrice" (I die for the one whose name is Beatrice — v. 14), and which to some extent resembles "Donna pietosa e di novella etate" ("A lady, tender in heart and young" — *Vita nuova* XXIII); the sonnet "Di donne io vidi una gentile schiera" (I saw a lovely group of ladies — *Rime* LXIX), which has several elements in common with "Tanto gentile e tanto onesta pare" (So gentle and so full of dignity appears — *Vita nuova* XXVI); or "Un dì si venne a me Malinconia" (One day Melancholy came to me — *Rime* LXXII), strikingly similar in its subject, the impending death of Beatrice, to "A ciascun'alma presa," the first sonnet of the libello (*Vita nuova* III).

Of Dante's work, *Vita nuova* has, second only to his *Comedy*, left the greatest mark on his readers. *Vita nuova* was copied by no less a hand than Boccaccio's, and until the time of Landino (the first major student of Dante to bring *Convivio* into play when he examines the *Comedy*), only the later *Monarchia* would challenge its status as Dante's second most frequently read work. It remains surprising that its readers, at least until the end of the nineteenth century, usually failed to bring concerted attention to Dante's unmistakable insistence on the religious valence of the work. This is a complex issue, not least of all because Dante himself is so (understandably) reticent to speak openly of his grand theological design. To speak briefly of matters of some complexity, the nub of the issue seems to be this: whereas poets who preceded him, beginning perhaps with Guido Guinizzelli, had spoken of their ladies as though they had some positive relation to a more-than-sensual goodness, or even as though they possessed a certain similarity to angelic perfection that might lead from an erotic impulse to a higher understanding,[28] none had suggested that his lady was centrally related to the Trinity. Boccaccio, who is pleased to make Dante a lover of the more usual sort, is only one among the earliest readers of *Vita nuova* who either does not understand or wants to deny its theological foundation.[29]

The plot of *Vita nuova* is arresting in its sparse and enigmatic detail. Just before he reaches the age of nine, Dante sees the eight-year-old Beatrice, dressed in red, and becomes the servant of the god of love. He sees her again when he is eighteen and becomes still more enamored (II). This second meeting is followed by a dream in which the god of love announces his lordship over the lover, as is reflected in the first sonnet of the collection (III). The lover's resultant change in appearance (he shows the signs of the typical lovesick swain of medieval erotic literature, pallor and distraction) causes others to take note of his changed condition (IV). Following the tradition of such writings, he finds a "screen lady" to deflect attention from his true beloved; observers believe that *she* (and not Beatrice) is the object of Dante's desire (V). When this "screen lady" leaves town, Dante is dejected because he fears that his deception may be discovered; he writes a sonnet, apparently about the second lady, but actually giving vent to his painful love for Beatrice (VII). The death of still another young woman offers Dante the occasion to write two sonnets about her, so honored because he had observed her in Beatrice's company, but again offering him opportunity to hide his true feelings (VIII). Since the first "screen lady" has still not returned to Florence, Love, appearing in Dante's mind, commands him to take a second such lady in the city; her reactions to the lover's attentions are unkind and she portrays him to others as vice-ridden; as a result, Beatrice denies him her *salute* (IX-XI). Dante, alone in his room, has a second dream of the god of love, who directs him to write secretly of Beatrice; he composes a *ballata* about her (XII). His thoughts divided about the benefits of being in love's thrall, Dante sees Beatrice at a wedding feast and nearly faints. His transfiguration is the cause of notice. He senses that he is the object of ridicule, and he wonders why he subjects himself to such embarrassment (XIII-XV). He remains in this condition (XVI) until he realizes that he can write no more in this vein and must find another (XVII). This is the conclusion of the first of the three "movements" of *Vita nuova*, this one dedicated to the pains of love in the spirit of Guido Cavalcanti.

The cause of the change in his poetic program is a conversation with a group of ladies who have penetrated his disguise and realize that he loves Beatrice. If so, they ask him, why are his poems about her so melancholic? From then on he determines to write nothing of Beatrice that is not in praise of her (XVIII). The difficulty of so lofty a theme holds him back, until one day, walking along a clear stream, he is inspired and plans his first canzone in praise of Beatrice, "Donne ch'avete intelletto d'amore" (Ladies who have understanding of love), which is clearly linked to the song of praise as practiced by Guido Guinizzelli (XIX-XX); the following sonnet is also in praise of Beatrice (XXI). The sense of mortality, which has been present in *Vita nuova* since its inception (III, VIII), becomes more insistent when death carries off Beatrice's father (XXII); and Dante himself is driven to his bed for nine days with an illness; he dreams that Beatrice is dead, as described in the second canzone, "Donna pietosa e di novella etate" (A lady, tender in heart and young), the mid-point (16) of the 31 poems gathered in the work, in which the analogies between the imagined dead Beatrice and Christ crucified are striking (XXIII). A few days later the god of love makes his last appearance in Dante's dreams, urging him to be joyful in his love of Beatrice; Dante sees her preceded by Cavalcanti's Giovanna, as Christ was preceded by John the Baptist (XXIV). The next chapter is devoted to Dante's decision to write in the vernacular (XXV). The height of Dante's praise, and perhaps the happiest earthbound moment in the libello, is found in the sonnet "Tanto gentile e tanto onesta pare" (So gentle and so full of dignity appears); two more sonnets continue this theme of praise (XXVI–XXVII). The beginning of the following chapter will reveal that we have finished the second "movement" in the libello, devoted to the praise of his lady under the sponsorship of Guinizzelli.

The next chapter begins with the Latin of the Lamentations of Jeremiah: Beatrice is dead. Dante will not treat of her death (this book is called the *New Life;* he is not up to the task, in any case; and to do so would, as he himself insists, inevitably involve praising himself). Instead, he will explain the significance of the number nine, which has been so closely identified with her (XXVIII–XXIX). Dante, grieving, writes a Latin letter to the rulers of the city (XXX) and the canzone "Gli occhi dolenti" (My grieving eyes—XXXI), and then a sonnet of grief at the behest of a brother of Beatrice (XXXII–XXXIV). A year to the day after her death he writes the "sonnet with two beginnings," with its conflicting heavenly and earthly views of Beatrice (XXXIV). And then, some days later, in his distress, he is seen by a beautiful lady at a window who shows pity for his plight; he writes four sonnets about her, even though he realizes that she—through no fault of her own—is the adversary of Beatrice (XXXV–XXXVIII). Finally, he returns to thoughts of Beatrice (subsequently, there will be discussion of the opinion of those who believe that the ending of *Vita nuova* is a *rifacimento,* a later revision), first in penitent shame (XXXIX–XL), then, in response to a request from two noble ladies that he send them some of his poems, in awareness of Beatrice's presence in heaven, as documented by the new poem he wrote for these two ladies (XLI), and finally in a vision, unaccompanied by verse, of his lady seated among the blessed in the presence of God (XLII).

♣ Dante's *Vita nuova* is thus divided into three main sections or movements: (1) the unhappiness wrought in him by his love for Beatrice (II–XVII), (2) his praise of his lady (XVIII–XXVII), (3) Beatrice *in morte:* his grief, backsliding, and eventual vision of her in Paradise (XXVIII–XLII).

As we have seen, in its brief compass *Vita nuova* tells a fairly complex story that is given focus by words charged with hidden meanings. On precisely the ninth anniversary of the day on which Dante first saw her, Beatrice, now dressed in white, bestows on him her greeting (*salutare*). Sermartelli felt obliged to replace the noun form *salute* (as in III, 4, "la donna de la salute") with one less theologically charged, *saluto*—a form that Dante uses "correctly," for instance, when he speaks of his own greeting (*saluto*) of his fellow poets, the *fedeli d'Amore* (III, 9) in the very same chapter (*Vita nuova* III, 13). Once they are introduced in III, 1, forms of the verb *salutare* or of the nouns *saluto* and *salute* occur some thirty-one times. In the prose, *salute,* for Beatrice's greeting, occurs, after this first use, four times in XI, once in XII (the occasion for the outburst is Beatrice's denial of her "dolcissimo salutare" in X, 2). In the first of these it is joined with *caritade* (a word that only appears this single time in *Vita nuova,* when Dante says that mere longing for the *salute* of Beatrice fills him with charity). The Christian meaning of her very special form of greeting seems clear. Various forms of *salutare/salute* occur nine times in the poems, but *salute* as Beatrice's form of *salutare* occurs first only in XIX, v. 39, and then six times more. It is probably significant that no poem written before his first "stilnovist" poem—according to Dante himself, "Donne ch'avete intelletto d'amore" ("Ladies who have understanding of love")—has this theologized sense of the word as it applies to Beatrice.

It is on this very day that Dante retreats to his *camera,* the room that is the setting for so many of his thoughts of Beatrice in *Vita nuova.* The word *camera,* used to indicate his room, occurs fairly often in the prose (III, 2 and 3; XII, 2, 3, and 9; XIV, 9; XXIII, 10 and 12), never in the verse, allowing us some sense of the atmosphere in which this work was forged, in a place apart, by a solitary figure meditating upon the meaning of his lady. Here the god of love first appears to him in a dream ("meravigliosa visione"—II, 3). In the first of the last nine hours of the night he writes his first sonnet about Beatrice. We can thus date at least the idealized beginning of Dante's career as poet of Beatrice with great precision: ten o'clock of an evening in late May 1283, since Dante saw her first just before his ninth birthday in 1274 (*Vita nuova* II, 2) and it is now precisely nine years later (III, 1).

The rest of the first section of *Vita nuova* presents Dante's reports of his unhappiness in love. As many have suggested, and as is accentuated by Dante's first reference to Guido Cavalcanti, respondent to his first sonnet and, in consequence, his *primo amico* (III, 14), the poems of the first part of the work (III–XVII), which give vent to the lover's unhappiness caused by the lack of response by his beloved, are essentially Cavalcantian in nature. His unhappiness in this fated love comes to the first crucial moment of recognition and the turning point of the work (had Dante known Aristotle's *Poetics,* he might have spoken of *anagnorisis* and *peripeteia*). Ladies who observe his tears of pain ask questions that force him to acknowledge that it is pointless to lament what he cannot have; happiness (Dante employs the more religious-sounding *beatitudine*—XVIII, 6) lies in praising his beloved for what she is. And from this moment on, the project of *Vita nuova* is changed. (Also changed is its subject, "matera nuova," according to XVII, 1 and 2, further characterized, twice in XVIII, 9, by the loftiness of the new "matera," praise of the lady.) *Vita nuova* XIX begins with Dante's description of a walk alongside a clear stream. He wants to write a poem. And then his tongue moves as if of its own volition. The canzone thus begun, "Donne ch'avete intelletto d'amore," becomes the defining moment in Dante's celebration of Beatrice, his discovery of "il dolce stil novo" (*Purg.* XXIV, 57). Both what he will later say (*Purg.* XXVI, 97–99; 112–14) of Guido Guinizzelli and the reference to the Bolognese poet in the next sonnet (XX, vv. 1–2), "Amore e 'l cor gentil sono una cosa, / sì come il saggio in suo dittare pone" (Love and the noble heart are but one thing—/ so says the wise man in his poem) make it clear that the second section of *Vita nuova* (XIX–XXVII) is under Guinizzelli's sign.[30] This state of relative bliss is disrupted, first by the anticipation of Beatrice's death (*Vita nuova* XXIII) in the central canzone (the sixteenth poem of thirty-one), itself anticipated by the death of Beatrice's father (XXII), but then clamorously and irretrievably by the actual death of Beatrice as reported in *Vita nuova* XXVIII. From this point on, it seems that *Vita nuova* no longer acknowledges a predecessor or patron, that the end of the libello is presented as having its sole human authority in Dante himself. For the pains of love Cavalcanti might serve as master;[31] for the praise of his lady, Guinizzelli; for the discovery of the true nature of a higher love than poets had heretofore expressed, only the discoverer could assume responsibility. The concluding section of *Vita nuova* is Dantean in every sense. Its new subject is Beatrice *in morte*, "la nuova materia" (*Vita nuova* XXX, 1) announced by the Latin words of Jeremiah (XXVIII, 1), its newness reflected also in the arrangements of the prose *divisioni*, which for all the rest of *Vita nuova* will precede rather than follow the verse (XXXI, 2), thus "widowing" that verse.[32]

Its first poetic component is the third and last canzone. It follows the three prose chapters (XXVIII-XXX) beneath the rubric of Jeremiah's lament for Jerusalem (which will be remembered again as the opening of Epistle XI, to the Cardinals of Italy), read by Christians as a pre-meditation, as it were, upon the death of Christ,[33] as Dante's own verses will later testify (*Inf.* XXXIV, 114-15), and including the surprising, even shocking, assimilation of Beatrice to the Trinity in XXIX. The canzone and the next three shorter poems offer expressions of grief (XXXI-XXXIV). The second part of this concluding section of *Vita nuova* begins with an astonishing event, given the work's exclusive concern with Beatrice (heretofore excepting only the "screen ladies," who in fact merely confirm her centrality): Dante relates that he fell under the spell of "una gentile donna giovane e bella molto" (XXXV, 2). Her rule over his heart is documented by four sonnets (XXXV-XXXVIII), showing how this consoling presence (and *consolar* is perhaps her key word, as *salute* is Beatrice's) mitigated his pain at the loss of Beatrice and finally, despite his guilt at having begun to forget his true love (XXXVII), accepts her consolation in his heart (his appetite, in the gloss), despite the objections of his soul (his reason, in the gloss). Thus the victory of the *donna gentile* is circumscribed by a necessary reawakening of Dante's reason. Barbi and, more recently, Marti have scotched the argument of those who have maintained, following Pietrobono (and then Nardi), that these chapters were added after Dante wrote *Convivio*, some ten years and more later.[34] It is an argument that is at the very least implausible, since the balanced structuring of the work (including the careful ordering of the poems) as well as its dissemination, which offers no instance of a truncated version, both adamantly oppose the likelihood of any such rifacimento. It is probably just to consider the case closed, even if some persist in opening it, most notably Maria Corti.[35] Despite her careful considerations, many continue to consider Marti's arguments conclusive.

The donna gentile is, as has been suggested, pivotally connected with the function of consolation for Dante's loss of Beatrice, both in verse (XXXVIII, v. 10) and in prose (XXXVIII, 2), where Dante's thought of her is accused of driving out thoughts of anything else—most damningly, those of Beatrice. Her desire or willingness to offer such consolation is never portrayed as base or wrong in any way. Dante's response to her, by contrast, is roundly condemned. It is important to keep this fact in mind: it is not easy to explain away the problem that it creates for the argument that he added this section to *Vita nuova* only years after he wrote the rest. For if Dante had been intent on putting a positive spin on his affection, not for a woman of flesh and blood, which might have been culpable, but for the entirely good Lady Philosophy, he never would have included his urgent condemnation.[36] If the lady's identity is lodged in the word *consolar,* his thought of her also is described by a key word: *vile.* This word, in the entire tradition of Italian amatory lyric, is perhaps the worst word that can be attached to a lover-poet. If the lady, *gentile,* can help him attain *gentilezza* or *nobiltà,* she will save him from the condition of *viltà.* The two words stand in polar contradiction, the last the very defining opposite of the first (we may turn to *Convivio* IV, xvi, 6, for Dante's restatement of the commonplace, " 'nobile' . . . viene da 'non vile' " ["noble" derives from "not vile"]). The word *vile* enters *Vita nuova* only with the appearance of the donna gentile, and departs with her (XXXV, 3 and v. 8; XXXVII, 1; XXXVIII, 4; XXXIX, 2). Dante leaves no

doubt about the strength of his self-denunciation in the penultimate of these passages. His thought of the lady is addressed in
verse as "gentile": "e dico 'gentile' in quanto ragionava di gentile
donna, ché per altro era vilissimo" (and I say 'noble' insofar as
it spoke of a noble lady, since in other respects it was most vile).
He now begins to repent the desire to which he has "sì vilmente"
(so vilely) given himself for "alquanti die" ("several days"—and
not thirty months, as *Convivio* will state); he has now driven
out "cotale malvagio desiderio" (so evil a desire) and returned
his thoughts to Beatrice, now named in the prose an eighteenth
and penultimate time. Had Dante composed this passage when
Pietrobono and Nardi claim he did, he surely would not have
said what he said: the love for the donna gentile was not, according to the author of *Convivio,* of such short duration, nor
was it "malvagio" or "vile."

The concluding chapters of *Vita nuova* reaffirm Dante's love
for Beatrice. "Contra questo avversario della ragione" (Against
this adversary of reason), begins XXXIX, locating the adversary
precisely in Dante's heart, "il cor" that spoke the last words of
the sonnet in XXXVIII, defending its love for the *consolatrice.*
The opponent of this adversary is the image of the eight-year-
old Beatrice with which the narrative began. Dante's heart now
repents. He is again in grief at the loss of Beatrice. The arrival of
pilgrims on their way to Rome (perhaps to see the Veronica, as
would be suggested by *Par.* XXXI, 104) causes him to desire to
make these pilgrims weep, not for the friends whom they have
left behind, but for "la sua beatrice" that his soul has lost. He
writes a poem in which his thought of Beatrice becomes a pilgrim to "quella Roma onde Cristo è romano" (that Rome of
which Christ is Roman—*Purg.* XXXII, 102), as "Oltre la spera"
relates.

And it is only now, in the wake of that partial vision of
Beatrice in bliss that, in some ten lines of prose, Dante an-

nounces that he has had "una meravigliosa visione" (XLII, 1), now not an imagining or a dream, but a vision, perhaps only understandable on the model of those granted St. Paul or St. John,[37] of Beatrice in Paradise. (Looking back to these moments in which he had visionary awareness of Beatrice from the vantage point of *Convivio*, Dante will indeed refer to his condition as "quasi rapito" [as though rapt], language that reinforces the parallels—*Convivio* II, vii, 6.) For the second time in the narrative since very near its inception (III, 1, where Beatrice's *cortesia* "è oggi meritata nel grande secolo" [is today rewarded in life eternal], the author uses the present tense to speak of Beatrice (as he has done in XL, 1) as the work concludes (XLII, 2–3): we learn that she knows that Dante is studying to be worthy of her and that she gazes upon God. This represents a sort of grammatical resurrection of his lady, no longer held by death in a longed-for past, but alive in grace. (The fact that the author is thus portrayed as having known the final significance of Beatrice from the beginning is of central importance in thwarting any argument that the author himself is in a changing state of development as he writes the work.) This culminating moment is an extraordinary one, although its force has escaped many readers who, like the protagonist, tend to look back to find Beatrice rather than forward. (Even *Convivio*, with its complicated relationship to *Vita nuova* and Dante's affection for Beatrice, refers to her in such a way as to reflect her living presence in heaven at the end of the earlier work: "quella viva Beatrice beata" is the phrase found at II, viii, 7.) The promise to write of her heavenly presence may well have been begun in Latin in the years before the exile.[38] But it is only finally fulfilled by the *Comedy*, although it would be difficult to argue convincingly that around 1293 Dante already had that work in mind. All we can say with certainty is that, when he wrote it, he knew very well what promise he was keeping.

The prose narrative of *Vita nuova* is strangely lacking in concrete detail. Few characters or places—even Florence—are identified except by circumlocution.[39] Dante refers in strikingly unconcrete ways to the city in which the solemn events that he records take place. If one comes upon the passage in *Vita nuova* XXX, 1, where Dante describes the grief of "la sopradetta cittade" (the above-mentioned city) after Beatrice's death and searches back through the text for an antecedent and explanatory naming, one finds instead merely the repetition of the phrase, first in XXII, 3, and again in XIX, 3, where Dante refers to his return to Florence in the following words: "ritornato a la sopradetta cittade." (We know it is Florence because we know this is Dante writing—but his name, too, is never given, although a lady once calls him by it—"chiamandomi per nome"— XIX, 3.) The path back leads to XIV, 3, where the phrase is again repeated, as it is again in IX, 1. This in turn leads us back to VIII, 1, with the same result, and then to VII, 1, with no improvement in our knowledge: the city is still "la sopradetta cittade." It is only when we turn all the way back to VI, 2, where the city is mentioned for the first time in the work, that we may learn its identity: "la cittade ove la mia donna fue posta da l'altissimo sire" (the city in which my lady was placed by the supreme Lord)—Florence losing every attribute but the fact that God has there put the blessed Beatrice. This effect is also achieved by Dante's final reference to the city, "la cittade ove nacque e vivette e morio la gentilissima donna" (the city where the most noble of ladies was born, lived, and died—XL, 1). Thus, in nine passages Dante refers to Florence in such a way as to make it and her coterminous, the city significant only in terms of his lady's life and death in it. A Christian might make similar sort of reference to Bethlehem or Jerusalem; a Florentine is more likely to name a landmark, as Dante himself would later do in *Inferno* XIX, 17, and *Paradiso* XXV, 9, referring to the baptistery.

If we were to ask whose name is found most often in the pages of *Vita nuova,* most would probably and understandably say that this honor falls to Beatrice. This is not the case. Amor, the god of love, is referred to just over one hundred times. (It is impossible to give a certain count, as there are two or three ambiguous namings, where either the god or the phenomenon of loving may be meant, but there are at least 105 namings of the god.) His large presence, dwarfing that of names of any others (Beatrice, the abstractions Morte and Pietade, Guido Cavalcanti's Giovanna/Primavera are the next most often named), is perhaps problematic. How are we to explain the presence of a pagan god in what certainly seems to be the celebration of a much different kind of love than is usually associated with Cupid? It is perhaps not accidental that Amor is mainly absent from the prose of *Vita nuova* once Dante has explained (*Vita nuova* XXV) that the god of Love is not a substance, but an accident inhering in a substance (thus repeating Guido Cavalcanti's most famous dictum on the subject, in "Donna mi prega," if with perhaps a far different intent). At least this is true with respect to Dante's love for Beatrice. After the death of Beatrice, beginning at XXVIII, new figures of authority are needed to respond to Beatrice's new being: Jeremiah (XXVIII, 1; XXX, 1), the Trinity (XXIX, 3), Jesus Christ (XL, 1), God Almighty (XL, 7), Aristotle (XLI, 6). Three things should be noted. First, Amor does not disappear from three of the concluding poems about Beatrice (XXXI, "Li occhi dolenti" ["My eyes that grieve"], v. 14; XXXIX, "Lasso! per forza di molti sospiri" ["Alas, by the violence of the many sighs"], v. 7; XLII, "Oltre la spera" ["Beyond the sphere"], v. 3), but his name is not mentioned in the accompanying prose. Second, Amor is only logically a part of both the poems and the prose dedicated to the "gentile donna giovane e bella molto" (XXXV, 2), when Dante has moved away from the love he owes Beatrice in heaven, as he himself later insists (XXXIX, 1). Third, the pivotal moment in his backsliding occurs in XXXIV, where the sonnet with two beginnings has him first writing of Beatrice, now "posta da l'altissimo signore / nel ciel de l'umiltate, ov'è Maria" (placed by the highest Lord in the heaven of humility, where Mary is), words that bring back to mind the opening circumlocution for Florence as "la cittade ove la mia donna fue posta da l'altissimo sire" (the city where my lady was placed by the highest Lord—VI, 2), but then returning to lament her loss to earth under the auspices of weeping Amore, as though he were trying to relocate her in the fleshly world inhabited by such creatures as the donna gentile that he will find gazing at him from her window in the next chapter. In short, Amor as patron of Beatrice has a brief, early role in this text, mainly concluded by chapter XII. And thus Amor's apparently controlling presence in *Vita nuova* is eventually limited and replaced by the God of Beatrice's heaven. Amor's relation to a semantic field reserved to love poetry is in potential conflict with his relation to the God who is Love. If there is one problem in this problematic work that seems to have exceeded Dante's grasp, it was how to resolve the opposing tendencies in this figure.[40]

After a two-sentence introduction, the narrative of the *Vita nuova,* begins by inscribing the name of Beatrice, "la gloriosa donna della mia mente, la quale fu chiamata da molti Beatrice" (the heavenly lady of my mind, who was called by many Beatrice —*Vita nuova* II, 1). No one would choose to argue that *Vita nuova* is not centrally concerned with, is not dedicated to, the memory of this woman—whatever her eventual significance. Nonetheless, it is interesting to consider how surprisingly absent the name of Beatrice is from the texts of the poems. Indeed, if we examine all of Dante's production as lyric poet and consider it apart from the prose of the libello, we find Beatrice's name in his lyric poems only four times: twice in XXV (*Vita nuova* XXXI), then once each in XXXVII (*Vita nuova* XLI) and in LXVIII. Other ladies, we might reflect, are "named" in as many poems in toto: "Fioretta mia bella" (LVI), "Violetta" (LVIII), "Lisetta" (CXVII), and this is not to take into account the "pargoletta" of *Rime* LXXXVII-LXXXIX. While one might explain the relative absence of his lady's name as being the result of that convention in medieval erotic lyric that concealed the name of the writer's beloved or hid it behind another name (the *señhal* of the troubadours), the point is that, had Dante not written the enveloping prose of *Vita nuova,* the extraordinary role played by Beatrice in the *Comedy* would have been terribly difficult to explain. But we have that prose. And the name of Beatrice moves literally from one end of it to the other, from the opening of the narrative to the reference in its concluding sentence to "quella benedetta Beatrice" (XLII, 3).

In comparison with the paucity of nominal reference in the verse, there is a veritable explosion of the proper noun *Beatrice* in the prose of *Vita nuova,* where it occurs nineteen times in all (II, 1; V, 2 and 3; XII, 6; XIV, 4; XXII, 1 and 3; XXIII, 3 and 13 [twice]; XXIV, 3, 4 and 5; XXVIII, 1; XXXI, 3 and 5; XXXIX, 1 and 2; XLII, 3). In the poems her name is spoken only in the final canzone of the work—where it occurs twice (XXXI, 10, 15) and where she is named only now that she is dead—and in the final sonnet's penultimate verse, after Dante's "sospiro" has seen her alive in beatitude. It is possible that these three occurrences are themselves significant, as Dante's own insistence on Beatrice's numerological meaning in *Vita nuova* might invite us to believe, for example, when he tells us that Beatrice "is" a nine ("questo numero fue ella medesima"—XXIX, 3):

Lo numero del tre è la radice del nove, però che, sanza numero altro alcuno, per sé medesimo fa nove, sì come vedemo manifestamente che tre via tre fa nove. Dunque se lo tre è fattore per sé medesimo del nove, e lo fattore per sé medesimo de li miracoli è tre, cioè Padre e Figlio e Spirito Santo, li quali sono tre e uno, questa donna fue accompagnata da questo numero del nove a dare ad intendere ch'ella era uno nove, cioè uno miracolo, la cui radice, cioè del miracolo, è solamente la mirabile Trinitade.

(The number three is the root of nine, since, without any other number, multiplied by itself it makes nine, as we plainly observe that three times three makes nine. Then, if three is the sole factor of nine and if the sole factor of miracles is three, that is, Father, Son, and Holy Spirit, who are three and one, so this lady was accompanied by the number nine in such wise that it may be understood that she was a nine, that is, a miracle, the root of which, that is, of the miracle, is the wondrous Trinity and nothing else—XXIX, 3.)

Reflecting her "nineness," Beatrice's appearances to Dante on the earth, though variously counted,[41] also are nine, and they are then augmented by his beholding her in the final vision [XLII], making her a perfect "ten" as well.[42] Recalling God's unity (10 = 1 + 0 = 1), ten is the perfect number, as Dante himself calls it ("lo perfetto numero"—*Vita nuova* XXIX, 1).

The resonances of the title of the work are numerous, running from its least dramatic association of Dante's first love for Beatrice with youth (both his and hers) to its most impressive, if half-concealed, claims for the relation of Beatrice to Christ. The words of a father of the Church, Quodvultdeus, were appropriate, if Dante knew them: "Omnis qui baptismum Christi desiderat, vitam novam concupiscit" (Everyone who longs for baptism in Christ desires a new life).[43] Dante's work wants to be taken as "new" in every sense: it is a first and youthful work, it is a new kind of literary creation, his lady is a new kind of literary lady, and she herself eventually comes to live in the "new life" in Paradise with Christ and leads her lover to that kind of love. Thus the new life is related to the life of the nine ("nove" and "nova" sound enough alike in Italian and Latin to help form the linkage).

For the architectonic shape of the arrangement of the poems of *Vita nuova*, discussed by Norton in 1859 and developed by various students of the problem since then, Mark Musa's elaboration of its design in 1962 is perhaps the most elegant that we possess.[44] In the diagram that he proposes, the larger roman numerals stand for the three finished canzoni, while the arabic represent the twenty-eight shorter compositions, the whole forming an elaborate chiasmus:

$$\text{1-9 I 1-3} \leftrightarrows \text{II} \leftrightarrows \text{3-1 III 9-1}$$

As for the shape of the work as a whole, that will depend on how the problem of Dante's division of the work into chapters is eventually resolved. As long as one accepts Barbi's division and numeration (forty-two chapters in all), one has available a numerologically pleasing and surely Dantean (or at least Dantesque) pattern: 31 poems + 42 prose units = 73 = 10 = 1. Further, the number forty-two is a particularly significant number in Christian exegesis of the Old Testament, especially in Num. 33, as interpreted by Peter Damian:[45] it is the number of the Exodus. Thus, if we knew that Barbi were correct, we would have little difficulty in knowing why Dante had chosen that precise number of chapters. However, and as the recent work of Cervigni and Gorni has reminded us, Barbi's numeration is his and not Dante's. We probably cannot easily accept their numerations either, since the very charge they lodge against Barbi—that any such ordination is the result of a modern interpretive reconstruction—may be lodged against them. The result is that we must live with an undefined formal structure for the prose, while sensing that it seems most unlikely that Dante would have left so important a formal element unresolved. The careful crafting of the poetic elements would argue that the prose had its numerical structuring principle as well, as would almost all of the rest of his work. Dante, as Thomas Hart has demonstrated most recently and convincingly, was a writer who was rarely without a sense of the numbers of his compositions.[46]

Written in "il libro de la mia mente" Dante finds inscribed the story of his love for Beatrice under the rubric "Incipit vita nova" (I, 1), the first of twenty-three Latin phrases in the work.[47] It is not without linguistic or theological interest that the libello begins and ends in Latin, its first inscription perhaps suggesting that not only the incipit but the following text was originally "dictated" in Latin (or might have been), as does the sudden switch into Latin in the last sentence of the work (XLII, 3), only the second Latin passage in the libello not to be set off from the Italian text as a quotation (the first is the passage from Jer., Lam. 1:1 that announces the death of Beatrice in XXVIII, 1). We are reminded by the use of Latin that Dante's linguistic choice of the vernacular for his self-commentary (the very existence of which is itself unheard of) is surprising. His Latin sentences and phrases serve the purpose of showing both that he could have written his commentary in the language of grammar rather than in the vernacular had he so wished and that his vernacular has the power and status of Latin, a point made with some force in his lengthy defense of the vernacular in *Vita nuova* XXV. But they also and often have significant biblical resonance.[48] At least one-third of them are explicitly drawn from the Bible, another third from what might be designated a generically "postbiblical" style of expression, and a third from classical literature, most particularly the six citations of the *auctores* in XXV, 9. Were the twenty-three Latin passages absent, *Vita nuova* would seem a somewhat different work. (We might reflect that a similar phenomenon is found in the *Comedy,* in which Dante's first spoken word as character in his poem [*Inf.* I, 65] is the Latin *Miserere* of Psalm 50, while Latin words and phrases run the length of the text, eighty-eight occurrences in all, ending with the *velle* that forms the first rhyme word in the final rhyme in the poem.) Latin would seem to be put to the service of raising the text's "seriousness." And its "Latinness" is not found only in the Latin words themselves, but in the many Latinisms in Dante's Italian prose, as well as in the style of that prose (and not the poems). Many have characterized this style as "scholastic," whether in its tone or in its manifestation of "clarification for clarification's sake" (the expression is Panofsky's [49]), evident primarily in the divisions of the sonnets (so troublesome to modern readers), but also in such passages as that dedicated to the elaboration of the three differing kinds of pilgrims (palmers, pilgrims, and Romers), where only one kind (the last of these) is referred to (*Vita nuova* XL, 7).

It was only in our own century that serious attention began to be paid to the distance that separates the author of the *Comedy* from his protagonist.[50] It is clear, or should be, that the same distinction operates in *Vita nuova.* For there also we must distinguish between the protagonist, and what he knows (and does not yet know), and the narrator, who is living and writing after the occurrence of the final vision that has transformed his understanding of his relation to Beatrice and of her eventual meaning. Just as is true with regard to the final vision described in *Paradiso* XXXIII, it is only in that final moment that the two beings become fused in one.

A further problem involves the historicity of the narrative

and, perhaps more importantly for some, of Beatrice herself. And once again the *Comedy* offers us a precisely parallel construction. As Singleton has said, "The fiction of the *Divine Comedy* is that it is not fiction."[51] We should probably understand that this is also the case in *Vita nuova,* which begins by asserting that the events it records are inscribed in the writer's memory, not invented by a writer. Dante, as scribe, will now only copy out things already "written" on his mind by experience, will be only the "scribe of a scribe," as it were. In *Vita nuova* Dante underlines his claim when he explains that, were he to record some of his youthful behavior, the result might seem "alcun parlar fabuloso" (mere fictive words—II, 10). And thus we are to understand that everything narrated in *Vita nuova* (and in the *Comedy*) is narrated as though it had actually occurred. This understanding in no way requires that we actually believe that all took place in actuality, as the text maintains, only that we grasp that the author claims historical validity for what we at the very least suspect is, indeed, fictive. (Dante did not, all will surely agree, actually see Geryon, for instance [*Inferno* XVI].) Beatrice did not appear, we also suspect, in conjunction with as many "nines" as Dante insists.

Words for nine or ninth occur twenty-two times in the work. *Nine* is the first word of the narrative ("Nove fiate"—*Vita nuova* II, 1): Dante was about to turn nine when he first saw Beatrice (II, 2); exactly nine years later she offers her *salute* (III, 1), at nine o'clock in the morning (III, 2); his vision of Love with Beatrice in his arms occurred at ten o'clock that night (the first of the last nine hours of night—III, 8); Beatrice's name appears ninth among the names of the sixty ladies of Florence in Dante's lost (if he actually wrote it) *sirventese* (VI, 2); his dream of Love appearing to him in his chamber occurred at nine o'clock in the morning (XII, 9); ill for nine days (XXIII, 1), he imagines, on the ninth day of his illness, that Beatrice is dead (XXIII, 2).

Finally, Dante promises to explain why the number nine has been "cotanto amico" (so friendly) to Beatrice (XXVIII, 3), and he mentions the adjective or the noun eleven times (including the last nine occurrences of the noun *nove* in the work, in perhaps intentional grouping) in XXIX, 1–3. How different a text *Vita nuova* might seem to a contemporary reader did it not contain these details or, even if it did, were there no such exposition as is found in XXIX. (That it is the constructing prose that governs Dante's shaping of the meaning of the poems of *Vita nuova* is made all the more clear by that fact that some of the key words of the work, like *nove* and *camera*, do not appear in any of the poems.)

If we are to grant that Beatrice is a "nine," are we also expected to believe that she actually existed? With regard to our understanding of *Vita nuova*, there are perhaps few less important issues than this. Over the centuries scholars have argued for various positions: some have held that Beatrice was a historical person, the daughter of Folco Portinari; but any number have insisted that she is only a symbol, with whatever valence. The text is so insistent on the factual nature of the narrative, as though it were a *sanctae Beatricis vita*, that we have no choice but to treat it, within its own convention, as nothing less or other than that.[52] In the end, it is less important whether these things are literally true than that Dante says that they are. For that tells us what sort of fiction—to the degree that the narrative is fictive—he was intent upon writing, one that cannot be separated from historical reality. (The same may be said of the *Comedy*.) For now, it is enough to say that, even were it to turn out that Dante's Beatrice had no historical existence (as is most unlikely to occur), we would still need to pay heed to the historical footing of the entire narrative. It seems more than likely, however, that Beatrice was in fact a real person with a particular history. As has been observed, Dante's use of her nickname, Bice, in the sonnet in XXIV, points in that direction, if perhaps not conclusively. And the precise dating of her death, 8 June 1290 (XXIX, 1), makes it seem clear that she was a particular person, not a figment of a poet's imagination. If she had not died precisely when Dante said she had, we can only imagine what protest his critics would have lodged against him for so grave an error. Although arguments *ex silentio* are not conclusive, it is difficult to forget that Dante had several detractors who left a public record of his supposed inconsistencies or other forms of foolishness. It is probably fair to say that, had Beatrice not been more or less as Dante said she was, either Cecco or Forese or Dante da Maiano (or Guido Cavalcanti?) would have been delighted to poke holes in the fabric Dante had spent so much time and energy weaving.

If Beatrice is herself, then, rather than a symbol of a quality, what does she signify beyond herself? There are, as a wag has put it, only two classes of readers that are deeply offended by Dante's claims for divine inspiration, believers and nonbelievers. And such is also the case with regard to Beatrice's status as "figura Christi" (or, more accurately, "postfiguration of Christ"). Nonetheless, the more we examine the text of *Vita nuova,* the clearer it becomes that Beatrice, like St. Francis before her (and without whose example one doubts that Dante would have had the daring to develop his Beatrice's filiations with Christ[53]), can be understood only as mystically related to God, both in His actions and in His being. Her coming to earth is, as it were, a "second first Coming," a coming analogous to that of Christ. No other understanding can justify the otherwise extravagant claims that Dante makes on her behalf. If she has, by showing herself to humankind, the power to bring those who look on her toward salvation (as Dante believes she brought at least himself), we have not many other alternatives, as uncomfortable as we may feel with such claims. In Dante's *vita Beatricis* the presence of the life of Christ behind her life gives the dominant significance to his lady. Until the *mirabile visione*, it is precisely that which he has failed to understand about her, even if at least some of the poems that begin with "Donne ch'avete" reveal those elements—for example, Beatrice's salvific mission to earth; God wanting his special creature back in heaven; the earthquake, darkness at noon, and other Good Friday events that are a part of Dante's imagining of her death. The writer, who knows of Beatrice's special status in grace from the opening pages of the work, has to wait for the protagonist to catch up to him, as occurs only in the final brief chapter of the work, when the two become one.

Few questions in the past fifty years have more troubled Dante studies than that which regards the nature of his relation to what we may refer to as "l'allegoria dei teologi" (*Convivio* II, i, 4). And while most of the battles that have been fought on this terrain involve the *Comedy,* the *Convivio,* and the epistle to Cangrande, it also seems clear to some that the discussion is not without relevance to *Vita nuova.* In this view Beatrice, as her actions are described in the libello (and, still more tellingly, in the *Comedy*), should be understood not as an idealized personification of an abstract idea, but as a figural projection developed with elements drawn from the life of Christ.[54] One of the crucial presences in this discussion is one that is not often remembered in the continuing debate: Mario Casella. In a recent study Francesco Mazzoni[55] has recapitulated the argument and underlined Casella's priority in planting the seeds of a theological understanding, not only of the source of Dante's later description of his own "dolce stil novo" (to which we shall turn shortly), but of a theologized understanding of Beatrice herself.[56] It is important to be aware that the leading American exponent of a theological approach to the meaning of Beatrice, Charles Singleton, studied Dante in Florence with Casella, as did Mazzoni, one of the leading Italian students of the ecclesiastical sources of Dante's thought. These two schools of thought, the so-called *scuola americana* and what might be called *la scuola fiorentina,* have had perhaps more arguments than agreements, though both approaches are primarily developed from Casella's discoveries and insights in the 1930s and both propose a basically theological reading of Dante's work. Singleton was preceded not only by Casella but by Auerbach (whose extensive work on figural allegory Singleton never mentioned). Once he became the predominant expositor of the position that made Dante the poet of fourfold exegesis, Singleton was followed by others, mainly also Americans (Freccero, Hollander, and Mazzotta). Figural allegory, establishing a connection between people (for example, Moses as "type" of Christ) or events (for example, the Exodus as linked to the freedom from bondage wrought by Christ), is, the Americans argued, the core of Dante's significative practice in the *Comedy*.[57] From Singleton's work on *Vita nuova,* although he does not say so explicitly, one might draw a similar conclusion: Beatrice is a "postfiguration" of Christ, precisely like St. Francis in this respect. Mazzoni, who objects to this view, follows Casella (and was joined by Contini) in developing a different theological basis for the understanding of Beatrice, deriving precisely from *Vita nuova* XXIX, the Trinitarian source of Beatrice's "nineness." This view plays down figural interpretation in favor of an argument based on another kind of analogy, spiritual rather than historical. More narrowly, Mazzoni insists on Casella's term *analogia entis* (analogy of being) as constituting the key to Beatrice's meaning. That is, her being is an analogue; Dante specifically says, XXIX, 3, "questo numero [nove] fue ella medesima; per similitudine dico" (she was herself this number [nine]; I mean by analogy). Thus, for Mazzoni, the American hypothesis misses the central point. Insofar as the "Americans" have not heeded this dimension of Beatrice's meaning, he is surely correct. However, Mazzoni's argument is in some difficulty when we turn our attention from Beatrice's being to her actions. For when these are described by Dante, they frequently do bring to mind things done by Christ, both in *Vita nuova* and, even more pronouncedly, in the *Comedy*. Each side in the debate (and we must remember that there is a large group of others who would deny either one its major premise) has failed to grasp, one might argue, the important contribution of the other. In the end, these two views are not so much opposed as complementary. Beatrice's actions, occurring in time and space, have a figural dimension; her being, existing beyond such boundaries, an analogical one. Her phenomenal life has figural connections, her noumenal existence stands in analogy with the Trinity.

As if this vexed question were not enough in itself, it is necessarily related to another, that concerning the nature of the dolce stil novo. When Dante looks back from the vantage point of *Purgatorio* XXIV (ca. 1311–12?) he declares that this "style" began when he composed "Donne ch'avete," around 1288–89. This declaration, whatever other consequences may be drawn from it, makes it clear that there was no group of poets who adopted the style before that time—if there ever was such a group at all. Much of Italian literary history of this period is based on the assumption that such a school existed; it has become difficult to state the obvious: the dolce stil novo, as it is described in histories or anthologies of Italian literature of the trecento, is a creation of the nineteenth century.[58] As far as Dante himself is concerned, all we can say is that he is a practitioner, and that at least one poet (the plural, as indicated by "le vostre penne" of *Purg.* XXIV, 58), was, in his opinion, a fellow practitioner.[59] But perhaps the major issue raised by the phrase is what it is really meant to indicate. The adherents of the two most popular current positions, which stand in polemical relation to each other, believe either that Amor is the traditional god of love, and that Dante is claiming that he wrote more accurately and honestly of his amorous feelings than did others, or that Amor is in fact the code name for the Holy Spirit and Dante is claiming that his celebration of Beatrice in the *Vita nuova* (and in the *Comedy*) is thus inspired. This debate, central to the question of the claims that Dante makes for his status as poet, both in *Vita nuova* and the *Comedy*, will undoubtedly continue. In Italy writers such as Maria Corti would blend the two positions, claiming that Dante was presenting himself in relation to Amor, as the writer of love poems, much as a soul that is filled with the Holy Spirit might speak.[60] The question is not easily resolved.

Whatever interpretive skills *Vita nuova* requires of its readers, it rewards even those who are without them. It was admired in its day—and is so still more in our own—by those who fail to pass beyond its veils of deeper meaning and remain content with its "love story," tragic in its tones and noble in its bearing. Others, more alert to literary signals, dwell on the technical innovations in this amazing little book, yet manage to avoid any significant encounter with the barely submerged religious meanings it contains. The fact is that readers, faced with this enigmatic work, have made their own texts out of whatever responsive capabilities they possess. It must be a measure of Dante's genius that he has been able to satisfy so many different kinds of readers with this libello, even those whom he would surely have disdained. *Vita nuova* has found an audience for more than seven hundred years. That audience consists of beings who disagree for the most part about what the text really means.

LATER LYRICS

The *Vita nuova* is the breakthrough work that made Dante's career as a serious writer possible. Once it was behind him, certainly no later than 1295 and perhaps as early as 1293, various future paths must have beckoned. The one that led to the *Com-*

edy, however, took at least twelve years to open out before him. As unswervingly as Dante seems ready to follow Beatrice as her poet at the conclusion of *Vita nuova*, he would not do so for some time. It is particularly interesting to observe that, even as he was writing *Vita nuova* or shortly thereafter, he was also writing very different sorts of poems indeed. Whether because he did not feel himself ready to write the work he claims to be readying himself to write at the conclusion of *Vita nuova*, or perhaps because his poetic instincts drew him elsewhere, we find perhaps his most powerful lyrics to date addressed to other concerns and, indeed, to other women. Once again we can sense in him the need to experiment. The years 1293–98, as he becomes more involved with his other great passion, politics, bring a comparatively smaller poetic output and no work in prose.

In the roughly five-year period of his remaining poetic activity in Florence Dante wrote some fifteen poems.[61] If the canzone "Voi che 'ntendendo" (O you who by intellection—LXXIX), later included in *Convivio*, can be accurately dated to the second half of 1293, and if *Vita nuova* was finished by then (both these hypotheses must be tentative, as indeed must many things that historians of Dante's career try to establish about this particularly obscure period of his activity), then we find in this canzone the first major result of his turning to new poetic themes. This poem, and the problems of its allegorical or literal nature, will be discussed in the consideration of *Convivio*, along with its companion poem, "Voi che savete" ("O you who know"—LXXX). Also to be included as members of a group of poems dedicated to the lady at the window of the conclusion of *Vita nuova* are "Amor che ne la mente" ("Love that in my mind"—LXXXI), the second canzone included in *Convivio*, and the sonnets "Parole mie" ("Words of mine"—LXXXIV) and "O dolci rime" ("O you sweet poems"—LXXXV). This group within the group offers a single major difficulty, which is debated to this day: As they are written, are they about a flesh-and-blood woman, the same one to whom Dante turned, according to the libello, when he let his affection fall away from Beatrice? Or is she the Lady Philosophy? It is extremely difficult to resolve the question.

A different order of difficulty pervades the three so-called *pargoletta* poems (LXXXVII–LXXXIX). Addressed to a young woman and managed with a stylistic lightness that stands out from the weightier manner of the previous group, these graceful poems are variously understood as addressing the donna gentile or another (and younger) woman, as the word *pargoletta*, or "young girl," would indicate. Nonetheless, it probably makes most sense to believe that she is presented as a woman distinct from any that Dante has written about before and that she is to be construed as a woman or girl who tempted the poet, a suggestion that may explain why Beatrice's reproaches of Dante in the Earthly Paradise include reference to a "pargoletta" (*Purg.* XXXI, 59) as unworthy of his attention after Beatrice died. Two other poems seem to be dedicated to yet another woman, one who may be distinct from any of those already mentioned: "Amor che movi" ("Love, who send down [your power from heaven]"—XC) and "Io sento sì d'Amor la gran possanza" ("So much do I feel Love's mighty power"—XCI). The latter is cited indirectly at *Purgatorio* XXX, 39, when Dante sees Beatrice on the chariot: "d'antico amor sentì la gran potenza." Is this self-citation used as self-criticism? Once again, it is difficult to be certain. "Le dolci rime d'amor" ("The sweet poems of love"— LXXXII), the final poem that Dante would ever include in another work (*Convivio* IV), marks a turning from the amatory staging of his poetic production to the "philosophic" consideration of the nature of true nobility. A companion piece of sorts is "Poscia ch'Amor" ("Since Love [has utterly abandoned me]"— LXXXIII), an ironic attack on courtiers (and others) who devote themselves to being "leggiadri" (Foster and Boyde translate *leggiadria* as "Charm"), seeking and performing the empty form of the good. To this period scholars also date the series of insults exchanged between Dante and Forese (which some believe not to be genuine), utterly different in tone and language from the love lyrics. And, most notably, he writes the remarkable and beautifully wrought "petrose," the four poems to the woman who, whether in fact or fancy we shall never know, drove Dante to more than usually frank sexual expression. In these poems (C–CIII) for many readers Dante reaches the height of his expressive powers as a lyric poet, turning back to the harsh and difficult verse of Arnaut Daniel to find a model for what was for him an entirely new, and carnal, voice.

The rime petrose (stony poems), numbers C–CIII in Barbi or 77–80 in Foster and Boyde, are generally considered as having been composed around 1296.[62] One of them ("Amor, tu vedi ben," CII [79]) is referred to in *De vulgari Eloquentia* II, xiii, 12. This poem and CI (78) are both, with their identical rhymes, developed from the example of Arnaut's sestina "Lo ferm voler," as Dante himself later indicated (*DvE* II, xiii, 2). All of them are characterized by a rougher, harsher poetic diction and an arrestingly frank sexual content. They all concern a "stony lady" who holds the poet in thrall and all express his vengeful desires for sexual release. While the authors of an important recent study argue for a cosmic and even harmonious reading of these erotically charged verses,[63] most who deal with them consider their meaning to reside in their open and violent sensuality and in their significance as technical experimentation, Dante's first homage to Arnaut (see *Purg.* XXVI, 115–48), reflecting the writer's mastery of a new poetic voice. Commentaries to *Inferno* XXXII, 1–6, frequently refer to the coincidence of lexical and stylistic traits that clearly reflect both Arnaut and the petrose. This "harsh new style," once added to Dante's virtuosic repertory, can be perceived in many moments in the *Comedy*, where they add a tonal register that well serves the poet who describes so much anguish and defeated longing in his *Inferno*.

Thus, if Dante's output slowed during this period of his first major involvement in the civic life of Florence, his ability as writer of verse shows significant improvement. The range and power of these works, only five of them short poems, is considerable. One might suggest that, without the structure of the surrounding prose, many of the poems in *Vita nuova* would not seem very impressive. Such a remark could not easily be defended with regard to the extraordinary poems that Dante wrote in the 1290s. He had become a great poet but was still nearly ten years away from his magnum opus.

Between 1298 and 1303 there seems to have been little literary activity on Dante's part. The years 1300-1302 were taken up with quite different matters, the sudden rise and equally precipitous fall of Dante Alighieri the politician. Probably in 1304 he wrote the sad, allegorical canzone of the exile, "Tre donne intorno al cor mi son venute" ("Three ladies have come round my heart"—CIV). A companion piece of sorts is found in the sonnet "Se vedi li occhi miei" ("If you see my eyes"—CV), Dante's only overtly political lyric, a lament for the death of justice at the hands of the pope. With its fairly clear references to Clement V and Philip the Fair of France, it was written sometime after the election of Clement in 1305, which led to the "Babylonian Captivity" of the papacy at Avignon, beginning in 1309. Foster and Boyde allow for the possibility of a much later date (1310-13), which would probably make it Dante's last preserved lyric. However, there is little reason it could not have been written in 1305 or soon after, as Dante became increasingly aware of Clement's collaboration with Philip and his plans to remove the papacy to France. "Doglia mi reca" ("Grief brings [boldness to my heart]"—CVI), probably written earlier than 1305 since it is referred to in *De vulgari Eloquentia* (II, ii, 9), is, like "Poscia ch'Amor," a barbed attack on a vice, in this case avarice. There has been considerable speculation that Dante would have used it to build his essay on the opposing virtue, liberality, that was to be the subject of the fifteenth and final treatise of *Convivio*. At this time we also have the poetic correspondence between the also-exiled Cino da Pistoia and Dante (CX–CXV). Dante's third epistle helps to date this exchange of sonnets as taking place after 1303 and before 1306. Their amatory matter is also reflected in "Amor, da che convien" ("Love, since I am forced [to grieve]"—CXVI), better known as *la montanina* because Dante so addresses it in his *congedo*. It was written perhaps in 1307 and is referred to in his fourth epistle (to Moroello Malaspina), which accompanied a copy of the poem, shortly thereafter. Its account of a desperate and impossible love has led to a number of theories about the identity of the woman whose coldness it describes.[64] Perhaps written after Dante had begun writing *Inferno*,[65] the montanina was possibly Dante's last lyric, or at least the last that has come down to us. The nine poems that he wrote in exile that have been preserved show him to be as various of voice as he is always—and remind us once more of how thoroughly he gave himself to whatever convention with which he happened to involve himself. Trying to make a single strand of these is a temptation best avoided.

CONVIVIO I

Dante's next large undertaking is notable both for its length and by the fact that it was never finished. Even as it stands, it is the most extended piece of Italian prose yet dedicated to a literary subject, some 150 pages in length in an unannotated edition. When we reflect that had it been completed, *Convivio* might have run some six hundred pages, we have some sense of the size of the projected undertaking. In his exile, effectively cut off from home and any other career but that of writer (despite his continuing efforts to involve himself in Florentine politics from a distance), Dante had settled on this vast, encyclopedic enterprise to make himself a major figure in the literary landscape of northern Italy.[66] Once again he turns to the hitherto unheard-of tactic of making his own poems the basis of his prose text, now a series of canzoni on differing themes. We know that the work was to have included fifteen *trattati*—all but the first, an introduction to the work as a whole, devoted to an elucidation of one of his own poems. Even as much as we have of *Convivio* reveals a work that is still in a state of flux as it is being written.[67]

"Sì come dice lo Filosofo nel principio de la Prima Filosofia, tutti li uomini naturalmente desiderano di sapere" (As the Philosopher says at the beginning of the First Philosophy, all men naturally desire to know—*Convivio* I, i, 1). Deployed through its first sentence under the banner of Aristotle's *Metaphysics, Convivio,* whatever might have been its eventual purpose, is clearly meant to praise the virtues of philosophizing, the "amoroso uso di sapienza" (the loving use of wisdom—III, xii, 12; IV, ii, 18). Writing probably between 1304 and 1307,[68] Dante completed only its first four *trattati*, a word we found used in *Vita nuova* to indicate the serious exposition of a weighty subject, from its first use (V, 3) to its last (XLII, 1).[69] The unfinished work has nonetheless a certain integrity, for at least those parts of it that Dante did complete are more or less finished, especially when we compare it with *De vulgari Eloquentia,* broken off in mid-sentence near the end of the second of its proposed four books. The forty-six manuscripts that have come down to us all descend from a single late and terribly insecure lost archetype. Simonelli proposes, with proper caution, that *Convivio* had a first disorderly (and perhaps partial?) diffusion (Vasoli indicates references to passages from *Convivio* in the so-called Ottimo Commento,

Pietro di Dante, Boccaccio, and Giovanni Villani),[70] followed by a later circulation of manuscripts of the work as we have it, from the late fourteenth or early fifteenth centuries, all showing clear evidence of that single lost archetype. (The text was first printed in 1490.) Following the introductory treatise, we find the next two conjoined in subject, a sort of extensive afterword to *Vita nuova* (*Convivio* II and III), followed by a quite different treatise on nobility (*Convivio* IV). As opposed to *Vita nuova*, which was known to a number of Dante's fourteenth-century readers, *Convivio* had little immediate afterlife, in part because it was unfinished, in part because Dante never put it forward himself as his own (for whatever reason—that is, whether he had wearied of it or whether he simply did not wish to publish the unfinished work). One of its most striking aspects is that it was composed for a reader well acquainted with *Vita nuova*.

From the four extant treatises we can deduce only a little about the eventual possible content of the projected magnum opus. We should not forget that it was to be precisely that for Dante, a text to magnify his reputation among the literate citizens of Italy, as his (surely overoptimistic) reference to the audience of *Vita nuova* as "quasi . . . tutti li Italici" (just about . . . every Italian—*Convivio* I, iv, 13) makes plain. Dante tells us only that each treatise was to be devoted to the exposition of one of his canzoni and dedicated to a single subject. From within his text we know that the penultimate treatise was to deal with that great concern of the *Comedy*, justice (IV, xxxviii, 11), perhaps, as Barbi suggested, presented as commentary upon the text of the canzone "Tre donne." The seventh (IV, xxvi, 8), it seems, was meant to address the theme of temperance. Dante's two references to the fifteenth and final treatise (I, viii, 18; III, xv, 14) leave it quite unclear what the surmounting topic was to be, though some think (finding the word in I, viii, 18) this would have been liberality. As for the canzoni to be included, only "Tre donne"

("Three ladies [have come round my heart]"—seems to have been assured a place—and even that is conjectural. Various other of Dante's existing canzoni have been proposed for one slot or another. Given the condition of our present (and of our likely future) knowledge, we must allow all such hypotheses to remain in the realm of utter speculation. It is perhaps best simply to restrain any instinct that would lead us to try to fill a lacuna that ought instead to be respected.

Dante's own introductory statement of the subjects of the fourteen canzoni offers only two: "Sì d'amor come di vertù" (*Convivio* I, i, 14). As for the virtues that are referred to as subjects or potential subjects in the work, there is reason to believe that at least one of the cardinal virtues, prudence, was not to be included, as we shall see shortly. And what of the theological ones? Dante does not seem to have planned to include them, either. Were they to be omitted because the work was inscribed under the heading of philosophy, the *ancilla* of theology, but not under that of theology itself? In Ulrich Leo's formulation, the essential differences between *Convivio* and *Comedy* are revealed in the facts that "the author of the *Convivio* had . . . submitted himself to the limits of mortal man, limits established also in the *Comedy*, in accordance with the Thomistic doctrine. But in the *Convivio*, he did not even try to 'see' anything beyond natural limits. In the *Comedy*, on the other hand, it has been granted the poet to overcome, in an ecstatic rush, those human restrictions."[71] (Dante speaks of theology as queen of the sciences and of them as her *ancille* at II, xiv, 20, but we hear little of her in the rest of the work, and there is no promise of any ulterior extended treatment, which probably would have been made if the work were eventually to have encompassed so exalted a subject.) The absent parts of the work, as well as Dante's reasons for leaving them unwritten, are irretrievably lost from our knowledge. Yet one passage does seem to promise at least a possible plan for what virtues were to be included (it seems dubious that Dante would have returned to the Lady Philosophy–Beatrice conflict, the *amor* of his formulation at I, i, 14, since it had been resolved by discussion in the second and third treatises). In the second half of the commentary to the third canzone, Dante lists the eleven moral virtues (IV, xvii, 4–6) put forward by Aristotle in his *Ethics*. Were these to be the subjects of the missing eleven trattati, one of them for each? Fortitude, Temperance, and Justice are all named, and the absence of Prudence is explained by Dante's statement that Aristotle considered it not a moral but an intellectual virtue (IV, xvii, 8). Is this chapter the guidepost to the eventual content of the work? It is possible, but only if Dante wanted to confine his subject to the moral virtues, of which the *Ethics* speaks (IV, xvii, 2). While these "fanno l'uomo beato, o vero felice" (make a man blessed, or truly happy—IV, xvii, 8) in the active life, Dante immediately goes on to speak of the higher contemplative life. Would the rest of *Convivio* have been limited to concerns with the active life? It is certainly possible. But we can say no more than that.

What, then, of the four parts that we do possess? They in fact form a work that has a certain sense of completeness. If Dante had left no precise record in the text of his vaster design, we would probably make more of *Convivio* than most currently do. For here is the first major extended literary project undertaken by Dante since around 1293. Few great writers have left so long an interval between their major efforts. This is not meant to downplay the accomplishment displayed in some of the intervening lyrics (the petrose, for example, are among the great lyric poems we have in Italian—or in any Western language), but only to underscore the seriousness with which Dante must have contemplated the choice of subjects for the vast canvas of *Convivio*. It, too, traverses a sea that offers "offers no passage for a little bark" ("non è pareggio da picciola barca"—*Par.* XXIII, 67).

The form of the whole as well as of the parts, as has been demonstrated by Simonelli, is significantly based on the number fifteen: fifteen treatises, each of the three that serve as commentaries also divided into fifteen chapters (II and III) or the sum of two fifteens (IV, which has thirty chapters). It is curious that Dante, who clearly did "number" his chapters,[72] as he had not in *Vita nuova* (where there is no reference to the actual or potential numeration of either prose or verse elements), allowed the first treatise to escape similar numerical ordination. (This fact may support a view that *Convivio* I and II are separated in time.) Simonelli's observations nonetheless remain inviting and probably convincing. Dante was not one to remain deaf to the call of numbers.

The introductory treatise has two extended aims, Dante's self-defense for speaking of himself (ii–iv) and for employing the vernacular in his prose commentaries (v–xiii). It begins, however, not defensively, but aggressively. Dante's pride at times reaches a level approaching or perhaps exceeding arrogance. Concluding the lengthy digression describing our earth, its elements, and the revolution of the sun, he turns to his flagging readers with the following characterization of their intellectual capacity (III, v, 22): "E voi a cui utilitade e diletto io scrivo, in quanta cechitade vivete, non levando li occhi suso a queste cose, tenendoli fissi nel fango de la vostra stoltezza!" (And you for whose profit and delight I am writing, in what great blindness do you lead your lives, not raising your sight to these things but keeping it fixed upon the mud of your stupidity!). Since God has formed us to seek our own perfection, and since knowledge is the ultimate perfection of our soul, in knowledge lies our ultimate happiness (a formulation that might not find favor with the author of the later *Comedy*). Leaving behind the herd of the ignorant, our author, having had time and occasion for study, not at the banquet table where the bread of angels is consumed,

but on the floor beneath, where the leavings from that banquet
have fallen from the lips of those who have so fed, will share that
knowledge with us in the form of meat (his canzoni) and bread
(his commentaries upon them). Thus Aristotle (with his inevitable companions, Albertus Magnus and St. Thomas)[73] comes
to the fore as the prime philosophical authority, while Solomon
looms as the major biblical presence behind this text. Having
established his purpose, Dante, as is his wont, inscribes the title
of his work near its beginning (see, by way of comparison, *Vita
nuova* I, 1; *De vulgari Eloquentia* I, i, 1; and *Monarchia* I, i, 5) but
does so in a way unique in his writings, by coupling it with that
of an earlier composition.

> E se ne la presente opera, la quale è Convivio nomi-
> nata e vo' che sia, più virilmente si trattasse che ne
> la Vita nuova, non intendo però a quella in parte
> alcuna derogare, ma maggiormente giovare per
> questa quella; veggendo sì come ragionevolmente
> quella fervida e passionata, questa temperata e virile
> esser conviene.

> (And if the present work, which is called *The
> Banquet,* just as I wish it to be, deals with its subject
> more maturely than did *The New Life,* it is none-
> theless not my intention to contravene the latter in
> any respect, but to support it in major ways with
> this one, since, where that work was understandably
> ardent and impassioned, it is fitting that this one be
> restrained and mature—I, i, 16).[74]

Here we find Dante, around 1304, looking back to the work he
had probably finished and circulated by 1294. Thus does he himself acknowledge the importance of *Vita nuova* and the balance
he needs to establish between the two projects, a major task of
the second and third treatises. He is content to consider *Vita*

nuova, written "a l'entrata de la mia gioventute" (at the beginning of my youth—I, i, 17), as a valid but less mature work, for this one is being written with that stage of his life behind him. Dante, having now passed the "colmo de la vita mia" (the midpoint of my life—I, iii, 4), regards *Convivio* as the more serious work. If it was the dolce stil novo that characterized the breakthrough writing found in "Donne ch'avete" and some of the other poems in praise of Beatrice, he now must seek a "più alto stilo" (higher style) in his commentary, to make it weightier and filled with greater authority ("per la quale paia di maggiore autoritade"—I, iv, 13).

The lengthy self-defense that fills the rest of the first treatise is clearly articulated. First Dante must cleanse his "bread" of two "accidental" apparent defects: his speaking of himself (I, ii) and the possibly too deep or difficult exposition of his poems. If the work is inscribed beneath the philosophy of Aristotle and the Scholastic method of St. Thomas (IV, xxx, 3, where Dante specifically mentions the *Summa contra Gentiles*), it finds its first models in Boethius and Augustine.[75] The example of Boethius serves as pretext insofar as Dante has also been unjustly accused; that of Augustine might also, insofar as his development from bad to good, from good to better, and from better to best, as recorded in his *Confessions,* would seem to parallel Dante's own record of his similar development. The Augustinian example might suggest this sequence, in Dante's case: the initial love for Beatrice (Cavalcantian lament), the second stage of that love (Guinizzellian praise), and the eventual affection for the donna gentile. These rather glorious precursors, Boethius and Augustine, more than excuse Dante and offer worthy models for his first two endeavors: namely, to escape infamy for having turned to the donna gentile, his feelings for whom will be revealed not as "passion" but as "virtue" (*Convivio* I, ii, 15-17); and to teach what others cannot teach (I, ii, 15). Next, he excuses himself for the seeming difficulty of his expositions (I, iii–iv). These "accidental" and apparent defects once disposed of, he can turn to a "substantial" objection—that is, one that is based on a real condition, his use of the vernacular in the prose part of the work. It is striking that he does not resort to the example of *Vita nuova* in making this defense, for it might have served him well. The rest of the first treatise is entirely devoted to a defense of his Italian prose commentary (where *De vulgari Eloquentia* will be devoted to a defense of his use of Italian in verse, a crucial distinction not observed by all who find this aspect of the two works contradictory).

Dante's *défense et illustration de la prose italienne* runs to some fifteen pages in a compact printing unadorned by notes. It is set under three headings (I, v, 2). He has chosen Italian rather than Latin out of a desire to avoid ordering things inappropriately (v–vii), out of generosity of spirit (viii–ix), and out of his natural love for his native tongue (x–xiii). It is the first of these arguments that has understandably received the most attention, both because of its greater pertinence to the actual choice between the two languages and because of its apparent lack of congruence with what Dante says in *De vulgari Eloquentia,* the work promised, indeed in this very argument (I, v, 10: "un libello ch'io intendo di fare, Dio concedente, di Volgare Eloquenza"—and thus, perhaps for the first time, the title of that work resounded in the world in Italian, not in Latin). The argument, if casuistic, is not difficult to follow. Because in the order of things a servant should be subject, obedient to his master, and because the commentary is, as it were, in service to the canzoni, it may not be in Latin. For Latin is noble (permanent and not corruptible, while the vernacular is corruptible and ever-changing), competent (Latin can express concepts the vernacular cannot), and beautiful (Latin follows the rules of art; the vernacular follows usage). Thus Dante employs negative arguments to defend his use of Italian in his prose in order the better to serve his verse. (We might wonder, if we took the argument at face value, why he did not translate the canzoni into Latin, for then he could have written Latin commentary to them.) His next two defenses are a good deal more positive. The vernacular allows him to reach more people, to be of greater use, and to offer a gift where none was requested. But it is when he puts forth his love for his native tongue (x–xiii) that we find the most positive reasons for his choice, culminating in the last sentence of the introductory treatise, where his affection for Italian prose is expressed in the following forceful terms: "Questo sarà luce nuova, sole nuovo, lo quale surgerà là dove l'usato tramonterà, e darà lume a coloro che sono in tenebre e in oscuritade, per lo usato sole che a loro non luce" (This [commentary] shall be a new light, a new sun, one that shall rise where the old one shall set and give light to those who live in shadow and darkness because the old sun does not shine upon them — I, xiii, 12). Discussion of the rest of *Convivio* continues after that of *De vulgari Eloquentia*.

De vulgari Eloquentia

Dating the composition of *De vulgari Eloquentia* in relation to that of *Convivio* is difficult. Since Dante's concerns for Italian prose, which conclude the first treatise, may have been what triggered his turning to the question of vernacular eloquence in verse, it seems reasonable to turn to *De vulgari Eloquentia* at this juncture. In any case, it is well to consider the Latin work in close conjunction with the defense of Italian prose put forth in *Convivio* I. If one follows the precisions of Barbi and of Petrocchi, Dante began *Convivio* in 1304 and finished the fourth treatise in 1307. The dating of *De vulgari Eloquentia* has been generally located as sometime between 20 August 1302 and February 1305, but there is no certainty to be had in this matter. (Corti has argued for dating the first three treatises of *Convivio* to 1303–4, the last to 1306–8, and *De vulgari Eloquentia* to between 1304 and 1306.[76]) It seems clear that *De vulgari Eloquentia* was written while Dante was composing *Convivio*. It is difficult to be sure, however, whether it is a companion to the first treatise or was written in the interlude between the third and fourth, as he changed the direction of his project.[77] This discussion assumes no position in response to that question, despite the fact that it engages *De vulgari Eloquentia* where it does.

Like his Dominicans and Franciscans in the heaven of the Sun in *Paradiso*, who praise the members of the other order rather than the members of their own, Dante praises Latin in Italian, Italian in Latin. The manuscript tradition, described fully by Mengaldo, is sparse: only three significant manuscripts have come down through the years.[78] It is rather doubtful that Dante circulated the work himself, though we do find reference to some of its *dicta*, first in Giovanni del Virgilio, in Dante's lifetime, then in Pietro di Dante, and most extensively in Boccaccio.[79] Still, that Dante refers to it in *Convivio* and that he seems to have disseminated some of his other work even before it was completed might account for a certain circulation. And, as was the case for *Convivio*, the fragmentary nature of the text would probably have given pause to some who might have seen it. It was translated into Italian by Trissino in 1529 and published in Latin only in 1577, in Paris. In short, as important as it seemed to Dante as he began to compose it, it did not become important for the vast majority of his readers until the sixteenth century.

The intended scope and contents of the work, which was broken off in mid-sentence near the end of the second book, are not clear. All we can say is that Dante planned at least four books. Yet he never gives any indication of what the subject of the third book was to have been, although he does make plain that the fourth was to discuss comedy,[80] and thus the low and middle style (as opposed to tragedy and the high style, discussed in the second book). We can therefore surmise that the third book was to have contained more about the *vulgare illustre*,[81] but we have little sense of what was left for him to say on that subject. Whatever else we may think about this text, however, what we have of it allows us to see that it is relentlessly self-promoting.

One of the major problems left us by *De vulgari Eloquentia* is to ascertain—as is also the case for *Convivio*—how much the pronouncements Dante makes about poetry should be understood as governing his thoughts on this subject when he composed the *Comedy*. It is probably not wise, in any case, to assume that Dante later agrees with everything he says in his treatise on eloquence in the vernacular.

The lengthy (eighty-two-word) opening period of the work weighs heavily on its reader. Beginning with the at least partially correct insistence that no one before him had ever made clear the *doctrina* of vernacular speech (true for Italian, if not for French and Provençal), Dante allows himself, despite the thoroughly elitist stance he will strike throughout the text, democratic vistas. He pledges to bring light to those who "tanquam ceci ambulant per plateas" (wander through the town square like blind men). This *discretio* that he proposes to offer to all, including women and children (he hedges by adding, "as far as their natures allow"), is similar to that promised at *Convivio* IV, viii, 1. He now hopes to be of help to the unlettered, that is, those without Latin, *vulgares gentes* (in *Convivio* I, ix, 5, he refers to those who are "volgari e non litterati"). Speaking in the formal first-person plural of scholastic discourse, which is dropped only unusually for *ego*,[82] Dante makes a remarkable claim. He will perform this task "Verbo aspirante de celis" (aided by the Word that breathes down from heaven). For Dante's presentation of Jeremiah as being inspired by God when he wrote his Lamentations, see Epistle XI, 2: "mentem Deo dignam viri prophetici per Spiritum Sanctum sua iussione impressit" (impressed the prophet's mind, worthy of God, at the bidding of the Holy Spirit). All those who believe that the *Comedy* is put forward under a disguised claim to have been inspired by divine revelation here find a less hidden claim, yet one that is generally neglected or treated as a mere gesture.[83] Dante will fill this great cup ("tantum poculum") for us not only with his own genius but with the best of the thoughts of others, to present us with "dulcissimum ydromellum," the honey of this second "convivio."

He proceeds to define the vernacular as the speech that infants, once they begin to articulate sounds, learn without benefit of grammatical rules, from those who nurse them, "sine omni regula nutricem imitantes" (I, i, 2). This form of speech is immediately distinguished from "locutio secondaria nobis, quam Romani gramaticam vocaverunt" (another tongue of secondary importance, that the Romans called "grammar"—I, i, 3). And here we are confronted by the contradiction of what Dante says in *Convivio* I, v-xiii, in which discussion he states, as part of his argument for his use of the vernacular in prose commentary, that Latin is not subservient to but sovereign over Italian "per la [sua] nobilità e per vertù e per bellezza" (by its nobility, its power, and its beauty— *Convivio* I, v, 7). Now, however, Dante seems to reverse himself: "Nobilior est vulgaris" (*De vulgari Eloquentia* I, ii, 4). To insist that there is no flat-out contradiction between the two passages would be disingenuous; however, to argue that the contradiction is of little concern to us and probably was of little to Dante himself, is another matter. This likelihood is enhanced by Dante's intention, announced as he looks up from this page of *Convivio* at us, to write a book about this unstable and corruptible vernacular, "di Volgare Eloquenza" (*Convivio* I, v, 10). Surely Dante knew that *Di Volgare Eloquenza* would elevate the vernacular above Latin, as indeed it does. We can say this not only because we sense it in his words whenever he speaks of the importance of the vernacular and its ability to rival or surpass Latin (for instance, in *Vita nuova* XXV), but because in *Convivio* I he ends up championing the vernacular in words even more excited and pugnacious than those we find in *De vulgari Eloquentia*.

In short, the only reason Dante says in *Convivio* I that "grammatical" speech is more noble, competent, and beautiful than the vernacular is to justify not using it in his "humble" commentary to his own vernacular poems. This limiting context does not merely modify the statement; it controls it. As we have seen, the second and third arguments for his use of vernacular in *Convivio* I, viii–xii, are entirely positive and contain no laudatory remarks about Latin at all. This first one is, as is plain, a negative argument, as though to say, to those who are disturbed by his use of Italian in a commentary on his own poems, that his use of Italian is more appropriate than the use of Latin would have been. The tactic is astute, partly because it takes our mind off what might be our strongest objection, namely that Dante should have dared to shape an encyclopedic treatise on love and virtue out of his own commentaries to his own poems. Instead, we are asked to quibble over whether Latin or Italian is the more fitting linguistic vehicle for his purpose. And if, as he composed those words, he should have happened to envision a doubting Thomas, we can imagine him addressing his imagined interlocutor with the words that Walt Whitman later addressed to his reader in *Leaves of Grass:* "Do I contradict myself? Very well then, I contradict myself."

Now it is the vernacular language of poetry that is Dante's subject, and it is, like the odes of *Convivio*, sovereign, not subject. As such, it is "nobilior," and for three reasons. It was the first language used by humankind; it is universal (whereas we are asked to believe that Latin or Greek or any other grammatical speech is local to certain cultures, vernacular is presented as a single universal speech—a casuistic but charming notion); it is natural, while grammar is artificial. This brief introduction (twenty-seven lines of Latin prose) serves to clarify the intentions of the perhaps prideful but nonetheless dedicated servant of the new literary vernacular that has up to that point enjoyed only little more than a century and a half of somewhat precarious life (*Vita nuova* XXV, 4). The rest of the first book of the treatise clarifies Dante's project. Speech, the property of humans, not of angels or beasts (I, ii, 2), has as its purpose "nostre mentis enucleare aliis conceptum" (to evince for others what our mind has conceived), a notion seconded not only by *Convivio*, "lo sermone . . . è ordinato a manifestare lo concetto umano" (language is ordained to make plain human conceiving—I, v, 12) but by many passages in which the word *concetto*, in its various forms, appears in the *Comedy*. (The words *concepire* and *concetto* are used seventeen times in the *Comedy*, fifteen of those in *Paradiso*, and indeed seven times in the last five cantos of that *cantica*, thus emphasizing their ascending importance as the poet's ability to conceive God's plan increases.) The nature of human intellect falling between that of the superverbal angels and that of the subverbal beasts, we communicate with other humans by signs that reflect our resemblance to the classes of beings both above and beneath us: "aliquod rationale signum et sensuale" (a certain sign at once rational and sensory—I, iii, 2), reflecting our very being, part angelic reason, part bestial instinct. These two chapters set the stage for what may seem to be a digression, discussion of the identity of the first human speaker.[84]

Reflecting a habit of mind of medieval encyclopedists that such writers as Rabelais and Cervantes would later greatly enjoy ridiculing, Dante turns back to the beginning. Who was the first human speaker? Genesis clearly indicates that it was Adam, when he named the beasts (2:19–20); only later (3:2–3) does Eve speak, responding to the serpent. For not the only time in his works Dante, finding his theory obstructed by the biblical account of events, rewrites Scripture, first bypassing the speech in which Adam named the animals (Gen. 2:19-20) and then disregarding the words spoken by his mate (I, ii, 6). Even if the Bible records as a fact Eve's precedence in speech, it is only reasonable to believe, says Dante, that Adam, not Eve, was the first speaker (I, iv, 2-3). Now, having added a text to Genesis, he embellishes it. Adam's first word was *El*, God's name pronounced in joy (I, iv, 4). Dante's consideration of the first speaker and the first language spoken, from its origin in innocence and joy to its fall in sin and sadness, occupies the first four chapters in what we must understand as Dante's attempt to establish his own version of the history of human language. As soon as the divine *afflatus* breathed in him (as it now breathes in Dante, we have been asked to believe), Adam responded by naming his Creator (I, v, 1). This he did perhaps before he was placed in the Earthly Paradise (I, v, 3). Now, in a brief digression, Dante asserts that each of us regards his own homeland as the most noble in the world and his "materna locutio" (mother tongue—the "parlar materno" of *Purg.* XXVI, 117) as identical with that first spoken by Adam (I, vi, 2).

As for Dante himself, despite his love for the city that has unjustly exiled him, he must testify that there exist, on the authority of the poets and other writers, many cities more noble than Florence and at least one language more pleasant and useful than Italian (I, vi, 3). It seems a strange sentiment in light of the claims to be made for Italian later on. However, the reference, most likely to French, given the words used to describe that language at I, x, 2, "facilior et delectabilior," seems to be an acknowledgment only that Italian, in its current condition, is inferior to French. Such a view is entirely consistent with his plan to reform Italian and make it worthy, as he claims it is destined to be. Returning to the main thrust of his argument, he asserts that Adamic speech remained intact through the sons of Heber so that Christ would speak in unfallen Hebrew, the language of the first created human being ("lingua gratie"), and not in "lingua confusionis" (I, vi, 5–6). Indeed, all would speak in the same Adamic vernacular had our race not suffered a linguistic "fall" to match the sin of Adam and Eve. The first sinner in this respect is the giant Nimrod (I, vii, 4), made centrally responsible for the confusion of tongues described in Gen. 11:7, which afflicted, in Dante's view of human activities as expressed from the standpoint of the guildsman, each order of the workers joined in the effort to build the tower of Babel. The happy few who escaped the linguistic consequences were those absent from the work and who derided it, the sons and daughters of Shem, Noah's third son (I, vii, 8). The subsequent diaspora populates northern and southern Europe, and Greece (I, viii, 2). The southern Europeans are divided into three large linguistic groups, the third of which receives Dante's fullest attention; it too is divided into three: "Yspani, Franci et Latini," with their respective ways of saying "yes," *oc, oïl,* and *sì.* This "ydioma tripharium" (triform speech) was once a single tongue, as its many basic words in common attest (I, viii, 5).

Having finished his speculative "history of the language," Dante devotes the rest of his first book (ix–xix) to more practical concerns, and these involve only the three European vernaculars *oc, oïl,* and *sì.* Their babelic condition (I, vi–x) explains why grammar became necessary: "que quidem gramatica nichil aliud est quam quedam inalterabilis locutionis ydemptitas diversibus temporibus atque locis" (which grammatical speech is nothing but a kind of inalterable language, unchanging no matter what the time or place). The brevity of the discussion of grammaticized language underscores Dante's determination to concentrate on the virtues of the vernacular. The argument put forward here so briefly (I, ix, 11) occupies three chapters in *Convivio* (I, v–vii), where Latin is praised as part of the negative argument that establishes the rightness of composing the commentary in Italian. Here, in three sentences, Dante puts forward Latin's invariable nature and its *auctoritas*. But it is not Latin that is chiefly on his mind; he wants to establish the superior literary worth of a single branch of the *ydioma tripharium*, Italian. From the outset it is clear that this is the tongue that will win the three-sided battle: it is presented as having been granted a certain preeminence by the founders of Latin grammar, whose word for "yes," *sic*, is closer to the Italian *sì* than to "yes" words in the other Romance tongues (I, x, 1). Dante then turns his attention to French, but only to French prose—historical works blending deeds found in the Bible with those of the Trojans and the Romans (for example, *Histoire ancienne jusqu'à César, Fet des Romains* [Mengaldo]), the beautiful adventures of King Arthur (such as the prose *Lancelot* and *Mort Artu* [Mengaldo]), and other historical or doctrinal works (for example, *Doctrina de compondre dictatz,* and *Doctrina d'acort,* not to mention Brunetto Latini's *Tresor* [Mengaldo]). It might seem strange that the author of *Il Fiore* and *Il Detto d'Amore* would not wish to mention the great source for these works, *Le Roman de la Rose,* or any other French works of poetry. This may be the result merely of his program here—he wants to avoid the problem of French primacy in poetry—or of a decisive change of heart with regard to French culture.[85] Or it may be that Dante's acquaintance with French lyric production was as limited as he here seems to indicate.[86] The question is an important one and requires further study. At the same time, one must observe that the treatment of French poetry in *De vulgari Eloquentia* is minimal. The king of Navarre is mentioned as the author of the canzone "De fin amor si vient sen et bonté" (I, ix, 3; II, v, 4) and of "Ire d'amor que en mon cor repaire" (II, vi, 6—but that poem is actually by Gace Brulé [Mengaldo]). He is the only French poet who is allowed to enter the assemblage of poets in the pages of *De vulgari Eloquentia*.

Turning to the language of *oc,* now clearly Provençal and not "Spanish" (as is further confirmed at II, xii, 3: "dico Yspanos qui poetati sunt in vulgari *oc*"), he says that the first practitioners of vernacular eloquence can claim as their tongue one that is more perfect and sweet (than French), offering Petrus de Alvernia as the first exemplar (I, x, 2). And then it is the turn of Italian, seen as affirming its own superiority by bettering *oc* on two grounds: In its service are some who have written more sweetly and subtly; it is written in greater accord with the rules of grammar. In *Vita nuova* XXV Dante had claimed for his Italian verse the same powers as the "grammatical" poets enjoyed. His claim here is still more emphatic, especially since it is conjoined with his boast of his own importance. Italian is superior because "qui dulcius subtiliusque poetati vulgariter sunt, hi familiares et domestici sui sunt, puta Cynus Pistoriensis et amicus eius" (those who have written poems in the vernacular most sweetly and subtly, like Cino of Pistoia and his friend, are its familiars and servants—I, x, 2). It is clear that Dante's "bella scola moderna" has changed its membership. The old "sweet style" featured Cavalcanti as "primo amico"; the new style fosters Cino in that role. Only he and "his friend"—our not-so-modest essayist (notwithstanding his preference for the first person plural) uses that locution for himself throughout the work—are seen as having achieved the height of lyric eloquence. Once the claim is lodged, Dante proceeds with his description of modern-day Italian poetry.

Dividing Italy at the Apennines so that it has a right and left side (as it faces us), Dante reviews the fourteen vernaculars of the western parts of the peninsula, from Rome to Sardinia, and finds them all lacking. The only partial exceptions he makes are for Sicily and Apulia. Sicily has shown, in some of its poetry and in some of its princes (Frederick II and Manfred), genuine nobility of spirit (I, xii, 2–4).[87] In both places the writers best demonstrating eloquence (Guido delle Colonne, Giacomo da Lentini, and Rinaldo d'Aquino) are presented as having departed from the local vernacular (I, xii, 9). As a result, we cannot say that the vernaculars themselves are *illustres*. Turning to his former homeland, Dante excoriates its speech. Guittone d'Arezzo, Bonagiunta da Lucca, Gallo Pisano, Mino Mocato da Siena, and Brunetto (Latini) of Florence are accused of writing not of *curialia* but of *municipalia* (I, xiii, 1). Dante then offers five examples of popular forms of this municipal speech, drawn from the five cities of the five writers he has just named (I, xiii, 2). Ranged against these five and their *turpiloquio* are three Florentines and one Pistoian: Guido Cavalcanti, Lapo Gianni, "unum alium" (Dante), and Cino (I, xiii, 4). That only four "good poets" are named from Tuscany probably underlines the care in Dante's choice, for his usual concern with balanced lists would have urged him to single out for mention the same number of positive as of negative figures. We can be fairly certain that Dante had given careful thought to both lists.

He now turns to eastern Italy and, in a single chapter, dispenses with Romagna (Forlì, Faenza, Brescia, Verona, Padua, Treviso) and Venice (I, xiv). What is left in Dante's survey of the peninsula? Trento, Turin, and Alessandria, all of which are "border cities" with mixed, corrupted speech; their inhabitants cannot be said to speak a true Italian (I, xv, 7). It is allowed that the Bolognese speak the most beautiful Italian, if only by comparison with everyone else. For had their language been "aulicum et illustre" (royal and illustrious), the good poets of Bologna would not have had to depart from it in their poems, as they had in fact done (I, xv, 6). And here Dante refers to Guido Guinizzelli as the greatest poet of that city, along with three others (Guido Ghisliere, Fabruzzo, and Onesto), this group of four paralleling the Tuscan foursome that is presented as superior to it (I, xiii, 4). Thus Guinizzelli, "maximus Guido Guinizelli," is given very high praise indeed, as he always is in Dante's references to him, but not the highest, which is reserved for Cino and for Dante himself.

Still on the hunt for the "panther" (I, xvi, 1) of the illustrious vernacular through the hills and dales of Italy, Dante has found that its scent is in every city but that it dwells in none. And thus the language that is at once "illustre, cardinale, aulicum et curiale" (illustrious, selective, royal, and courtly—I, xvi, 6) remains for Dante to define. It is clear that we have been led on a "wild panther chase." Our panther will be a beast of Dante's own devising. He spends the next two chapters defining the four terms. "Illustre" (xvii) is that quality which, wrapped in light, enlightens all it falls upon. Not surprisingly, examples of *illustres,* in addition to Seneca and Numa Pompilius, as philosopher and wise ruler, respectively, are Cino and Cino's "friend." The second pair may be in parallel relation to the first, for we shall eventually discover that Cino is presented as the poet of intellectual love; Dante, of rectitude. The following chapter (xviii) defines the other three key terms, *cardinale* as derived from *cardo,* the hinge on which swings the "door of language," admitting and excluding the fit and unfit tongues of Italy, so that the whole herd (*grex*) of municipal vernaculars moves and halts according to its pivotal movement; *aulicum* as the de facto "royal house" of Italy, which has no king besides its language; *curiale,* in similar fashion, as the true "court" of Princess Italy. The first book concludes with the praise of the *doctores illustres* (the illustrious teachers) who have already created that language. We should reflect that such praise is primarily self-praise, that the sweet-smelling panther we seek has already been found, leaving his scent in city after city, yet dwelling in none. Dante never uses his own name in this work. But it is clear that he is the panther whom we seek.

The second book of *De vulgari Eloquentia* begins with the observation that the "latinum vulgare illustre" may make its presence known in prose as well as in verse (II, i, 1). However, since writers of prose take their cues from poets, and not vice versa, Dante will first deal with poetry. His words do not make it clear whether he meant to take up the question of prose in *De vulgari Eloquentia* at length (he does devote part of one chapter to it— II, vi, 2-5). But we surely remember that in *Convivio* he gave over most of the first treatise to the defense of Italian prose. In a sense, if the composition of *Convivio* I preceded that of *De vulgari Eloquentia*, as seems probable, he had already supplied that treatment. That he, perhaps strangely, does not refer it in this passage, as one might well have expected him to do, lends support to those who argue that *De vulgari Eloquentia* was written earlier than (or early in the composition of) *Convivio*.

The vulgare illustre is not open to all, but must be exercised by a qualified élite, just as the best horses require the best riders— those in whom reside, in their *conceptiones,* "scientia et ingenium" (II, i, 8). To the select nature of these hypothetical writers is joined the select nature of their potential subjects (II, i, 1). Whether all subjects are worthy of being treated in the vulgare illustre ("utrum omnia ipso tractanda sint aut non") is a question, answered in the negative, that leads to a brief excursus on *dignitas* (II, ii, 2-5). The three potential subjects for the vulgare illustre reflect a familiar medieval topos, the three souls possessed by every human being, a subject frequent enough in many a writer, and surely in Dante.[88] The vegetative soul pursues the useful; the animal soul pursues the pleasurable; the rational soul pursues the *honestum.* The three souls are associated, then (in order), with plants, beasts, and angels (II, ii, 6). They in turn are redefined as self-preservation (*salus*), sexual pleasure (*venus*), and virtue (*virtus*). These are the three *magnalia* of the vulgare illustre, now still further defined as "armorum probitas, amoris accensio et directio voluntatis" (prowess at arms, ardor in love, and uprightness of the will—II, ii, 7). Who are the practitioners of these three magnalia?

	Provençal	*Italian*
arma:	Bertran de Born	———
amor:	Arnaut Daniel	Cino da Pistoia
rectitudo:	Giraut de Bornelh	Cino's friend (Dante)

Dante concludes by emphasizing that no Italian has yet written of arms (II, ii, 8), a lacuna that Boccaccio will gratefully seize the occasion to fill with his *Teseida* (XII, lxxxiv, 6–8), perhaps thinking he had already begun to do so with his *Filostrato*. The composition of his own that Dante presents as exemplary is the recent "Doglia mi reca." He is now the poet of moral virtue that he will be again in *Convivio* IV, a congruence that lends potential support to the view that *De vulgari Eloquentia* and *Convivio* IV were composed during roughly the same period and are to be considered companions.

What are the formal metrical requirements of the vulgare illustre? Of canzoni, ballate, and sonnetti, only the first form is deemed worthy (II, iii, 3). As for the second two, they will be treated when Dante offers his discussion of the *vulgare mediocre* in the (unwritten) fourth book. Now he turns to the definition of poetry itself, arrogating to vernacular rhymers the distinguished Latin term *poeta* (as he has already done in *Vita nuova* XXV, 4 and 7). *Poesis* is nothing other than "fictio rethorica musicaque poita" (fashioning expressed in verse following the laws of rhetoric and music—II, iv, 2). This definition has caused disagreement among dantisti. Does Dante intend us to understand that poems are fictive, literally untrue? Or does he mean only that they are "made," and may thus be constructed of reality, as it were?[89] Some, encouraged by Dante's claims in the *Comedy* (to leave aside what is said in the letter to Cangrande) to have the power to reveal literal truth, incline toward the second reading. However, given what he says of allegory in *Convivio* II, i, and his allegorizing in *Convivio* II and III, which, precisely, reveals him treating his poems as fictions (whether we consider them so or not), it is difficult to believe that a word that has such importance in Dante's discussions of poetry does not here mean exactly what it seems to mean. No matter what "history," what *facta*, may constitute the occasions for his *poesis*, when the writer makes his poem, it is he who creates its *fictio*. This is not to say that the author of the *Comedy* is constrained by this definition (he may be), but only that the author of *De vulgari Eloquentia* is.[90]

Realizing that he has (again, as he did in *Vita nuova* XXV) transgressed a boundary by equating *dicitori per rima* (writers of verse) and *poetae*, he immediately considers the distinction between great poets (*magni poetae*) and himself (and perhaps his fellow practitioners of the illustrious vernacular): the former use words and an art of writing both of which are governed by rules, exactly what had been lacking in the tradition of the vernacular—the reason, we understand readily enough, for his composing *De vulgari Eloquentia*, with its rules for the inclusion and exclusion of certain words and for establishing the groundwork for the illustrious vernacular. And so, rather than forget or reject the great Latin poets, Dante wants to imitate them: "quantum illos proximius imitemur, tantum rectius poetemur. Unde nos doctrine operi intendentes doctrinatas eorum poetrias emulari oportet" (the more closely we imitate them, the more apt our poetizing. As for us, then, who aim at creating a doctrinal work, we must emulate their poems, which are rich in doctrine). The passage (II, iv, 3), if it may be seen as also referring to others who compose in the vulgare illustre, is meant to refer principally to his own work, which he has just associated with "rectitude." The phrase "nos doctrine operis intendentes" would clearly seem to refer to Dante's own moral canzoni and to nothing else. He then (II, iv, 4) refers to Horace's *Ars poetica*, vv. 38–40, a passage he will also cite in *Paradiso* XXIII, 64–66, in such a way as to make the reader once more aware that in enunciating his general precepts, he has a most particular poetic career in mind: his own.

His next subject is the possible style of the poems to be written in the vulgare illustre. (Here, and in almost every discussion of what the illustrious vernacular must be if Dante can define it and then pursue it, we realize that the future tenses are employed incorrectly to the extent that Dante has already both defined and pursued it.) There are three possible styles to select from: tragedy, the higher style; comedy, the lower; elegy, still lower— the *stilus miserorum* (the style of those in misery). Dante's "wheel of styles," this *rota Dantis,* is based on ideas that were never developed as an entity, for his promise to deal with comedy in relation to tragedy in the fourth book, repeated here (II, iv, 6), was not kept. In order to make elegy the lowest style, he allows it only the low stylistic register, while comedy will at times make use of the middle, and at times the low, style. But it is tragedy that is his ultimate concern, and tragedy and the vulgare illustre are made coterminous (II, iv, 6). Indeed, the tragic style receives his full attention for the rest of the chapter (iv, 7–12). Tragedy is only truly present when seriousness of thought is matched by the magnificence of the verse, the height of the construction, and the excellence of the words.[91] This is the style in which one must sing "salus, amor et virtus" (arms, love, and virtue—II, iv, 8). Those who have the capacity to do so are few, and to be capable of such a lofty enterprise, they must have cultural and technical preparation. These are the ones whom the poet, in the sixth book of the *Aeneid,* calls "Dei dilectos et ab ardente virtute sublimatos ad ethera deorumque filios, . . . quanquam figurate loquatur" (the sons of the gods, those whom God has loved and raised up to the heavens because of their ardent virtue, . . . even if he is speaking figuratively). This is the first citation of Virgil (of only two, the other found at II, viii, 4) in the text, and it is found also in *Convivio* IV, xx, 4, in much less developed form. Seen in the light of the *Comedy,* the passage may seem to speak of a divinely chosen author. Here Dante pulls us back toward earth. Virgil, he says, speaks only figuratively. As the new Aeneas of literary Italian, Dante has a mission that, although it is inherited from Adam, is more circumscribed than it will be in the later poem.

Having discussed the necessary *gravitas* of the illustrious poet's subject, Dante, turning to the magnificence of his verse, defends the hendecasyllable as the most splendid poetic line (II, v). His practice is to list examples, here of the openings of canzoni, the form he is forced to choose, given his argument in II, iii. The exemplary poets are Giraut de Bornelh, the king of Navarre, Guido Guinizzelli, Guido delle Colonne, Rinaldo d'Aquino, Cino da Pistoia, and, unsurprisingly, Cino's friend, who somehow nearly always finds a way to be the culminating example of excellence in vernacular composition. Since Cino was almost certainly younger than Dante, we cannot imagine that the order of their mention is anything but deliberate. (This second self-citation is of the canzone "Amor, che movi tua virtù da cielo" ["Love, who send down your power from heaven"— *Rime* XL.)

The following chapter of *De vulgari Eloquentia* is dedicated to the construction of the tragic canzone, the order and effectiveness of words in statements. Moving from the childish *constructio* "Petrus amat multum dominam Bertam" (Peter loves very much mistress Bertha), Dante illustrates the mature construction of fully developed speech in the artificial, cadenced, and figurative language of the following aggressive and self-serving Latin sentence: "Eiecta maxima parte florum de sinu tuo, Florentia, nequicquam Trinacriam Totila secundus adivit" (Once the greater part of your blossoms, Florence, were torn from your breast, in vain did the second Totila make his way to Sicily—II, vi, 4). Dante's nasty reference to the French agent of his exile, Charles of Valois, and praise of himself as one of Florence's "fiori" reveal his serious playfulness. These examples lead to still others, once again the incipits of canzoni: Giraut, Folchetto di Marsiglia, Arnaut Daniel, Amerigo di Belenoi, Amerigo di Peguhlan, the king of Navarre, il Giudice di Messina, Guinizzelli, Cavalcanti, Cino, and the author of "Amor che ne la mente mi ragiona" (II, vi, 6). He could, he says, have offered examples from the *poetae regulati,* Virgil, Ovid (author of the *Metamorphoses*—in other words, the more illustrious Ovid), Statius, and Lucan, Dante's main precursors in "epic" in the *bella scola* of *Inferno* IV. These four "grammatical" poets are seconded by four other *regolati,* writers of prose: Livy, Pliny, Frontinus, and Orosius. The chapter's content is shaped chiastically:

> four examples of contemporary "constructed" Latin prose;
> eleven examples of "modern" canzoni;
> four examples of ancient Latin poets;
> four examples of ancient Latin prose writers.

This is the only chapter of *De vulgari Eloquentia* in which prose has a significant presence. It gives us some sense of the seriousness of purpose behind Dante's announced intention to speak of it (II, i, 1). The chapter, otherwise so aesthetically ordered, ends with a vicious swipe at Guittone d'Arezzo, ridiculed for his popularizing bent, revealing in Dante what a twentieth-century reader like Harold Bloom might refer to as anxiety of influence.[92]

The final topic announced in the discussion of the four aspects of the tragic style (II, iv, 7) is *excellentia vocabulorum* (the excellence of its words). The liveliness and particularity of Dante's treatment of the vocabulary allowed to the vulgare illustre (II, vii), while in fact fairly conventional in its adherence to various medieval handbooks on versification (as Mengaldo's notes demonstrate), has made it a favorite text of contemporary readers. From the vulgare illustre are proscribed the following sorts of words:

childish (*puerilia*)	*mamma, babbo* (and *mate, pate*)
	(mommy, daddy)
womanish (*muliebria*)	*dolciada, piacevole*
	(sweetness, pleasing)
rural (*silvestria*)	*greggia, cetra*
	(herd, lyre)
urban (*urbana*)	*femina, corpo*
	(woman, body)

Championing his vulgare illustre, Dante has already objected to certain "municipal" locutions in the Tuscan vernaculars. The first two words he offers as exemplary of Florentine barbarity are *manichiamo* (let's eat) and *introcque* (at the same time—I, xiii, 2). Yet each appears in the *Comedy* (*Inferno* XXXIII, 60; XX, 130). Now he adds eight more. Six of these eight words, specifically proscribed by the author himself, then appear in his masterwork, and not a few times: *mamma* (five), *babbo* (one); *greggia* (five), *cetra* (one); *femina* (five), *corpo* (fifty-six). What do we make of the fact that words here excised from the vulgare illustre appear a total of seventy-five times in the *Comedy?* It certainly would suggest that, however we eventually define the style of the *Comedy*, it is not likely to be the lofty style as it is defined here.

Having proscribed, Dante now turns his attention to some of the metrical feet, sounds, and words that are to be welcomed in the vulgare illustre (II, vii, 5-7). It is time to bind the gatherings of his harvest (II, viii, 1) in consideration of the canzone, the vehicle for vernacular eloquence in poetry, whether the "active" work the poet himself composes or the "passive" one that he or someone else recites once the work is finished (II, viii, 3-4). The canzone is represented by a sole exemplar, Dante's "Donne ch'avete intelletto d'amore" (II, viii, 8), and is discussed with regard to its stanzaic form (II, ix), its melody (II, x), its *habitudo* (disposition), or the relation between the melody and the rhyme (II, xi—exemplified by Dante's lost canzone "Traggemi de la mente amor la stiva" ("Love sets my mind to plow with him"— xi, 5), and further consideration of poetic meter (II, xii) and of rhyme (II, xiii), beginning with stanzas that make use of a series of unrhymed words, the sestina, with Arnaut Daniel and himself serving as the final exemplars to be recorded in the unfinished treatise, Dante represented by "Al poco giorno" ("To the short day"). Having sufficiently treated these two subjects, melody and division of parts of the canzone, he turns to the third and final one promised in II, ix, 4, "de numero carminum et sillabarum" (the number of verses and syllables—II, xiv). A dozen or so lines of text later *De vulgari Eloquentia* comes to its abrupt end.

We cannot say what we have lost. Like Aristotle's *Poetics*, Dante's unfinished treatise on poetry tells us about tragedy, but not about comedy, each author having promised exactly such an eventual discussion. What we would have learned might have been of great interest in our understanding of what he thought about the theory of comic expression in the poem called, indeed, *La comedìa*. But we cannot even be sure of that much, since Dante seems to have changed his mind about so many positions that he took in his earlier works when he later looked back to them. If he is anything, Dante is a reviser, a reshaper of earlier formulations, even to the point of contradiction. Perhaps the later poet who is most strikingly like him in this is Goethe, who is not only always changing, developing, but who makes that very change and development one of the important subjects of his work. Whether or not he said on his deathbed "nun kommt die Wandlung zu höheren Wandlungen" (now begins the change to higher changes)—the "standard version" has him dying at his desk, asking for "more light"—the characterization of his past writerly life as changeful seems right. And we should see that Dante's development, similarly, was extraordinarily changeful. Not only was he a poet in search of constant experiment, revealed in the strikingly diverse aspects of his work, as in the "sweet" canzoni composed alongside the petrose; he was also a writer who built a new substance out of earlier efforts almost every time he wrote. The prose of the *Vita nuova* supplies meanings for some of the earlier poems that do not seem to be easily extracted from the poems themselves; the prose of *Convivio* does so in still more striking manner; *Convivio* and *De vulgari Eloquentia* approach the question of language from apparently different or even contradictory positions; the *Comedy* frequently engages its precursors in the continuing process of growth and self-definition. If there is one thing of which we can be certain in the difficult task of trying to find consistency in this elusive writer, it is that we cannot point to an earlier statement in the expectation that it can explain a present one. Another tradition of deathbed utterance tells that Calderón's last words were, "Dante, why were you so difficult?" Whether or not the anecdote is true or not, the lament is fitting.

Convivio II and III

The next two trattati of *Convivio* are closely related and have numerous similarities. Each devotes eleven chapters to the literal exposition of a canzone of Dante's; each also devotes most of four others to an allegorical exposition of that poem;[93] and each, in keeping with the encyclopedic ambitions of its author, introduces significant digressions as part of each section of the commentary.[94] Further, each is significantly linked to *Vita nuova*, the second by clear references both in text and in gloss, the third less directly.

The last three trattati of *Convivio*, despite their close attention to the texts of the author's canzoni, are all heavily marked by digression. (At one point Dante, who frequently uses the word to describe his sallies into various fields of knowledge, acknowledges that "le mie digressioni sono lunghe"—IV, viii, 10.) With his wide range of subject areas, the author is present as something of a philosopher himself. It is difficult to form a list of these "digressioni," since they are at times brief additions to arguments, perhaps thrown in for the sake of establishing the writer's knowledge and thoroughness (for instance, the listing of the four cardinal virtues at IV, xxii, 11), whereas on other occasions they form extended essays that actually do reflect and continue the thought of the verse (for example, IV, xi–xiii, the excursus on the *viltà* [vileness] of riches, which expands on the thought "le divizie . . . vili son" [riches are vile]—vv. 49–51 of the canzone). In all, there are some thirty such passages in the work, "set pieces" that are not necessary for the explication or interpretation of the poems but that do open the horizons of the text to wider perspectives. This technique, seen rarely in *Vita nuova*, will serve Dante well and often when he composes the *Comedy*.

The first canzone of *Convivio*, "Voi che 'ntendendo il terzo ciel movete" ("O you who move the third heaven by intellection") is probably datable, by its stylistic characteristics, its subject, and the external evidence found in the gloss, to the period in which Dante wrote the four poems to the donna gentile of *Vita nuova* XXXV–XXXVIII, probably no earlier than 1293 and probably no later than early 1294. The canzone seems to be connected with the visit of Charles Martel to Florence later that year, since Charles refers to it in *Paradiso* VIII.[95] In every respect but one, it is a fitting companion to the poems (and to the commentary to them) about the donna gentile found in *Vita nuova:* it recounts not Dante's dubiety about his new love, but his yielding to her and forsaking Beatrice. That, even as he was writing about the new lady, he was having a difficult time deciding whether she should replace Beatrice in his affection is reflected in the companion sonnets (*Rime* LXXXIV and LXXXV), each of which takes a different view of the matter. In the climactic stanza of the canzone (vv. 40–52), a "spiritel d'amor gentile" (gentle spirit of love) assures Dante that he will now experience such lofty miracles ("sì alti miracoli") that he will speak the following words on behalf of his soul: "Amore, segnor verace, / ecco l'ancella tua; fa che ti piace" (Love, true lord, behold your handmaid; do as you please). These last two verses are left without comment twice, in both literal and allegorical gloss (*Convivio* II, x, 11; II, xv, 12). Surely the reader is led by such avoidance to supply one. The "miraculous" Beatrice has been replaced by a new miraculous lady; the true God has remetamorphosed into the god of Love; and Dante is called on to serve this new lady from now on. We thus have no difficulty in understanding why the poem could not be included in *Vita nuova*, even if it was written in time to be so. The canzone has retraced, now with a quite different result, the struggle between Dante's soul (his reason) and his heart (his appetite—*Vita nuova* XXXVIII, 5). But whereas in *Vita nuova* it is the heart's thought of the new lady which is *vilissimo* (most vile—XXXVIII, 4), now it is Dante's soul that is accused of being *vile* for holding back its affection from the donna gentile (*Convivio* II, i, v. 45). The process, which is a mirror image of that recorded in *Vita nuova* XXXVIII, has a totally different result, Beatrice losing out to the donna gentile in Dante's affection.

The literal exposition of the first stanza of the canzone is clear: Dante's soul (*anima*), still commending the memory of Beatrice, is assailed by the "spiritel novo d'amore" (*Vita nuova* XXXVIII, v. II), now referred to as "l'altro spirito" (the other spirit — *Convivio* II, vi, 8) in that "battle" between his thought of Beatrice and the new thought that opposes it (*Convivio* II, ii, 3), the language once again specifically reminiscent of *Vita nuova:* "la battaglia de' pensieri" (the battle between my thoughts — *Vita nuova* XXXVIII, 4). The triumph of the donna gentile is not, if we have *Vita nuova* in mind, as we are so clearly meant to, what we expect, given the insistence on the *viltà* of Dante's susceptibility to the allure of the new lady in *Vita nuova*. It is no wonder that the end of the canzone tells us that those who hear the poem will find its speech "faticosa e forte" (intricate and difficult). It is narrating, from the point of view of *Vita nuova,* the unthinkable. Reading the writing over the gate of hell in *Inferno* III and responding, we are led to believe, to its apparent command to abandon hope, the protagonist of the *Comedy* turns to Virgil to say, "Maestro, il senso lor m'è duro" (Master, for me their meaning is hard). Here Dante has his canzone proclaim itself "difficult" (*forte*) and explains, " 'forte,' dico, quanto a la novitade de la sentenza" (difficult, I say, with respect to the newness of its meaning — *Convivio* II, xi, 7). The allegorical exposition that will follow tells us that this was no lady who triumphed over his memory of Beatrice, but the study of philosophy. But we are still in the literal exposition, and this strange new meaning would seem to be pertinent to the literal sense itself: an explicit account of his abandonment of Beatrice for the lady at the window. This is a "hard" reading indeed, for Dante has previously assured us that, in *Convivio,* "non intendo però a quella [*Vita nuova*] in parte alcuna derogare, ma maggiormente giovare per questa quella" (I do not intend in any way, however, to contravene [the *Vita nuova*], but instead to lend it support —

I, i, 16). The question of this new lady's ontological status (was she a woman or an allegory of philosophy?) is crucial; and Dante gives us, as we have seen, absolutely no help in his commentaries to the poem in forging an answer. As Barbi, however, long ago pointed out, her *grandezza* (greatness—v. 47) makes an allegorical identity more likely, as *grande* was never used by Dante as an adjective to describe a mortal woman in one of his lyrics.[96]

The allegorical exposition (*Convivio* II, xii–xv) reveals what we could never have guessed from the pages of *Vita nuova*: the donna gentile represents or signifies the study of the lady of the philosophers Dante read after the death of Beatrice (*Convivio* II, xii, 6). The gloss goes on to explain how he spent some thirty months studying philosophy at the schools of the religious.[97] Dante offers a striking revisitation of the moment of inspiration for the first poem—as he will later proclaim—that he wrote in the "dolce stil novo" (*Vita nuova* XIX, 2; *Purg.* XXIV, 49–57): "Allora dico che la mia lingua parlò quasi come per se stessa mossa, e disse: 'Donne ch'avete intelletto d'amore' " (I say, then, that my tongue spoke as though it moved of its own initiative, and said, "Ladies who have understanding of love"). Now, moving from the thought of his love for Beatrice to that of his new lady, "quasi maravigliandomi apersi la bocca nel parlare de la proposta canzone" (as though marveling, I opened my mouth to speak the words of the canzone set forth above—*Convivio* II, xii, 8). Pernicone observes closely and well the elements within the poem that parallel those found in "Donne ch'avete."[98] "Voi che 'ntendendo" is thus presented as a similarly inspired latter-day account of Dante's "conversion" to the praise of his new beloved, and as De Robertis has pointed out,[99] of his rediscovery of the style of praise in the next "treatise" (III, i, 4). But now, for the first time in Dante's history of his affections we hear (twice) a new and crucial word: *fictitious* (*fittizia*—II, xii, 8 and 10). This is the first time, even in the exposition of this canzone, that we are asked to believe that the donna gentile was no lady at all. Dante the allegorist of philosophy has replaced Dante the historian of Beatrice. The ending of the trattato is triumphant in tone:

> E così, in fine di questo secondo trattato, dico e affermo che la donna di cu' io innamorai appresso lo primo amore fu la bellissima e onestissima figlia de lo imperadore de lo universo, a la quale Pittagora pose nome Filosofia.
>
> (And thus, at the conclusion of this second treatise, I say and affirm that the lady with whom I fell in love after my first love was the very beautiful and chaste daughter of the emperor of the universe, to whom Pythagoras gave the name Philosophy—II, xv, 12).

It is difficult to accept Dante's earlier claims that *Convivio* is not meant to take anything away from the praise of Beatrice that marked the pages of *Vita nuova* so indelibly.

Looking back at the second treatise from the beginning of his commentary in the third, Dante explains that it was in order to defend himself against those who might have blamed him for his flightiness in turning from his first love to another that he composed, or so he now explains, "Amor che ne la mente mi ragiona" ("Love, speaking in my mind"—III, i, 11). This canzone offers fewer difficulties to its interpreters in at least one particular: it is not itself in explicit rivalry with Beatrice. But its apparent literal sense is centrally involved with the god of love (who, as we have seen, reappears only when, in the final section of *Vita nuova*, Dante moves away from thoughts of the celestial Beatrice toward more earthbound feelings, whether for her, or more often, for the donna gentile). The second stanza, however, does offer several phrasings similar to those found in the sonnet "Tanto gentile" (*Vita nuova* XXVI), leaving a reader at least curious about how and why that lady has been replaced by this one, whoever she may be. For, while the first canzone of *Convivio* clearly associated the donna gentile with the lady at the window in poems and prose of the *Vita nuova,* such is not the case here. If the commentary makes the two ladies identical, it is not possible to say the same thing about the text of the two poems. Whether the second poem was originally composed to honor the donna gentile, as Dante now says it was, or is now simply made to fit that purpose is not clear from the evidence within the text of the canzone.

That the lady of "Amor che ne la mente" was almost certainly not Lady Philosophy when Dante first wrote the poem is underscored by its description of her physical attractiveness (vv. 33–36), so great that, like Beatrice, she draws forth sighs from her beholder. The prose disposes of this physical encumbrance with understandable tact and celerity, insisting that her body is under the sign of the soul, a soul which "riceva miracolosamente la graziosa bontade di Dio" (miraculously receives the gracious goodness of God—III, vi, 12). A similar insistence is found in vv. 39–54, once again reminiscent of elements found in "Tanto gentile" (and what is said sounds much like what is said there of Beatrice's effect on those who see her physical beauty). The prose explains how the lady's physical aspect is such that "la nostra fede è aiutata" (our faith is given aid), sounding more like passages in the prose of *Vita nuova* than we might expect. Her miraculous mortal flesh, like that of Christ crucified, may direct us toward salvation (III, vii, 16). It is difficult to reconcile such text or such commentary with the overlying allegory of Lady Philosophy. Was she "ordinata ne la mente di Dio in testimonio de la fede a coloro che in questo tempo vivono" (ordained in the mind of God in testimony of the faith for those alive in this time—III, vii, 17)? The next chapter will establish that her physical beauty is most present in her eyes and in her smile (III, viii, 10-11), and the allegorical exposition will further explain that these are the demonstrations and persuasions, respectively, of Sapienza (III, xv, 2). In the poem, this lady, like Beatrice, is associated with paradise more than with Athens. What is perhaps most surprising about the first two canzoni of *Convivio* is how different they are in style and content. It is only Dante's prose that makes them seem to be about the same woman. The prose, however, concludes by equating her body with "le virtudi morali" (the moral virtues—III, xv, 11), and with "morale filosofia" (moral philosophy—III, xv, 14). And that will be the subject to which Dante turns in the fourth trattato.

Convivio IV

"Le dolci rime d'amor" ("The sweet poems of love"), the last canzone of *Convivio,* was composed some years after "Voi che 'ntendendo." Foster and Boyde suggest that the date was nearer to 1295 than to 1300, but almost certainly between these two dates. Its style, content, and tone all convey the impression that it was composed later than the previous canzoni with which it is necessarily connected by Dante's choice to include it where he did. And where the prose will begin and intermittently continue to make it seem a part of the same enterprise, on its own terms the verse has a way of appearing not quite amenable to such a purpose. The literal sense, the narrative line established by the canzoni themselves, thus presents three stages: "Voi che 'ntendendo" records the triumph of the donna gentile over Beatrice in Dante's soul; "Amor che ne la mente" offers a song of praise for his new lady, closely modeled on Beatricean elements in "Donne ch'avete" and in "Tanto gentile." "Le dolci rime" opens by narrating a change of heart in the lady, who now has "chiusa la via / de l'usato parlare" (barred the path of my usual speech—vv. 7–

8). The conclusion of "Amor che ne la mente" refers to another poem of Dante's, also composed for his new lady, which apparently contradicted what he had said about her humility in the canzone, that she was "fera e disdegnosa" (harsh and scornful— v. 76). He explains the situation more fully in the prose: before he wrote "Amor che ne la mente," since the lady appeared to be "fatta contra me fiera e superba alquanto (somewhat harsh and haughty), "feci una ballatetta ne la quale chiamai questa donna orgogliosa e dispietata" (I composed a little ballad in which I called her prideful and pitiless—III, ix, 1). The *ballata* in question, all agree, is "Voi che savete ragionar d'Amore" ("O you who know how to reason about love"—*Rime* LXXX). Indeed, in it the poet says that his lady will not share the love that her noble lord has put into her eyes with one who seeks that love; she is described as "disdegnosa" (disdainful—v. 3) and "fera" (fierce— v. 23); and she says of herself (vv. 13-14), "Io non sarò umile / verso d'alcun che ne li occhi mi guardi" (I will not be humble before anyone who looks into my eyes), thus withdrawing the *umiltà* ascribed to her in "Amor che ne la mente": "e qual donna gentil questo non crede, / vada con lei e miri li atti sui" (and let any noble lady who does not believe this accompany her and contemplate her bearing—vv. 39-40); "miri costei ch'è essemplo d'umiltate" (gaze at this lady, the very model of humility—v. 70). It is no wonder that, both in the verse and its accompanying gloss (III, xv, 19), Dante feels called upon first to note and then to explain the apparent contradiction (the fault lay with him for not yet being able to grasp either her persuasions or her demonstrations). The contradiction is, in fact, more than apparent.

It is striking to see that the third canzone, only several lines down the page from this assurance that his lady is humble (*umile*) and not "disdegnosa" and "fera," repeats the precise formulations found in "Voi che savete": "li atti disdegnosi e feri, / che ne la donna mia / sono appariti, m'han chiusa la via / de l'usato par-

lare" (but the disdainful, harsh bearing now apparent in my lady
has barred the path of my usual speech—vv. 5-8). It turns out
that the *ballatetta* (III, ix, 1) is closer to the truth than the gloss
on the canzone (III, xv, 19). Indeed, the first stanza of "Le dolci
rime" is primarily a recasting, in identical terms, of the drama
narrated in "Voi che savete ragionar d'Amore." The donna gentile, within the narrative established by the poems and without benefit of gloss, after winning his affection away from dead
Beatrice, now denies him access to her. And it is thus that, in
"Le dolci rime," Dante puts off "lo mio soave stile, / ch'i' ho
tenuto nel trattar d'amore" (that sweet style of mine that I have
held to when writing of love—vv. 10-11). The first treatise of
Convivio promised that Dante would treat "sì d'amor come di
vertù" (both of love and of virtue—I, i, 14). It is at this precise moment, in the record supplied by the poems themselves,
Dante's imagined or actual "autobiography," that he turns from
the one to the other: "e dirò del valore, / per lo qual veramente
omo è gentile, / con rima aspr' e sottile" (and I will speak instead
in harsh and subtle rhymes of the quality by which man is truly
noble—vv. 12-14). The rest of the canzone is in a style surely
more "aspro" than "dolce," and on a subject more relevant to
"virtue" than to "love." Rather than praise of the Lady Philosophy, we find here a treatise in verse dedicated to a "philosophical" subject, the nature of true nobility. The argument, which
has a long history in the poetry that celebrates so-called courtly
love, here strikingly lacks that usual aspect. The gentility here
defined is not restricted to that found in the heart of a lover-poet
but enjoys a more ample purview. Written against the opinion
of Frederick II that nobility (*gentilezza*) resides in wealth and
luxurious display and of those who believe that it is conferred
by birth, the first part (stanzas 2-4) of the lengthy (146-verse)
canzone is spent attacking these notions. The second part (stanzas 5-7),[100] now that it has been established what nobility is not,

is dedicated to the definition of the nature of true nobility, put forward beneath the aegis of Aristotle's *Ethics* (which is referred to by name in the text at v. 85). Whatever we make of the eventual relationship among the three canzoni of *Convivio*, we must surely acknowledge the difference between the first two and this last one, as well as the more subtle distinctions that separate the first two from one another.

Dante's gloss to the third canzone is lengthy and contains a number of significant digressions. Its first chapter links it to the allegorical presentation of his lady as philosophy found in the first three treatises, as though there were to be no real change in the subject of the prose, no matter how great the change recorded in the verse may be. Dante uses the occasion to make three main points. As lover of philosophy, he had begun to love what she loved, to hate what she hated, particularly, in the latter category, widely shared and false opinions regarding the true nature of nobility ("nobilitade"—IV, i, 7). This concern apparently brought him to consider the difficult theological (or metaphysical) question of prime matter, a major ground for debate among the more "orthodox" of Christian thinkers, who had to deny that anything could pre-exist God's Creation, and those who followed such thinkers as Averroës in believing that God formed what had already existed with Him.[101] Finding his lady unwilling to enlighten him, he attacked the less metaphysical problem—the nature of nobility—on its own terms (IV, i, 8). And thus he decided to write this canzone, speaking not "sotto alcuna figura" (in some sort of figurative speech) but openly, with the result that the commentary here requires no allegorical exposition (IV, i, 10-11). Whether or not we believe that the first two canzoni were originally conceived "sotto figura," we can surely see that this one is mainly not so conceived.[102] Its essence is "moral philosophy" in verse, joining Dante to the tradition of Guittone d'Arezzo,[103] whether Dante, always hostile to Guittone, would like us to believe so or not. Not explained away—as they were in the third treatise, when Dante went out of his way to discuss "Voi che savete," a poem not included in the text of *Convivio*, but referred to in "Amor che ne la mente" as negating his praise of his lady—are the "atti disdegnosi e feri" that we find present again in the third canzone (v. 5). The absence of an allegorical exposition offers a possible reason for the failure to rescind the description. And we may choose to understand, supplying the "allegory" ourselves, that his absence from her when he poses his question (IV, i, 8) reflects that verse in the poem. Thus Dante is called upon to explain that she only seemed to reject him, with implicit reference to the tenth chapter of the last treatise, where he addresses this problem. Nonetheless, it is as though the entire allegorical machinery, so insistently proclaimed in II, i, and then resolutely practiced in II, xii–xv, and III, xii–xv, has fallen to pieces. As Beatrice was banished from further mention in II, viii, 7, so does the word "allegoria" now disappear after IV, i, 11. But in this respect Dante is equally disingenuous. Thoughts of Beatrice in her rivalry with the donna gentile continue after II, viii, and Dante does in fact repeat his allegorical understanding of the Lady Philosophy, in IV, ii, 17–18. This is, however, the last time such a formulation occurs with regard to the poem. The text of the commentary itself, perhaps surprisingly, offers three major exceptions to his promise not to allegorize further: IV, xxii, 15: the three Marys who come seeking Christ in his tomb are allegorized in unprecedented ways (they represent the Epicureans, the Stoics, and the Peripatetics in their search for truth);[104] IV, xxvi, 8–11: although unacknowledged, an allegorical understanding of the actions recorded in the *Aeneid* is clearly present; IV, xxviii, 13–19: Marcia is allegorized as the noble soul and Cato as God, in an extended and striking passage.

The vexed question of the precise nature of Dante's allegory is made still more complex by Dante's discussion of the subject in *Convivio*. (This problem is related to the issue of how we are meant to understand the process of signification in *Vita nuova*, touched on earlier.) In the opening chapter of *Convivio* II Dante outlines what he takes to be the principal differences between poets' and theologians' allegorical procedures. Much to everyone's relief, he asserts that in *Convivio* he intends to follow the practice of the poets. What has not often been noted is the striking nature of his claim that he indeed had a choice, a claim that is not only unusual but unacceptable by any usual standard. Whatever the allegory of theologians was understood to comprise, no competent judge would assent to the notion that fourfold exegesis of the Bible could be reassigned to the interpretation of odes about ladies. Dante's claim here should trouble more readers than it has.

Once we are nominally, at least, freed from allegory's yoke, the fourth treatise brings us into what for the reader may seem familiar territory: the real world of moral choice. It seems likely that the rest of *Convivio* was to be devoted to the lower order of philosophy, as it were, although the shifts we have seen in the work as it has come down to us make any such prediction precarious. In any case, in *Convivio* IV we have moved from Aristotle's *Metaphysics*, with which we began in the very first line of the text, to the *Nicomachean Ethics*, at which point the incomplete work ends. Indeed, it may have been meant to end there even if it had been completed—at least if we can credit the new design of which we can see the outlines in the fourth treatise.

Why Dante never finished *Convivio* is at once easy and impossible to say. He wrote the *Comedy* instead. In the words of Ulrich Leo, he responded to "the urge to take the step to poetry and vision, away from reason and prose." [105] We shall never know exactly how or why he came to that crucial decision, only that he did. Perhaps one sign of his movement away from Amore, the

Lady Philosophy, allegorical exposition, and self-commentary as the prime instrument for the forging of his thought, is found first in *Convivio* IV, iv–v, where, for the first time in his life as writer, he turns to the question of Rome and its authority as the seat of empire.[106] This concern will next echo in the first and second cantos of *Inferno,* and then again as the central concern of *Monarchia.* It is presented in the fourth trattato as part of a larger question, that of philosophical and imperial authority, yet it is clear that the imperial aspect of the argument is not necessary to its main thrust—is a "digression." It thus stands out all the more as being of new and pressing interest, as representing Dante's first major overt concern with the world of political reality, even if in its ideal form.

Dante's discovery of the classical world as a touchstone for his immediate concerns has been discussed by Ulrich Leo, in an important article. He argued, on the basis of stylistic evidence, that Dante, by the time he composed *Convivio* IV, xxv, had returned to a study of the great literary works of Rome's golden and silver ages. Leo claims that citations of this nature appear only at the end of *Convivio;* recalling Statius (xxv, 6 and 10); Virgil (xxvi, 8, 9, 11, 13, and 14); Ovid (xxvii, 17-20); Lucan (xxviii, 13-19); and also Juvenal (the only *auctor* not later to be included in the "bella scola," *Inf.* IV—94, xxix, 4 [twice], and 5). We have seen nothing like this amount of precise and zealous citation of Latin literary texts in Dante heretofore. Leo's intriguing surmise is that the last six chapters of the last treatise of *Convivio* reveal a rekindled affection for classical poetry and a careful rereading of these texts.[107] The *Comedy* will continue to exploit this rich vein of material.

The project of *Convivio,* no matter how Dante would eventually regard the work, was immense. It was his attempt to put into one place all human knowledge—from both experience and reason—of substances, accidents, and their relations ("sustanze e accidenti e lor costume"—*Par.* XXXIII, 88). Perhaps no one has better, or more affectionately, described the greatness of the desire that lies behind the unfinished banquet than Peter Dronke. The second chapter of *Dante's Second Love*, which concerns the syncretizing and universalizing ambitions that produced *Convivio*, helps us to see what is difficult to see, since we come to *Convivio* either from *Vita nuova*, with which it is at odds in crucial and undeniable ways, or, more likely, from the finished and magnificent *Comedy*, which necessarily dwarfs the earlier, unfinished work, and which also has crucial complaints to lodge against it. If we read *Convivio* on its own terms, with a sympathy that some of its readers would argue Dante himself does not later authorize, the accomplishment, daring, and beauty of thought and expression mark it as one of the richest and most intriguing abandoned works that we possess.

Nonetheless, whatever Dante's view of the overall project that was *Convivio* as he looks back at it from the standpoint of the *Comedy*,[108] it is clear that in any number of instances a particular judgment is found incorrect and is publicly modified. This self-correcting is always done in such a way as to be clear only to a reader of the earlier text, because Dante never names the work. Although *Convivio* was probably not published by Dante, it is apparent that the work did circulate, since it did not perish along with its author. In any case, it is true that Dante himself was keenly aware of what he had said in it, and he took the trouble to set things right when the occasion demanded. The brief enumeration that follows does not include less-than-obvious occurrences or only potentially hostile revisitings of *Convivio*, but only some oppositional confrontations that reveal clear corrections of previous views:[109] (1) the damnation of Guido da Montefeltro in *Inferno* XXVII and (2) that of Bertran de Born in XXVIII stimulated Castelvetro, in his commentary on *Inferno* XXVIII, 134, to conclude that Dante has thereby contradicted, in each case, what he had suggested about these two men in *Convivio* (IV, xxviii, 8, and xi, 14, respectively), namely, that they had turned to God at the end of their lives; (3) in *Purgatorio* II we find the passage in which Casella sings Dante's second Convivial ode and eventually draws Cato's rebuke down on his listeners, which has seemed to some an urgent self-criticism on Dante's part for his turning from Beatrice to the Lady Philosophy;[110] (4) *Paradiso* II is usually understood to counter the theory that accounts for the spots on the moon offered in *Convivio* II, xii, 9;[111] (5) the eighth canto of *Paradiso* includes a correction of *Convivio*. It is administered by Charles Martel in the most courteous of chastisements. In the first Convivial ode, addressed to "Voi che 'ntendendo il terzo ciel movete," the order of angels associated with the heaven of Venus, Dante addressed, as the commentary at *Convivio* II, v, 13, makes plain, "Thrones"; but now Charles informs Dante that his angelic mates while he is in this heaven are Principalities ("Noi ci volgiam coi principi celesti" [We revolve with the celestial princes]—v. 34), *not* Thrones. (Dante's greater "error" here is potentially far more disturbing: the abandonment of Beatrice for the Lady Philosophy, to whom the poem is addressed[112]); (6) the angelological problem is insisted on again and far more frontally in *Paradiso* XXVIII, 121–35, where Dante's Convivial ordering of the angelic hierarchy is shown to have been led astray (more in fact by Brunetto Latini than by Gregory the Great, who had only Principalities and Virtues confused) in the placement of four of the nine orders (Powers, Principalities, Dominions, and Thrones). It is impossible to take Gregory's supposed smile of recognition at his fault as not being Dante's as well.

The case can be made for other passages in the later poem that "correct" those in *Convivio*, such as the ultimate simile of *Paradiso* (XXXIII, 133–38), which compares Dante, desiring to understand the relations among the three persons of the Trinity, to the geometer who wishes to discover the principle by which he might square the circle. *Convivio* (II, xiii, 27) is clear about this: "lo cerchio per lo suo arco è impossibile a quadrare perfettamente" (because of its arc, the circle cannot be perfectly squared). In the concluding verses of *Paradiso* XXXIII we are told that Dante's impossible desire was answered by a flash of lightning (*fulgore*) that fulfilled his wish; the implication is that, against the rationalist confines of *Convivio,* the *Comedy* allows a mystical possibility for the "squaring of the circle."

The point of this assemblage of evidence is not to see how often in the *Comedy* Dante is in polemic with his own previous work, only that he sometimes is. It is not convincing to say that when we read the poem, we are not licensed to consider the text of *Convivio* as relevant to its meaning—either because in 1300, within the fiction, Dante had not yet written it and could not make its contents part of his consciousness as character in the poem, or because the work had little or no diffusion.[113] It is more helpful to observe that the later poem at times tackles the task of clearing the record of errors in *Convivio.* And it is clear that some of these are not trivial.

COMMEDIA

It probably took no more than an instant for Cervantes to conceive the simple, fruitful idea that produced *Don Quixote:* take a middle-aged, down-at-the-heels landowner, fill his brain with the entire tradition of chivalric romance, and then have him ride forth into the world as a knight errant. What publisher would have bought that idea for a book, had Cervantes consulted one before he began writing? Dante's *Comedy* is possibly the result of a similar sudden inspiration, one based on a perhaps even less defensible pretext: take a not-very-successful (though respected), soon-to-be-exiled civic leader and poet, then send him off to the afterworld for a week. One cannot imagine many publishers today, despite the enormous popularity of a poem based in this pretext, who would want to take a chance on so absurd a contrivance.

We shall never know what brought the work to life in Dante's mind or what was his first awareness of a plan. But we can see to what degree the *Comedy* departs from his previous extended work, for all its thematic and stylistic links to his literary past. *Vita nuova, De vulgari Eloquentia,* and *Convivio* all put prose in the service of controlling and explaining verse. (We might want to reflect on what that eventually indicates about Dante's earlier sense of his own powers as a poet or of the relative worth of poetry.) Some ten years of lyric production (1283-93) are followed by the publication of *Vita nuova* (1293?). Another ten years of lyrics (1294-1304), fewer now (a political career has its costs) but still more masterful, are followed by *De vulgari Eloquentia* and *Convivio* (1304-7?). Poetry, followed by an excited turn toward prose in order to put forward what the writer obviously feels are new and commanding subjects—a beloved lady different in her spiritual meaning from all earlier poets' ladies (*Vita nuova*); a second lady, celebrated in his canzoni, under whose auspices he will bring philosophy into Italian for the first time (*Convivio*); and the first treatise ever dedicated to the subject of Italian vernacular poetry (*De vulgari Eloquentia*). From 1307 until the end of his life Dante will eschew the *prosimetrum,* the form of *Vita nuova, De vulgari Eloquentia* (in a certain respect), and *Convivio,* in favor of verse alone (*Comedy, Eclogues*) or prose without verse (*Monarchia, Questio*).[114]

The history of the *Comedy*'s making is a difficult subject. In Petrocchi's view, it falls into the following stages: *Inferno* (1304-8—but mainly 1306-8); *Purgatorio* (around 1308-12); *Paradiso* (1316-21).[115] Many current students of the problem are in basic accord with Petrocchi's dates for the stages in the poem's production and dissemination. Continuing debate about the matter is, however, inevitable, given our possibly permanent ignorance of so many crucial details. Nonetheless, most discussants today agree that *Inferno,* with few exceptions, reflects events that took place no later than 1309; *Purgatorio,* no later than 1313. The major exception is the possible, even probable, reference to the death of Pope Clement V in 1314 (*Inf.* XIX, 79–84). The singularity of so late a date, rather than confirming the thesis that *Inferno* was completed only after 1314, supports Petrocchi's notion that it represents a rare later major reworking of the text.[116]

The manuscript tradition of the poem is vast and complicated.[117] Nonetheless, and despite all the difficulties presented by particular textual problems, the result of variant readings in various manuscripts, it must be acknowledged that in the *Comedy* we possess a remarkably stable text, given that we do not possess an autograph (and what Dantist does not dream of its one day being discovered? but then many of us would be revealed to have been fools many times over) and that the condition of the codices is unyieldingly problematic. On the other hand, we know that Dante left us precisely 14,233 verses arranged in one hundred cantos, all of which contained precisely the number of verses we find in them today in every modern edition.[118] Those are not small things to hold for certain — many a twentieth-century text is more problematic than this one.

The earliest diffusion of the poem (first printed by Johann Neumeister in 1472) is evidenced around 1315. In Petrocchi's judgment, Dante released the first two cantiche together, or at least within a year of each other, in 1314–15. Once it began to establish a readership, the *Comedy* was an enormously popular text. The wide and rapid diffusion of manuscripts, the profusion of early commentators, the extensive citation in works of other major writers (Boccaccio, Petrarch, and Chaucer are perhaps the most notable) — all these signs indicate that Dante's gamble on that perhaps disconcerting motivating idea of an otherworldly journey had been astute, a bet that bought him literary immortality. At least we can say that the first 250 years of the poem's life were filled with use and praise. But we should remember that the rich and long-lasting initial florescence of the *Comedy* was followed by a fairly abrupt dessication in the last quarter of the sixteenth century. Relative neglect was the general condition of the poem, in Italy and in the rest of Europe, for two centuries after that. It was only in the last quarter of the eighteenth century that Dante once again began to find a large audience. The past two hundred years have turned him into one of the most famous and best loved of all writers, in Europe and indeed in all the world.

The reader will note that the following treatment of the poem differs from the treatments of Dante's other works in this volume. To a certain degree, some knowledge of the text is assumed; the reader is imagined as having come from an experience with the *Comedy* wanting to know more about Dante's development as a writer. The discussion is presented as a series of subjects or themes. Obviously, there could have been many others. One cannot write a short book about Dante's "intellectual biography" and include in it a treatment of the *Comedy* that would parallel in length discussion of the other works, for it would overwhelm the book, as the poem overwhelmed everything else that Dante wrote.

The *Comedy* is set in Easter week of the year 1300, although we are also asked to consider that the narrative action of the work begins on 25 March, two weeks before the actual occurrence of Good Friday in 1300.[119] Inner references (for example, *Inf.* XXI, 112–14; *Purg.* II, 98–99) point to *both* dates. And study has shown that Dante was almost certainly using Profacius' star charts for 1301.[120] These three pieces of information do not reveal confusion or self-contradiction, but indicate that, as usual,

Dante is making things work out the way he wants them to for maximum poetic effect. In these and in many other details, the reality of Dante's physical world is dependent on its portrayal in the poem. For instance, do physical laws exist in Dante's afterworld? They do, and they do so absolutely—unless Dante chooses to suspend them. How can Virgil, who is a shade, carry Dante, who is corporeal? Because his doing so makes for a better scene. We might think of Cervantes again, for he too was a writer who enjoyed playing collaborative games with his reader. "That could not have occurred," he knows his reader will object at any number of moments. And he knows that the reader will go on to realize that the only one empowered to decide what "occurred" is the author himself. It is Dante's book, and we are allowed to share it only on condition that we become his willing collaborators, not merely choosing to understand that a given narrated event is "impossible," but learning to comprehend why the author is asking us to grant its "truthfulness."

Truth and Poetry

The question of the veracity of the *Comedy*'s narrative is never far from the reader's attention. In the first invocation of the poem (*Inf.* II, 7), the poet requests the aid of the Muses (the rules of grammar and rhetoric?) and of "alto ingegno" (lofty genius—either, somewhat implausibly, the poet's own capacities, or, more probably but also rather disconcertingly, that of a higher power). A claim (and not an "invocation") immediately follows: the poet's memory will be able to provide an exact record of his weeklong visionary journey: "O mente, che scrivesti ciò ch'io vidi / qui si parrà la tua nobilitate" (O memory, that set down what I saw, here shall your worth be shown—

II, 8–9). Dante would seem to be acknowledging his need for two kinds of external assistance: that conferred by what one can learn about poetic discourse (figures of speech, rhetorical devices, rhyme, and so on), and that conferred by God to allow the poet to conceive the meaning of his experience. (The words *concepire* and *concetto* occur at many important moments that stress the necessity of such higher understanding, one beyond usual or normal human powers, including three of the nine invocations of the poem,[121] those occurring in *Inferno* XXXII and *Paradiso* XVIII and XXXIII.) From this first insistence that what is narrated as having occurred is to be treated as having actually occurred, it is clear that Dante expects us not to believe that this journey really took place, but rather to note that he has claimed that it did. The central difference between the *Comedy* and medieval allegorical visions lies precisely in this. At such moments, we sense, the poet realizes that his readers will not grant for an instant that such things have indeed taken place (for example, the advent of Geryon in *Inferno* XVI, when Dante stakes the truthfulness of his entire *comedìa* on his having seen this most fabulous of creatures), but that those readers will recognize why the poet must make the outrageous claim: his poem is not a mere fiction, like those condemned by Aquinas and other theologians, when they hold that poets are liars.[122] We can discern exactly the same tactic when, in *Inferno* XXIX, Dante compares his victims of a plaguelike ailment in their eternal damnation to those described by Ovid on the island of Aegina, who were replaced by "ant-people"—"secondo che i poeti hanno per fermo" (as the poets hold for certain). That dig at Ovid—that no one will (or should) believe what a lying poet says—is a risky joke we share with Dante. For at heart we know that the sinners he portrays are as fictive as Ovid's Myrmidons. By claiming total veracity for his poem, Dante conquers St. Thomas's objections and at the same time smilingly capitulates to them: he is, after all, only another lying poet, but one who always insists that he is more than that, whether he is claiming that the poem is literally true or that his subject is eventually of the highest purpose and seriousness. Dante, on this subject as on so many others, has things as he wants them. There are of course any number of moments at which he seems altogether serious about the truth claims he makes for his vision. Yet his careful (and generally amusing) undercutting of their full impact makes the poem's readers far more comfortable than they would be were such passages not present. They allow for utter seriousness when the author needs to establish it (one cannot imagine such playfulness being allowed in the climactic series of visions in *Paradiso* XXXIII), and they permit readers to think that Dante is at least as sane as they are. It is difficult for visionaries to seem reassuring to those to whom they present their visions. Dante, while as stern a moralist as one is likely to find, is a surprisingly restrained visionary. And it is in exactly this spirit that he describes the six wings adorning each of the four biblical beasts representing the authors of the Gospels in *Purgatorio* XXIX. Dante assures us that the wings of each were six in number (Ezekiel's cherubic creatures had only four [1:6]), that is, as many as are found in John's description of the same cherubic creatures (Rev. 4:8). Verse 105 puts this in an arresting way: "Giovanni è meco e da lui si diparte" (John sides with me, departing from him). No one but Dante would have said this in this way. "Here I follow John" would have been the proper way for a poet to guarantee the truthfulness of his narrative. Not for Dante. Since the pretext in the poem is that he indeed saw all that he recounts having seen, that experience, according to good Thomistic procedure, is prior—he knows this by his senses. And so John is *his* witness, and not vice versa. It is an extraordinary moment.[123]

Allegory

Almost anyone coming to the *Comedy* for the first time has probably heard two things about its larger strategies—it is the most Christian of poems and it is "an allegory."[124] But an allegory of what? And what is allegory in the first place?[125] The most simple medieval definition of allegory is found in the seventh-century Spanish encyclopedist, Isidore of Seville (*Etymologiae* I, xxxvii, 22): "Allegoria est alieniloquium, aliud enim sonat, aliud intelligitur" (Allegory is "otherspeech," for it occurs when one thing is said and another is understood). This definition, which may be taken as being either global or narrowly particular (it is in fact offered as a definition of one kind of irony by Isidore), is frequently referred to in discussions of allegory and is thus included here. In fact, however, it does not resolve the problem in a helpful way, especially for students of Dante, who himself referred to two kinds of allegory, the one employed by poets, the other by theologians in their interpretation of the Bible (*Conv.* II, i, 3-4). If we can understand what Dante meant in his discussion, we may be able to understand better what he did in his poem.

Allegory, as practiced by poets, may generally be described as possessing the following characteristics. An allegorical work (1) is to be understood as being fictive and as not even possibly recording events that have actually occurred (for instance, the *Romance of the Rose*), while also (2) being developed as an extended metaphor (for example, the Christian life portrayed as a continual "war," a struggle against inner temptations and external forces ranged against the would-be Christian—as in the *Psychomachia* [around 405] of Prudentius). In concert with these two characteristics, allegory of the poets (3) presents its action as being internal, as taking place in the mind or soul of a single figure (say, Prince Arthur in Edmund Spenser's *Faerie*

Queene [1596]) or of an anonymous "everyman" (Pilgrim in John Bunyan's *Pilgrim's Progress* [1678]). Further, allegorical fictions (4) tend to rely heavily on the use of personifications, generally of vices (such as Incontinence, Despair) and virtues (such as Continence, Hope), "ladies" who perform physical actions in battle with other "ladies," as in the *Psychomachia*. (Abstractions in Latin generally take the feminine gender—for example, *continentia, spes.*) Not every allegorical work has all these characteristics; all, however, possess some of them.

Now let us examine Dante's definition of allegory in the opening pages of the second treatise of *Convivio:* "L'uno si chiama litterale, [e questo è quello che non si stende più oltre che la lettera de le parole fittizie, sì come sono le favole de li poeti. L'altro si chiama allegorico,] e questo è quello che si nasconde sotto 'l manto di queste favole, ed è una veritade ascosa sotto bella menzogna. . . . Veramente li teologi questo senso prendono altrimenti che li poeti; ma però che mia intenzione è qui lo modo de li poeti seguitare, prendo lo senso allegorico secondo che per li poeti è usato" (The first [sense of a text] is called the literal, and this is the sense that does not go beyond the surface of the letter, as in the fables of the poets. The other is called the allegorical, and this is the one that is hidden beneath the cloak of these fables, and it is a truth hidden beneath a beautiful lie. . . . Indeed, the theologians take this sense otherwise than do the poets; but since it is my intention here to follow the method of the poets, I shall take the allegorical sense according to the usage of the poets—*Conv.* II, i, 3–4). For Dante, the distinguishing element in the allegory of the poets is that it is based on texts that are literally untrue. Such a view may disconcert us. Are not all poems literally fictive?[126] Before attempting to respond to that question, one might consider what Dante believed to be the distinguishing mark of theological allegory, the way in which "the theologians take this sense otherwise than do the poets."

It is clear that he is now speaking of a privileged and limited class of texts, the historical passages in the Bible that medieval exegetes believed to possess four senses. The four senses (and not, as all too often in modern discussions, "levels") of the Bible are generally put forth, especially in the wake of Thomas Aquinas (*Summa theologiae* I, i, 10), as follows: (1) historical/literal, (2) allegorical, (3) moral or tropological, and (4) anagogical. It is helpful to understand that these senses unfurl along a a historical continuum. For instance, the *historical* Moses, leading the Israelites out of captivity, gains his *allegorical* meaning in Christ, leading humankind out of bondage to the freedom of salvation. His *moral* (or *tropological*) sense is present now—whenever "now" occurs, in the soul of the believer who chooses to make his or her "exodus," whereas the *anagogical* sense is found only after the end of time, when those who are saved are understood to have arrived in the final Promised Land, the blessed life in heaven. To offer a second example, one favored by Dante's early commentators: Jerusalem was the *historical* city of Old Testament time; it points to the *allegorical* Jerusalem in which Jesus was crucified; it is the *moral* or *tropological* "city" (whether within a single believer or as the entity formed by the Church Militant now) at any present moment; it is, *anagogically,* the New Jerusalem, which will exist only at the end of time. How the formative principles of this method of biblical interpretation inform the *Comedy* will be addressed below. For now we observe only a single and crucial particular. As opposed to the literal sense of poet's allegory, the literal sense of theological allegory is historically true, found only in events narrated in the Bible (the fall of Adam and Eve, Moses leading the Israelites during the Exodus, the birth of Jesus, the Crucifixion). In his discussion in *Convivio* II, Dante not surprisingly goes on to say that he will employ the allegory of the poets to elucidate the meaning of the "allegorical" personification, Lady Philosophy. As has been noted, it is astounding that he claims that he *could have* employed theological allegory in his analysis of his poems. In the Middle Ages the line separating the two kinds of allegorical exegesis was clearly drawn. All imaginative literature, as one would expect, was considered fictive and not historical. In medieval rhetoric there did exist a category to describe "realistic" fiction, called *argumentum,* as opposed to *fabula* (things clearly untrue) or *historia* (things that have clearly occurred). *Argumenta* are things that, although they have not actually occurred, could have done so.[127] Further, theological allegory was limited to a single use, interpreting the several meanings found in certain (though far from all) historical passages in Scripture. Dante, in one rather alarming step, had crossed that line—in theory if not in practice. Nonetheless, the claim he had staked when he wrote *Convivio* (around 1304–6) lay ready to be mined when he moved on to the *Comedy* (around 1307).

Later in his life Dante wrote a letter to one of his most important supporters, Cangrande della Scala, a sort of preamble to his *Paradiso,* in which he explained many of the essential strategies of the *Comedy,* and most particularly its use of allegory. It must immediately be said that, since 1819, the authenticity of this document has been hotly debated. Most often, those who deny that Dante wrote it find that the contents of the epistle do not accord with their view of Dante's opinions or stylistic practice. Certainly the most astounding and controversial assertion in the epistle is that the fourfold interpretation of texts used to elucidate the historical meanings of the Bible is the very method to be used to understand the *Comedy.* This is surely the stuff of heresy.[128] For the position at the very least and unmistakably implies that the literal sense of the poem is historical, that is, that Dante's seven-day visit to the afterworld is to be treated as historical fact. Whether or not Dante wrote the letter, some contemporary students of the issue make the point that his practice in the poem is such as to indicate that the epistle, whoever wrote it, merely makes explicit what has already been accomplished in the poem.[129]

Dante, faced with theologians' strong opposition to the idea that secular literature had any meaningful claim to be a purveyor of truth, made a bold decision. Rather than employ the allegory of the poets, which admitted—even insisted—that the literal sense of a work was untrue, he chose to employ the allegory of the theologians, with the consequence that everything recounted in the poem as having actually occurred is to be treated as "historical," for the poet insistently claims that what he relates is no less than literally true. If we can acknowledge that the poet makes this claim, we have come a long way toward demystifying the subject. However the four senses of theological allegory may function in the *Comedy,* we can agree to the pretext that it is to be read historically.

If the *Comedy* is to be understood as being intimately related to the allegory of the theologians, in what precise ways should we understand that Dante has adapted its methods?[130] The main technique he borrows from the theologians centers on the relation between the first two senses, historical/literal and allegorical. These two senses have several sets of synonyms, among which the two most commonly used are "type and antitype" and "figure and fulfillment." In addition, historical events are sometimes referred to as "shadows" of things to come. Theologians refer to Moses as the "type" of whom Jesus is the "antitype" (a warning: this word is often misused in discussions of Dante's allegory); to the sacrifice of Isaac, intended by Abraham, as the "figure" of which the Crucifixion is the "fulfillment"; to Jonah's three days in the innards of Leviathan as the "shadow" of Christ's three-day sojourn under the earth between the Crucifixion and the Resurrection. While all these historical senses may have corresponding moral/tropological and anagogical ones, most discussions are directed to their second meaning, the allegorical (or "figural" or "typological") sense. Those who believe that Dante borrowed this technique of ordering meaning historically contend first and foremost that his appropriation of the first two senses offers the clearest indication of this indebtedness. One could indeed argue that Dante sees each sinner or saved soul as the fulfillment of the earthly life that brought him or her to the afterworld—this is the view advanced most significantly by Auerbach. To this formulation one might reasonably respond that, if it is true, it is also not very interesting, except insofar as it guarantees the exceptional claim the poet makes for his poem, that its mode of signifying is to be understood as being that of the allegory of the theologians. Some recent discussions of the question have centered on the far more interesting typological, or figural (these words, one should remember, are synonyms), relationships exhibited by persons in the poem to other persons. To take one instance, drawn from the report of an early-fifteenth-century reader of Dante (Filippo Villani), the Florentines referred to Guido da Montefeltro (canto XXVII) as the "new Ulysses."[131] In such an observation, about laymen reading a historical being "figurally," we can observe the adaptation of a theological technique to a secular understanding.[132] In Dante's poems one finds any number of such moments. The soul referred to in *Inf.* III, 59–60 (probably Pope Celestine V, if we accept the most convincing arguments[133]), is the "antitype" of others before him who showed a similar form of cowardice, such as Pontius Pilate; Francesca, reading a book in the company of a man named Paul (Paolo) that leads to her "conversion" to an adulterous love that leads to death, is the "negative antitype" of St. Augustine, reading a book by Paul that leads to his conversion (*Confessions* VIII, xii);[134] Cato, the guardian of Purgatory, is presented (cantos I and II) in ways that portray him as the pagan antitype of Moses and the type of Christ.[135] Statius, rising from his purgation ready to ascend to heaven (*Purg.* XXI, 7-10), has long been understood to play the role of a "postfigured" resurrected Christ, because the language of the poem makes this view of the matter seem necessary. The main point is that the reader is essentially freed from reading the poem as an allegory, at least as literary allegory is traditionally defined. Cato is not the personification of an abstract virtue but a historical being whose looks, actions, and significance all point to other historical entities and actions. This way of reading him is no easier than the traditional method of allegorical exegesis, but it is much more satisfying. This observation underscores the importance of heeding Dante's choice of theological allegory, an option denied him by every authority but which he simply made his own.

Framing the question in this way has the crucial result of freeing readers from their interpretive shackles—those imposed when they accept the allegory of the poets as the basic interpretive approach to the poem. And that exactly has been its fate from the time of the earliest commentators. An example may help. When Virgil enters the poem in the first canto, the vast majority of early commentators (and the phenomenon, surprisingly, persists) treat him as an abstraction, an allegory (often of "Human Reason" or something similar). But even a cursory reading of the text that presents him (*Inf.* I, 67-75) reveals that he stands before us as the historical Virgil.[136]

If a student wrestling with this difficult matter for the first time takes only this much away from the discussion, it should be of considerable aid. The poem does not call on the reader to see Virgil as Reason, Beatrice as Faith (or Revelation), Francesca as Lust, Farinata as Heresy. One may banish such abstractions from mind, unless Dante himself insists on them (as on occasion he does—for example, the Lady Poverty, beloved of St. Francis [*Par.* XI, 74], who is not to be confused with any historical earthly woman but is to be regarded as the Christian ideal of renunciation of the things of this world). It is a useful and pleasing freedom that such a reader may enjoy: "The allegory of the *Comedy* is not allegory as the commentators urge me to understand it. I may read this poem as history and understand it better." That, at least provisionally, is probably a good way to begin reading the poem.

The Moral Situation of the Reader

One of the most difficult problems for a twenty-first-century reader of the *Comedy* is to find a moral point of view from which to consider the actions portrayed in the poem. Finding one is not quite as problematic for readers of the last two cantiche. There, those on their way to becoming saints and those who are already among the blessed contribute to the establishment of an unmistakable moral ground. Even a non-Christian reader cannot overlook the essential "orthodox" moral meaning of these parts of the work. *Inferno,* by contrast, seems, at least, to be a far less morally defined space. Indeed, debates about how we are meant to respond to the most attractive sinners we meet in hell were frequent features of nineteenth- and twentieth-century discussions of the poem. The following paragraphs will not be an attempt to review that debate, but only to describe its most salient features.

The rediscovery of Dante in Europe at the end of the eighteenth century brought his poem into a context that tended to reformulate its moral argument. Later Romantic readers only amplified this tendency. The understanding of Dante that we find in many authoritative late nineteenth-century critics (for instance, Francesco De Sanctis) and early twentieth-century critics (for instance, Benedetto Croce) does not, we can probably agree, conform with the text its author left us. How can we define this view of the poem? In keeping with some of the most attractive tenets of Romantic artistic values—spontaneity of expression, vividness of portrayed emotion, gravity of subject matter, integrity of the writer's feeling—Dante became almost a contemporary of the Romantics. The core of such a view is located in the moral stance of the critic, not in that of the poem. In a not-very-exaggerated shorthand, Francesca, one of the most beguiling of Dante's sinners, replaces the sainted Beatrice as the guarantor of the poem's (and the poet's) greatness; Dante becomes the unrivaled portraitist of Great Feeling. The current debate over the moral exigencies of the poem has its roots in the Romantic rediscovery of Dante, one based particularly on readings of the most moving figures in the *Inferno:* Francesca da Rimini (canto V), Farinata degli Uberti (canto X), Pier delle Vigne (canto XIII), Brunetto Latini (canto XV), Ulysses (canto XXVI), and Ugolino della Gherardesca (canto XXXIII). Of those, Francesca, Ulysses, and Ugolino represent perhaps the three most treasured and discussed of Dante's infernal characters.

No one could reasonably disagree that Dante's "sympathetic sinners" are indeed sympathetic. Still, it seems evident that we, as readers, are meant to avoid the trap into which the poem's protagonist himself several times falls. We should try to honor the distinction clearly drawn in the text itself: that between the narrator, who has taken a journey through the created universe, culminating in his vision of God, and who as a result understands all things about as well as a human being can, and a protagonist who moves, like St. Augustine before him, in Dante's own formulation (*Conv.* I, ii, 14), "di non buono in buono, e di buono in migliore, e di migliore in ottimo" ("from not good to good, from good to better, and from better to best"—the last when he becomes the narrator (*Par.* I, 1–36). Dante's poem creates some of its drama from the tension that exists between the narrator's view of events (in *Inferno* often represented by Virgil's interpretive remarks) and that of the protagonist. What makes our task difficult is that at some pivotal moments neither the narrator nor Virgil makes clear judgmental statements of a moralizing kind. Instead, the poet uses irony to undercut the alluring words of sinners who present themselves rather as victims than as perpetrators of outrage in the eyes of God. Guido da Pisa's gloss (to *Inf.* XX, 28–30) puts the matter succinctly: "Sed circa miserias damnatorum, Sacra Pagina attestante, nulla compassione movetur. Et ratio est ista: In isto enim mundo est tempus misericordie; in alio autem, est solum tempus iustitie" (But the suffering of the damned should move no one to compassion, as the Bible attests. And the reason for this is that the time for mercy is here in this world, while in the world to come it is time only for justice). If it was John Milton's task to "justify the ways of God to men," Dante had already taken on the responsibility of showing that all that is found in this world and in the next is measured by justice. Everything in God is just; only in the mortal world of sin and death do we find injustice—the mark of Cain on most human agents. It is small wonder that Dante believes that only few of those alive in his time will find salvation (*Par.* XXXII, 25–27). The words *justice* and *just* recur frequently in the poem, the noun some thirty-five times, the adjective thirty-six. If one were asked to epitomize the central concern of the poem in a single word, *justice* might embody the best choice.

In the *Inferno* we find insistence on the justice of God from the opening lines describing hell proper, the inscription over the gate of hell (III, 4): "Giustizia mosse il mio alto fattore" (Justice moved my maker on high). If God is just, it follows logically that there can be absolutely no question about the justness of His judgments. All who are condemned to hell are justly condemned. Thus, when we observe that the protagonist feels pity for some of the damned, we are meant to realize that he is at fault for doing so. This is perhaps the most available test of us as readers. If we sympathize with the damned, we follow a bad example. In such a view, the protagonist's at times harsh reaction to various sinners—for example, Filippo Argenti (canto VIII), Pope Nicholas III (canto XIX), or Bocca degli Abati (canto XXXII)—is not (even if it seems so to some contemporary readers) a sign of his falling into sinful attitudes himself, but proof of his righteous indignation as he learns to hate sin.

If some readers think that the protagonist is occasionally too zealous in his reprobation of sinners, far more are of the opinion that his sympathetic responses to others correspond to the reactions that we ourselves may legitimately feel. To be sure, Francesca is portrayed more sympathetically than Thaïs (canto XVIII), Ulysses more so than Mosca dei Lamberti (canto XXVIII), and so on. Yet it also seems to some readers that Dante's treatment of Francesca, Ulysses, and others asks us to put the question of damnation to one side and leaves us to admire their most pleasing human traits in a kind of moral vacuum. It is probably better to believe that we are never authorized by the poem to embrace such a view. If we are struck by Francesca's courteous speech, we note that she is also in the habit of blaming others for her own difficulties; if we admire Farinata's magnanimity, we also note that his soul contains no room for God; if we are wrung by Pier delle Vigne's piteous narrative, we also consider that he has totally abandoned his allegiance to God for his belief in the power of his emperor; if we are moved by Brunetto Latini's devotion to his pupil, we become aware that his view of Dante's earthly mission has little of religion in it; if we are swept up in enthusiasm for the noble vigor of Ulysses, we eventually understand that he is maniacally egotistical; if we weep for Ugolino's piteous paternal feelings, we finally understand that he, too, was centrally (and damnably) concerned with himself.

Dante's risky technique was to entrust us, his readers, with the responsibility for seizing on the details in the narratives by these sympathetic sinners in order to condemn them on the evidence that issues from their own mouths. It was indeed, as we can see from the many readers who fail to take note of this evidence, a perilous decision for him to have made. Yet we are given at least two clear indicators of the attitude that should be ours. Twice in *Inferno* figures from heaven descend to hell to further God's purpose in sending Dante on his mission. Virgil relates the coming of Beatrice to Limbo. She tells him, in no uncertain terms, that she feels nothing for the tribulations of the damned and cannot be harmed in any way by them or by the destructive agents of the place that contains them (*Inf.* II, 88–93). All she longs to do is to return to her seat in Paradise (*Inf.* II, 71). And when the angelic intercessor arrives to open the gates of Dis, slammed shut against Virgil, we are told that this benign presence has absolutely no interest in the situation of the damned or even of the living Dante. All he desires is to complete his mission and be done with such things (*Inf.* IX, 88, 100–103) a reminder to us of Beatrice's similar lack of interest in the damned. This message is immediately reinforced once the poem enters the realm of salvation, for there Cato shows not a shred of sympathy for or even interest in the condition of the soul of his wife, Marcia, in Limbo (*Purg.* I, 85–90). Such an attitude may seem harsh to contemporary readers. To Dante it obviously seemed both proper and just.

Such indicators should point us in the right direction. It is a continuing monument, both to the complexity of Dante's poem and to some readers' desire to turn it into a less morally determined text than it is, that so many of us have such difficulty wrestling with its moral implications. This is not to say that the poem is less successful because of its complexity—precisely the opposite. Its greatness is reflected in its rich and full realization of the complex nature of human behavior and of the difficulty for living mortals of moral judgment. The *Comedy* asks us, like the protagonist, to learn as we proceed.

The Moral Order of the Afterworld

The three realms of the poem are organized by related yet evidently differing moral principles. Hell is essentially defined by three degrees of sinfulness (Incontinence, Violence, and Fraud, the last divided into two segments, "simple fraud" and treachery). Purgatory, the most clearly organized, features seven terraces that purify the seven capital vices (Pride, Envy, Wrath, Sloth, Avarice [along with Prodigality], Gluttony, and Lust). *Paradiso* is governed by the nine orders of angels that correspond to each of the nine heavens and, in a less patent scheme, by the seven virtues, moral and theological.

While we expect the first two canticles to be organized according to moral principles, we probably believe that the order of *Paradiso* should reflect the essentially intellectual development of the protagonist—the pivotal matter treated in it. However, and as Ordiway has shown,[137] the each of the first three spheres of *Paradiso* (Moon, Mercury, and Venus) represents a marred version of a theological virtue (Faith, Hope, and Charity, in that order); the next four correspond, as many have noted, to the four moral virtues, Prudence (Sun), Fortitude (Mars), Justice (Jupiter), and Temperance (Saturn). All three of the theological virtues (Faith, represented by St. Peter, Hope by St. James, and Charity by St. John) reappear, in their perfected form, in the Fixed Stars. This is not to deny that the angelic orders, as enumerated in *Paradiso* XXVIII, are reflected in their heightening ranks by the intellectual development of the protagonist. The order of the last *cantica* is developed along this axis, and prominently so. Yet here, too, a moral order gives the heavens some of their meaning.

Of *Purgatorio,* commentators have less to say, because its ordering principles so manifestly typify opposition to the seven capital vices. After the prologue in Ante-Purgatory, where the excommunicated and late-repentant do their time before being allowed to get on with their purification, each terrace of this magic mountain does its work exactly as announced. The Earthly Paradise, exposited as an "eighth terrace" by Lansing,[138] like the Empyrean, both lies outside the organizing principles of its cantica and subsumes them. In Eden all sins have been made good; in the Empyrean, love and knowledge, mutually reflective, irradiate the souls of the blessed in their loving knowledge of God. Will (expressed by love) and faith (expressed as true knowledge) are the twin wheels that move the poem from its outset to its last tercet, which, as Pertile has argued,[139] refers to *two* wheels, not to one alone, despite the singular form of *rota* in v. 144.

Strangely enough, the greatest debates among those who attempt to make sense of the moral order of the poem involve the first cantica, the one in which the design of evil is given the longest exposition—the entire eleventh canto—that such matters occupy anywhere in the poem. The essential ordering structure of the punishment of sin is not what we will find in *Purgatorio.*[140] Rather, it is derived from pagan sources, mainly Aristotle, with some Cicero thrown in for a crucial definition.[141] The following reading, developed from a recent commentary, is an attempt to bring the question into focus.[142]

Perhaps the key passage for our understanding of the organization of lower hell occurs in Virgil's words in *Inferno* XI, 22–27: "Every evil deed [*malizia*] despised in Heaven / has as its end injustice [*ingiuria*]. Each such end / harms someone else through either force or fraud. / But since the vice of fraud is

man's alone, / it more displeases God, and thus the fraudu-
lent / are lower down, assailed by greater pain." All sins punished
therein are sins of *malizia,* malice, in the sense that these sinners all willfully desire to do harm (those who are incontinent
in their desires may indeed end up doing harm to others or to
themselves, but their desire is for another kind of gratification
altogether, essentially only self-harming). Heresy, because it lies
within the iron walls of Dis, and is thus also punished as a sin of
the will rather than of the appetite (surely it seems closer to malice than to appetite), is perhaps less readily considered a desire
to harm others (even though it assuredly, to Dante's mind, does
so). *Ingiuria* thus has both its Latin meaning—injustice, acting
in opposition to the law (*iniuria*), and its other meaning—the
doing of harm. As Mazzoni points out,[143] Daniello was the first
commentator explicitly to link this passage with its almost certain source in Cicero (*De officiis* I, xiii, 41), a passage that defines
iniuria as having two modes, force or fraud, with fraud meriting
the greater disdain.

Here malice is divided into two subgroups, force (violence)
and fraud. Fraud itself will shortly be divided into two subgroups
(vv. 65-66), but for now Dante has simply divided the sins of violence (cantos XII-XVII) and of fraud (cantos XVIII-XXXIV)
into these two large groups. As for malizia, Mazzoni has pointed
out that for Dante, who follows St. Thomas, the word *malizia*
reflects *voluntas nocendi,* the will to do harm.[144]

At vv. 28-33 Virgil divides the sins of violence (synonymous
with those of force) into three subsidiary "rings" (*gironi*). These
are, in order of their gravity, violence against God (cantos XIV-
XVIII), against oneself (canto XIII), and against one's neighbor
(canto XII). Vv. 34-51 flesh out this analysis.

Turning at last to fraud (vv. 52-60), Virgil now divides it into
two kinds, depending on whether it is practiced against those
who trust in one or not. He first describes the second and lesser

kind, "simple fraud," we might say, committed by those who are punished in the eighth Circle, which we shall learn (*Inf.* XVIII, 1) is called Malebolge after the ten "evil pockets" that contain them (cantos XVIII–XXX). Here Dante, for whatever reason (to keep his readers on their toes?), allows Virgil to name the sins in no discernible order, meanwhile omitting two of them: (6) hypocrisy, (2) flattery, (4) divination, (10) counterfeiting, (7) thievery, (3) simony, (1) pandering [and seducing, not mentioned here], and (5) barratry; totally omitted from mention are (8) false counsel and (9) schismatic deeds. The second form of fraud (vv. 61–66), that which severs not only the tie of affection that is natural to humans but also that even more sacred one which binds human beings in special relationships of trust, is referred to as treachery (v. 66). Such sinners occupy the ninth Circle (cantos XXXI–XXXIV).

Virgil finally summarizes and clarifies (vv. 76–90) the situation. (Alas, the net effect has been anything but clear.) Aristotle, he says, in the seventh book of the *Ethics,* treats the three dispositions of the soul that Heaven opposes. These are incontinence, malice (the *malizia* of v. 22), and "mad brutishness" (*matta bestialitade*—vv. 82–83). The clarity of this statement should not have left so much vexation in its wake as it has. (For a thorough review of the debate and a solution of the problems that caused it, see Francesco Mazzoni's lengthy gloss on these verses.[145]) "Malice," just as it did when it was first mentioned, identifies violence and simple fraud; "mad brutishness" refers to treachery. As Mazzoni demonstrates, both in Aristotle's *Ethics* and in Thomas's commentary on it (and elsewhere in his work), "bestiality" is one step beyond malice, just as it is here in Dante; in Thomas's words, it is a "magnum augmentum Malitiae" (a major increase in Malice)—that is, a similar but worse kind of sin. Nonetheless, there are those who argue that, since *malizia* eventually comes to encompass *both* kinds of fraud (those punished in *both* the eighth and ninth Circles), *matta bestialitade* cannot refer to treachery. Yet if they considered the way in which Dante has handled his various definitions, they might realize that he has done here just what he has done at vv. 22–24: he identifies "malice" with violence and fraud and then (at vv. 61–66) adds a third category (and second category of fraud), treachery, just as he does here. Triolo has offered a strong and helpful summary of the debate in English, with arguments similar to and conclusions identical with Mazzoni's.[146]

The reader should be aware that the foregoing discussion is at odds with many others, and certainly that of Cogan. The single most troublesome aspect of Virgil's presentation involves the *three* orders of sins of the hardened will. (Sins of incontinence obviously also involve the will—any human action does. The distinction is between intermittent willfulness and more or less constant willful preoccupation—for example, between the frame of mind of a casual shoplifter and that of someone planning an elaborate holdup of a bank: the first does not wake up in the morning planning to steal a ribbon from a department store; the second awakens with a plan in mind.) In his first description (vv. 22–27) there are only two classes: sins of malice involving violence (cantos XII–XVII) and those involving fraud (cantos XVIII–XXXIV). Where does matta bestialitade (vv. 82–83) fit into this pattern? Where Mazzoni and Triolo (and the present writer) are sure that the answer is clear, that the phrase refers to treachery, the second degree of fraudulence, most commentators to this day believe that it refers to violence. The listing of the summarizing elements of sin in this passage present, in order, incontinence, malice, and mad brutishness, in such a way as to raise the question. Those who are in accord with Mazzoni read the tripartite division as incontinence, violence and "simple fraud," and treachery, a worse form of fraud. The opposing view has the scheme as follows: incontinence, fraud, and violence.

Two immediate and obvious problems with the second hypothesis are that it erases the first definition of malice (vv. 22–24) as including *both* violence and fraud; that it gives the three dispositions in a strange order: 1, 3, 2. We can realize that what was intended by Dante as a clear presentation of the moral order of the sins of *Inferno* has become the cause for an endless squabble among those who deal with the question. This is hardly the only time that commentators have made the poem more difficult than it is.

Virgil

Concerning the minor works composed before the *Commedia*, one can say that, with the exception of the last treatise of *Convivio*, which should probably be understood as having been composed in a moment of considerable pressure and of a consequent change in direction toward a new writerly identity, there is little evidence in Dante's texts of his having been deeply engrossed in the reading of Latin literature.

If one considers the question from a later vantage point, however, one can hardly overestimate the importance of Virgil for Dante. Here is Ernst Robert Curtius' assessment: "The 'awakening' to Aristotle in the thirteenth century was the work of generations and took place in the cool light of intellectual research. The awakening of Virgil by Dante is an arc of flame which leaps from one great soul to another. The tradition of the European spirit knows no situation of such affecting loftiness, tenderness, fruitfulness. It is the meeting of the two greatest Latins."[147] There can be no doubt that Virgil played an essential role in many aspects of Dante's composition of the *Comedy*, and probably in his very decision to write an "epic" poem, leaving incomplete his two treatises, *Convivio* and *De vulgari Eloquen-*

tia, in order to attach himself firmly to the great Latin tradition of writing about serious things in verse. As has frequently been pointed out, Virgil's example may be considered seminal for many aspects of Dante's poetic strategies in the *Comedy:* to write a poem that prominently features a visit to the underworld (Dante did not know Homer's texts, even if he knew about them, and can thus behave as though Virgil were uniquely qualified to serve as his model); that celebrates the Roman concept of political order as exemplified in the empire; and that is narrated by a poet who has been granted prophetic powers.

Virgil is one of the principal characters in Dante's poem.[148] That he should have been chosen to serve as guide in this most Christian of poems is something of a scandal. It is at least possible that puzzlement about Dante's reasons for choosing him for this role is at the root of the early commentators' tactic of treating the poem, not as the "history" of an actual experience that Dante claims it to be (with a consequent treatment of Virgil as a historical figure, as he is so clearly meant to be considered), but as an allegorical fiction. Although the introductory information processed in the poem (*Inf.* I, 67–75) makes Virgil entirely and recognizably historical (Mantuan parents, approximate dating of his birth and career, his authorship of the *Aeneid*),[149] commentators responded (and sometimes still respond) by interpreting Virgil as "Reason" or some related allegorical characteristic of the human psyche. The poem created by such interpretation is thus meant to be considered the record of an internal struggle of a threatened Christian soul, as represented by the contending forces of appetite (whose role is supposedly played by the character Dante) and those of reason (personified in Virgil). While the *Aeneid* itself was subjected to such readings by interpreters like Fulgentius and the author of the commentary attributed by some to Bernard Silvester, it seems clear that Dante himself, at least when he was composing the

Comedy, neither read Virgil's poem in this manner nor wrote the *Comedy* with such criteria in mind. Dante's treatment of the greatest Latin poet makes his Virgil a problematic character for the earliest interpreters of the *Comedy.*

Other problems, not of a commentator's devising, afflict our attempt to come to grips with Dante's choice of Virgil as the guide in his poem. And these problems arise from Dante's own troubled perception of his pagan poetic hero. One tradition of Christian reception of Virgil, which is at least as old as the emperor Constantine, held that his much-discussed fourth Eclogue actually foretold the coming of Christ. Had Dante believed that, his choice of guide might have troubled us less. However, we can be certain from *Monarchia* (I, xi, 1) that Dante knew that Virgil's "virgin" was not the blessed Mary but Astraea, or Justice. Any number of passages within the *Comedy* make it plain that Dante did not consider the Roman poet a Christian avant la lettre. We must conclude that he deliberately chose a pagan as his guide, leaving us to fathom his reasons for doing so. In recent years a growing number of Dante's interpreters have been arguing that Dante deliberately undercuts the Latin poet, showing that both in some of his decisions as guide and in some of his own actual texts he is, from Dante's later and Christian vantage point, prone to error.[150] If this is the case, we must not forget that Dante is at the same time intent on glorifying Virgil. And we might consider the proposition that Dante's love for him, genuine and heartfelt, needed to be held at arm's length and gently censured, perhaps revealing to a pagan-hating reader that Dante knew full well the limitations of his Virgil. Yet Dante could not do without him. Virgil is the guide in Dante's poem because he served in that role in Dante's life. Once Dante rediscovered the texts of the Roman poet, he seems to have made of him a central source for much of his own identity as supporter of the imperial ideal and as poet of weighty subjects. It was the works of Virgil, and not those of Aristotle or Aquinas, that served as model for the *Comedy;* it was Virgil who, more than any other author (although Ovid's role is far more important than it is often seen to be), helped to make Dante Dante.

Throughout this theologized epic, verses from Virgil make themselves heard with greater frequency than any other sources except for the Bible and the texts of Aristotle.[151] In the opening action of the first two cantos, as has been argued,[152] Dante carefully (and unobtrusively) weaves strands from the first book of the *Aeneid* into his narrative fabric. And this pattern of quotation, while not as persistent later in the text (roughly one-fifth of all Dante's citations of Virgil occur in his first five cantos), runs through it in its entirety, even after Virgil leaves the poem as a character in *Purgatorio* XXX. We are therefore not surprised when Dante has his character Virgil inform us that the younger poet knows his master's poem by heart (*Inf.* XX, 114). Virgil as a figure of medieval legend, subject of tales of magic that pleased the popular imagination,[153] is essentially missing from the highly literary focus of Dante's reading of Virgilian text. Whatever Virgil meant for Dante, that he was a poet seems to have meant the most to him. It has not been emphasized enough that the rereading of the *Aeneid* reoriented Dante from writing in mixed verse and prose to composing a lengthy poem intended to stand entirely on its own feet.

Yet Dante's great affection for Virgil does not get in the way of his careful sifting of the work of his *maestro* and *autore* for what he considers problematic in it. In recent years, some of Dante's readers have been pointing out that, if Virgil is allowed an honorable afterlife in Dante's pages, his standing is nonetheless frequently undercut in ways that point up the distance from him of even his greatest medieval admirer. This effect is noticeable in the poem in two kinds of situations: at moments in which the authority of Virgil as guide is undermined and in instances where his texts are found to be defective in one respect or another. In *Inferno* we find several examples of Virgil's fallibility as a guide: he is denied entrance to the city of Dis by the rebellious forces that guard it (VIII); he gives a confused and Empedoclean explanation of the Crucifixion (XII, 37–45); he offers several incorrect interpretations of the wicked intentions of the *Malebranche* and subsequently experiences annoyance at having been tricked by them (XXI–XXIII). In *Purgatorio* we see Virgil chastised by Cato, along with the saved souls who lent their ears and hearts to Casella's song (II and III); we find him indirectly but unmistakably compared to the loser in the simile that opens the sixth canto, in which Dante is like a winner in a game of dice; we observe the difficulty he has in understanding how Statius, who is accounted a Christian by none but Dante, could have been saved (XXII). These scenes, and others like them, are presented because Dante wanted to make his readers aware that he as a Christian poet had not "gone over to the other side" in his veneration of Virgil.

The same may be said with respect to the second category, in which we are given to understand that the works of Virgil likewise require correction, from a Christian point of view. In *Inferno* I, 125, we learn from Virgil's lips that he was "ribellante" against God's law. And even if his regret over the grounds for his perdition may make him overstate his guilt, signs of the wrongness of Virgil's work are frequent in Dante's text. If we limit ourselves to two examples from each cantica (and, in this category as in the other, additional significant examples could be mentioned), in *Inferno* we find the authority of Virgil's text gently questioned when the protagonist's formulation intrinsically compares the truthfulness of his newfound guide to that of the Bible (II, 25, 28): Virgil, as author, gives Aeneas the right to boast about his voyage to the otherworld, whereas Paul requires no such authorial intervention: he simply went there ("Andovvi poi lo Vas d'elezïone"); moreover, when Virgil retells the tale of Manto (not to mention that of Eurypylus), he does so in such a way as deliberately to contradict the narrative details found in the *Aeneid* (X, 198–203). In *Purgatorio*, in the very canto in which he is intrinsically compared to a loser in a game of chance, Virgil is also put in the position of having to explain how the message of the *Aeneid* (VI, 376), which would clearly seem to deny the efficacy of prayer, is not in fact at odds with Christian doctrine (VI, 28–42). In another extraordinary passage (XXII, 37–42), Statius informs the protagonist (and the listening Virgil) that the denunciation of avarice in *Aeneid* III, 56–57, was to him in fact a call for restraint in prodigality, a curious interpretation that anticipates a still more central and deliberate misreading of a Virgilian text, the opening of the fourth Eclogue (XXII, 67–72). Statius read this text as a prophecy of the coming of Christ, while we know that Dante believed it to have concerned Astraea, not Mary. In *Paradiso* we find the deliberate and otherwise unnecessary questioning of Virgil's veracity when he described the welcoming gesture of Anchises to Aeneas in Elysium, "se fede merta nostra maggior musa" (if our greatest muse deserves belief—XV, 26). Still more dramatic is the insistence on the salvation of Ripheus (XX, 67–69), in Virgil the most just of the Trojans, if abandoned by the gods to his lonely death ("dis aliter visum" [to the gods it seemed otherwise]—*Aen.* II, 428). In these and in other passages we perceive that Virgil's authority, not only as guide but as author, is held up to frequent and persistent scrutiny.

The linking of Virgil with tragedy (*Inf.* XX, 113) and of Dante with comedy (*Inf.* XVI, 128; XXI, 2) not only associates Virgil with the lofty style and Dante with the low style intrinsic in his choice of the vernacular for his poem but, as few currently acknowledge, associates the *Aeneid* with a tragic plot, one that ends unhappily, and the *Comedy* with a "comic" and positive ending. Most today do not believe that this was Dante's understanding. Yet the description of Virgil's poem as "l'alta mia tragedìa" (XX, 113) would involve a pleonasm if the noun does not stand for something different from the adjective: if the noun refers only to the (high) style of the Latin poem, the adjective is unnecessary. What Dante is making Virgil say is that his poem is exalted in style and unhappy in its conclusion.[154] The nineteenth-century commentator Raffaele Andreoli put the matter succinctly in his gloss to this verse: Virgil's poem is a tragedy "pel tristo fine dell'*Eneide* terminante con la morte di Turno, e per la nobile lingua usata da Virgilio" (both because of the sad ending of the *Aeneid*, which concludes with the death of Turnus, and because of the noble language used by Virgil). Both Jacopo della Lana and Francesco da Buti had previously made similar points, but Andreoli's view was and remains very much a minority position, especially among Italian Dantists. It is difficult to say why, especially since Dante himself, in *Monarchia* (II, ix, 14), acknowledges the possibility that the *Aeneid* could have had a "happy ending" had Aeneas not observed the offending baldric that Turnus had stripped from Pallas and decided not to exercise clemency.

For Dante, Virgil is the most welcome of sources, the most needed of poetic guides. It is simply impossible to imagine a *Comedy* without him. And no one before Dante, and perhaps very few after, ever loved Virgil as he did.[155] At the same time there is a hard-edged sense of Virgil's crucial failure as poet of Rome, the city Dante celebrates for its two suns, Church and empire, but which Virgil saw only in the light of the one (and perhaps even then not clearly). For Dante, that is his great failure. As unfair as it seems to us, so much so that we frequently fail to note how often Virgil is criticized by the later poet who so loved him, that is the price Dante forces him to pay when he enters this Christian precinct. And it may have been the price that Dante exacted of himself, lest he seem too receptive to the beautiful voices from the pagan past, seem less resolute as the poet of both Romes. The Virgilian voice of the poem is the voice that brings us, more often and more touchingly than any other, the sense of tragedy that lies beneath the text of the *Comedy*.

Beatrice

The *Comedy* begins in medias res. We hear the resonance of the epic convention in its opening phrase, "Nel mezzo del cammin" (Midway in the journey).[156] But the narrative skein actually begins only in canto II, where we hear of the council in Heaven that results in Beatrice's visit to Limbo to speed Virgil on his way to aid Dante, lost in mortal fear and danger. For those who come to the *Comedy* conversant with Dante's earlier work, this is a stunning moment. If from the ending of *Vita nuova* we knew of Dante's revivified love for Beatrice in Heaven, from *Convivio* we learned that Dante's affections had later moved in a different direction. Yet it is not the donna gentile who presides over the *Comedy*, but his first love. Readers tend to be so pleased by this resumption of that first "love story" that they fail to realize that this moment, intrinsically at least, is a sort of rifacimento of *Convivio*. As we have seen, the *Comedy* is often set to the task of countering or modifying particular ideas or attitudes expressed in *Convivio*. The reinstallation of Beatrice as his lady here, at the outset, at least suggests that the enterprise of *Convivio* (with its representation that the Lady Philosophy has superseded Beatrice as the object of his affection and reverence), is ipso facto to be regarded with caution. The debate over this issue divides Dantists, perhaps unnecessarily. Many readers find the writer of the *Comedy* and the champion of the Lady Philosophy frequently at odds; but some critics decry as absurd the suggestion that Dante rejected the Lady Philosophy at any time or in any form. There are three responses to such views: (1) it is true that Dante never stopped studying or thinking about philosophy; (2) Dante *did,* however, stop loving the Lady Philosophy; and (3) by turning his attention in the *Comedy,* to philosophy as the handmaid of theology, Dante corrects the central problem left by *Convivio,* which presents philosophy as his only lady. The division that separates the two works is not so much a debate between philosophy and theology as it is a discussion of the relative roles of the two. And it is significant that Lady Philosophy herself finds no place in the poem. In a sense, she is represented by the ancient philosophers gathered in Limbo and by the philosophic discourse we hear spoken by such authorities as Virgil, Marco Lombardo, and Thomas Aquinas. In every case we realize that the the insights offered by philosophy, practiced according to the proper rational procedures, are necessarily less than those which revelation makes possible, as Virgil himself several times attests. This does not make philosophizing unnecessary but makes it relatively less valuable. In the *Comedy,* David and Aquinas both know more that is essential than Aristotle does, but Aristotle can aid us in the effort to know as they know.

The next time that we see Beatrice, she appears in *Purgatorio* XIX, in Dante's dream of the lady, "holy and alert" ("santa e presta"—v. 26). This is a controversial statement. The identity of this lady in Dante's second purgatorial dream is much and hotly debated.[157] However, as a handful of twentieth-century commentators have observed, the most natural understanding is that Dante is here reprocessing the event of Virgil's encounter with Beatrice in *Inferno* II. In 1300, ten years after her death, she miraculously descends to Limbo to "harrow" Virgil (as his familiars, Homer and the other poets, apparently believe, only to realize that he is now back where he belongs: *Inf.* IV, 81, "l'ombra sua torna, ch'era dipartita" [his shade returns that had gone forth]).¹⁵⁸ And so, in a remarkably restrained and understated moment (what other poet would have relegated so dramatic a return of the heroine of his work to an offstage conversation with a "supporting actor"?) Beatrice returns to Dante's life and work as the centering presence once and for all. Here, it seems plausible or even probable, Dante's dream reflects the scene that initiates his guided journey through the afterworld. As Virgil will reveal to Dante the nature of sin in hell, so in the dream, encouraged by Beatrice, he strips the garments from the stinking belly of the Siren. The text makes plain that the *femmina balba* (stuttering woman—XIX, 7) is to be equated with the *antica strega* (ancient witch—XIX, 58), who represents the three excessive loves of the things of the world purged on the three upper terraces (avarice, gluttony, lust).

Beatrice's climactic appearance, now finally to Dante directly, occurs in *Purgatorio* XXX, when she calls him by name as her first act (XXX, 55), echoing the conclusion of the fourth Georgic, the unique occasion on which Virgil inscribes his own name within his three major works.¹⁵⁹ From here on, until she returns to her seat in the Empyrean, she will oversee Dante's instruction. But first it is time for a scolding. For if Dante showed promise in his youth ("ne la sua vita nova"—XXX, 115), as soon as Beatrice was dead, he gave himself to another (126),¹⁶⁰ only to pursue (still other?) false images of the good ("imagini di ben seguendo false" [131])—the phrase rehearsing the definition of the three excessive loves represented by the *strega* as these were described in canto XVII, 133: "Altro ben è che non fa l'uom felice" (there is another good that does not make man happy). Beatrice's harangue against the sinful Dante runs well into the next canto, until his confession is accepted and he is drawn through the waters of Lethe. Exactly what he is charged with is difficult to say. According to Beatrice, he gave himself to someone else (XXX, 126) and followed (still other?) false versions of the good

(XXX, 131); according to Dante, "presenti cose" (things near at hand) led him astray; Beatrice seems to allude to these as well when she speaks of *le serene* (XXXI, 45), for the stuttering woman in the dream referred to herself as "dolce serena" (sweet siren—XIX, 19), and Virgil equated her with the antica strega (XIX, 58). The objects of Dante's ill-directed affection are then referred to as "qual cosa mortale" (what mortal thing—XXXI, 53), "o pargoletta o altra vanità" (whether a young girl or other vanity—59–60). Whatever Dante's sins were, they must have involved sexual liaisons, for neither avarice nor gluttony, at least in his opinion, has touched him, and that would eliminate all but the sins of the Terrace of Lust. It is more than likely that the donna gentile of the *Vita nuova* is the "altrui" to whom he confesses that he turned after Beatrice's death, who is now returned to the carnal identity that she had in that text; however, given the various forms in which his transgressions are framed by Beatrice, it is difficult to be certain of more than Dante's self-confessed sin of lust.

Beatrice is first present in the poem in the role of moral preceptor rather than of guide to truth. But once we enter *Paradiso,* that is precisely her role. It is no wonder that Romantic readers insisted that they found her less attractive a character than Francesca. (And many today, following De Sanctis and Croce, want to turn the poem into something it is not.) Dante's heavenly preceptor sounds like a doctor of the Church, exactly as Dante wanted her to. Her role, some have argued, is to supervise the correction of Dante's intellect. (In such a formulation Virgil supervises the correction of Dante's will in *Inferno* and the perfection of his will in *Purgatorio,* while Beatrice plays a similar role in the correction of Dante's intellect in the first nine heavenly spheres, and Bernard presides over the perfection of Dante's intellect in the Empyrean.) [161] That role makes her Scholastic distinctions seem only reasonable. No one has ever poeticized theology at greater length or with better art than Dante has done in *Paradiso*.

Beatrice addresses many large theological and philosophical subjects. (In *Convivio* Dante might have referred to them as *digressioni*—and in *Paradiso* XXIX, 127, he again uses that word.[162]) This is not to consider those discussed by Justinian, Charles Martel, St. Thomas, Cacciaguida, and still others. Beatrice's topics include the following: the paradoxical nature of heavenly "gravity," which draws one up and not down (*Par.* I); the spiritual reason for the spots on the moon (II—another refutation of material found in *Convivio* [II, xiii, 9]); the information that saved souls do not return to their star (as Plato said they did in the *Timaeus*) but to the Empyrean (IV); the relation between absolute will and conditional will (IV); the repayment of broken vows and the freedom of the will (V); the *primum mobile* and the roots of time (XXVII); the order of the angelic hierarchy (XXVIII); the nature of and reason for God's creation of the universe (XXIX); the fallen angels (XXIX); members of religious orders who teach false doctrines (XXIX); the numberless ranks of the angels (XXIX); the blessed and the empire (Henry VII and his opponents—XXX). This last passage, with its rancor against the enemies of imperial Rome, has disturbed many readers, who find it inappropriate as Beatrice's last words. Such a response disregards the thoroughgoing political concern of the poem. It also pays no attention to the pattern that frames either end of Beatrice's appearances in the text. In *Purgatorio* XXX her first utterance was "Dante" (v. 55); her last, in the next canto numbered thirty, is the circumlocution for Dante's most hated enemy, Boniface VIII.[163]

Once she has finished her task, she reassumes her place in Heaven, next to Rachel (XXXII, 8–9). Having ceded her glorious office, Beatrice becomes more distinctly herself in her total absorption in her love of God. Now that she has restored Dante's soul to health, as he recognizes (XXXI, 89), he can for the first time address her as herself. When first he saw her, in the Earthly Paradise, he saw in her the memory of his former love; for that reason he is rebuked by her angelic choir (*Purg.* XXXII, 9): "troppo fiso!" (too fixedly!) is their exclamation. In an only apparent paradox, Dante begins his new "new life" with Beatrice in a subordinate role, addressing her by "voi," in recognition of her divinity, yet construing her as she was, a beautiful girl in Florence. By the time she has finished instructing him, he has learned how to love her in his love for God. His final words to her take the form of a prayer (XXXI, 91) and reveal the total success of her mission: Dante now fully understands that she lives in Christ, the cause of his being drawn from his sinful life when she descended to Limbo. He prays that she will keep alive in him his soul's new-found understanding, lest, once he is again on earth, his lower appetites return (XXXI, 78–90). During these, his last words to her, the one who has made everything possible for him (including, we may reflect, this poem), he now for the first time addresses her by the "tu," so enthusiastically, in fact, that second-person pronouns and second-person verb endings occur eleven times in these twelve lines. It is worth noting that a similar pattern in the naming of Beatrice is present in *Vita nuova*, where she is rarely addressed at all, and then as "voi" only in the poems (and not in the narrating prose, where she is always "she"): for example, in chapters XII, XIV, XV, XVI. It is only with his first imagining of Beatrice's death, in the penultimate verse of "Donna pietosa," that her soul in Heaven is addressed as "tu": "Beato, anima bella, chi te vede" (fair soul, blessed is he that sees you — *VN* XXIII, v. 83). After her actual death, in the third canzone, "Li occhi dolenti," the same phenomenon is apparent: "chiamo Beatrice, e dico: 'Or se' tu morta?'" (I call to Beatrice and say, "Are you then dead?" — *VN* XXXI, v. 55), as it is a final time in the sonnet in XXXIV, v. 14: "oggi fa l'anno che nel ciel salisti" (today marks a year since you arose to heaven). In *Vita nuova*, Beatrice on earth or, in the *Comedy*, out of the Empyrean and interacting with mortal Dante, is given the "voi"; only when she is at one with God, where and when there are no human hierarchies, does she become "tu." When she resumes her undeflected love of God, Dante is ready for his final ascent.

Bernard

It is perhaps not surprising that we pay less attention to St. Bernard of Clairvaux as a Dantean mentor than to Virgil, whose presence as guide in this Christian poem has the power to fascinate—and does so. The personalized nature of Dante's choice of his second guide, Beatrice, nevertheless renders that selection a challenging gesture. As a Christian saint, Bernard seems somehow a less surprising guide in a fourteenth-century poem than Virgil or Beatrice, and this apparent suitability for his role combines with the brevity of his presence in the poem (for less than three full cantos—XXXI, 58-XXXIII, 50—St. Thomas, Cacciaguida, the loquacious eagle in Jupiter, all have speaking parts that continue longer than his) to draw concerted attention away from him.

If the schema for Dante's growth as protagonist proposed earlier (correction and then perfection of the will followed by correction and then perfection of the intellect) does indeed correspond to the intentions of Dante the writer, then Bernard occupies the most elevated and crucial position among Dante's several guides. Under his tutelage Dante is prepared for the culminating visions that occupy the final ninety-one verses of the *Comedy*, for seeing first the universal relations of all things in God, then God as and in Himself, and finally the principle of the Trinity. Bernard himself is no longer necessary after his last smile, in a cantica filled with smiling, guides Dante's eyes upward (XXXIII, 50).

In a poem that infrequently features favored Frenchmen, Bernard occupies the highest possible position despite his ultramontane origin and life. Bernard, born in 1090, entered the monastic life at Citeaux in 1111 and, having been quickly recognized for his devotion and zeal, was asked to found a new monastery with twelve monks at Clairvaux in 1115. In 1128 he helped to form the order of Templars, Christian soldiers encouraged to fight in the Holy Land. The last quarter-century of his life was filled with political activity, both within the Church and in its relations with the French king. He was a rabid supporter of the ill-fated Second Crusade. His Cistercian order grew all the while: at the time of his death the number of its houses approached one hundred, all founded within a span of less than forty years (he died at Clairvaux in 1153). That a man so deeply embroiled in the realities of ecclesiastical politics, so heavily committed to Christian soldiering, could find time to write as much as he did is in itself remarkable, bringing to mind the unsurpassed example of St. Augustine. That his writing was, in the main, mystical and devotional may almost seem surprising. His major works include *De diligendo Deo, De laudibus novae militiae, De gratia et libero arbitrio, In laudibus Virginis Matris, Sermones super cantica Canticorum,* and *De consideratione.*[164]

Dante's citations of Bernard are few and far between; the only one that is name-specific is found in the epistle to Cangrande (28): "legant Bernardum in libro De Consideratione" (let them read Bernard's book *Concerning Contemplation*). That very sparsity provides the occasion for still another dispute about the authenticity of the epistle. As a result, there has traditionally been a certain puzzlement over why Dante should have turned to him as his guide in the concluding portion of the poem. Various answers have been given. Dante chose him only because he recognized him to be the leading figure in mystical theology, not because of any firm grounding in his works.[165] Another view, frequent in modern commentaries, is that it was Bernard's devotion to the Virgin that led Dante to choose him as guide.[166] Still other critics hold that it was instead from Franciscans (such as Bonaventure) and other mystical thinkers (such as Joachim of Flora) that Dante knew, more or less indirectly, the reputation of Bernard as mystic.[167] While insistence that the absence of recognizable citations of the works of Bernard in those of Dante would suggest that Dante did not have firsthand knowledge of them, recent work has now indicated that in Dante we find important elements of a Bernardan "culture," reflecting either actual texts or their tradition, a phenomenon that should now receive closer and more extensive study.[168]

Politics

Dante's political views are related to two extended periods in his life. The first, dating to the last five years of the thirteenth century and the first five of the fourteenth, involved practical considerations: his own political career and then his involvement in the united attempts of the exiled White Guelphs and Ghibellines to regain power in Florence; the second, beginning with his disavowal of his unsuccessful and squabbling allies after the disaster of the battle at La Lastra in 1304, is marked by a new spirit, global and theoretical, which endures, essentially unchanged, for the rest of his life. None of Dante's writings between 1283 and 1305 or so shows any marked interest in political ideas, despite his vigorous involvement in Florentine civic life between 1295 and 1301. His Guelph identity, which seems to have been a given, never gave rise to any theoretical justification of his views. Once he formulated his new understanding of

Rome's centrality in any larger political theory, that is, once he adopted an essentially Ghibelline view of Italy's future course, in which the empire was the cornerstone, his insistence on the theoretical justification for any political program became pronounced.

Unlike his earlier work (with the exception of *Convivio* IV, iv–v), the *Comedy* shows deep engagement with a political view of the human condition.[169] The first unmistakable note is struck in Dante's insistence on the "two Romes" (*Inf.* II, 19–24). Dante's formulation here is in no way divergent from what we will find in *Monarchia*. It is also true, however, that the imperial vision will be absent for the most part from the rest of *Inferno,* where Dante's political concern touches on events in Florence and other northern cities.[170] Although no passage in the first cantica voices concern over the sorry state of the empire, once we reach Ante-Purgatory, we hear frequent and insistent references to the importance of realizing the imperial dream shared by Dante and some languishing Italian Ghibellines. The civic discord of early fourteenth-century Florence is, however, very much on the poet's mind and is first seen in *Inferno* VI, the first "political canto" of the work. Its "Florentineness" is underscored by the relative absence of Virgilian citation for the first time since the poem began and by the emergence in the *Comedy* of Dante's "municipal style," writing characterized by its immediacy and frankness of expression. What had been condemned in *De vulgari Eloquentia* now reappears as a powerful voice, one that joins with the lofty style of Limbo and the courtly voice of Francesca to expand the range of styles available to this poet. Once it is heard, it is heard often.

The characterization of Filippo Argenti (VIII) is marked by Dante's sense of his riven city, divided, among other things, by the differences in wealth among its citizens. But Dante's political involvement in the life of the city comes back most forcibly in the character of Farinata (X), a Ghibelline with a party but no emperor (one can imagine how differently Dante might have handled this scene after the descent of Henry VII into Italy). Pier delle Vigne does bring us into the world of an emperor's court,[171] but it is one that has been gone for fifty years and is not lamented. Frederick II was the last emperor to come to Italy to rule; nothing in Dante's text indicates a hope for an imperial return. Had this scene been written during or after Henry's coming, we can imagine how much it, too, might have differed from the one that we know. As it stands, it has none of the immediacy of the imperial hope that we will find in *Purgatorio*. We return to the political life of Dante's city at some length (XV, XVI) with Brunetto, so important for Dante, whether as his guide in a life of politics, as here, or as his intellectual "father" for a career in Italian versifying, and then with the Florentine homosexual politicians—the most courteously treated of all sinners beneath the Limbus.[172] The usurers also reflect the political problems of the city (XVII), as, doubtless, do the simoniac popes (XIX): their avarice has altogether too many political consequences, as Dante could testify perhaps better than he would have liked. But no other scene in *Inferno* more vividly conveys the atmosphere of political corruption in the cities of Italy than do cantos XXI–XXII. We do not have to follow nineteenth-century interpreters in finding verbal associations between the Malebranche and actual Florentine politicians at the time of Dante's exile to sense the connection between the brutal games played in the pitch and Dante's last memories of home.[173] Similarly, the *bolgia* of the thieves (XXIV–XXV), with its five Florentines, gives us a further sense of the corruption in the lives of individuals that lies behind the decline in the city's civic values. Ulysses' canto begins with these five, and offers a bridge between theft and the false counsel practiced by Guido da Montefeltro, known, according to Filippo Villani, as the "new Ulysses."[174]

Ulysses is associated with Lucan's villain Julius Caesar by his quotation, in the first line of his address to his men, of Julius' first line of address to his troops.[175] Ulysses is further linked in canto XXVIII to Curio, whose tongue was sliced out in reprisal for his evil advice to Julius. The canto of the schismatics, like that devoted to Ulysses, thus intrinsically raises the issue of the empire, which Dante now presents rather as the destroyer of the Roman republic than as a sacred institution (his more usual view). Returning to Florentine problems, Dante shows us Mosca, whose schismatic impulse is political rather than religious (XXVIII), resembling in this the motives of Bertran de Born. In the next canto Dante describes his shame at not having avenged the death of his relative Geri del Bello (XXIX), as schism yields to vendetta as the subject of the poem. In the ninth Circle we find Bocca, traitor to the Florentines at Montaperti, and, in its final political image, Brutus and Cassius in Satan's mouths in punishment for the treason committed against the Roman Empire in the person of Julius. (Here Dante returns to the notion of the sacred empire.) Thus only the first and final political gestures in *Inferno* evoke a positive image of the empire, very much in keeping with the sentiments expressed in *Convivio* IV; these moments hardly reveal a writer who has many practical hopes for restoration of the empire in his Italy.

The opening two cantos of *Purgatorio* offer no obvious political interest, even if the figure of Cato necessarily summons up remembrance of republican virtue; Manfred, however, the victim of Guelph forces at Benevento in 1266 (*Purg.* III), reminds us that the Ghibelline principle had recently been extinguished as a vital force in Italian political maneuvering; so does Buonconte, dead at Campaldino after taking up arms against Dante and the Florentine Guelphs (V). The encounter with Sordello occasions the first outburst in the poem in favor of a reinvigoration of the empire in Italy. Heretofore we have heard only of its recent defeats; now Dante castigates Albert (who died in 1308 but was ruling at the time of the vision) and calls for a new emperor to rule over the Italians (VI, 88–126). It seems more than likely that these lines were written after Henry VII was selected but before he actually came into Italy.[176] The probable reference to Henry in v. 102, where Albert's successor is mentioned, is only guardedly optimistic, without enthusiasm. If the passage was written before Henry's advent in 1310, as is at least possible, Dante had no reason to be more hopeful than this passage would indicate that Henry would come to Italy. The same might be said for the much-debated verse in canto VII (96): "sì che tardi per altri si ricrea" (with the result that she will be belatedly restored by another).[177] Just as the emperor Rudolph (1273–91) could even then have saved Italy from "death," so now another will have the opportunity. The two passages are congruent and would seem to point to Dante's awareness of the new emperor and uncertainty about the path he would choose. Thus the *Purgatorio* would seem, as Petrocchi argues, to have been written almost exactly during the years corresponding to Henry's reign, from 1308 to 1312. It seems likely that Dante was writing this part of the poem as Henry's presence began to be felt in Italy. It is certain that his three "political epistles" were composed in 1310 and 1311.[178] All of them reveal a supporter of the new emperor whose hopes were, at least at first, ignited by the new and encouraging events. They offer some wider sense of Dante's political concerns as he was writing *Purgatorio*. To these we now turn.

Epistle V, addressed to the leaders of Italy by "humilis ytalus Dantes Alagherii fiorentinus et exul inmeritus" (the humble Italian Dante Alighieri the Florentine, unjustly exiled) in the autumn of 1310, as Henry was entering Italy, was written at a rhetorical pitch that takes one's breath away. Henry is said to be not only the Messiah—"Leo fortis de tribu Iuda" (the mighty lion of the tribe of Judah—Gen. 49:9) but a new Moses, leading his people to the "land of milk and honey" (V, 4). Described as "clementissimus" (V, 5—the word probably calls to mind, by antiphrasis, the sitting pope, Clemens, named at V, 30, and perhaps Aeneas as well, whose "clementia" might have spared Turnus according to *Mon.* II, ix, 14), this leader is poised to restore Italy to its proper role as the child of Church and empire. It is difficult not to feel the wave of enthusiasm flooding through the exiled poet-politician, only years after his "conversion" to an imperial view of the political possibilities for Italy, as he witnesses the advent of a new and anointed leader. In its conclusion, the epistle reveals Dante's awareness of the one reason to doubt the coming success of the new Augustus. Christ sanctified the principle of rendering unto Caesar the things due him (Matt. 22:21), "quasi dirimens duo regna" (as though to set apart the two kingdoms—V, 27); Peter seconded the idea when he said "regem honorificate" (honor the king—I Peter 2:17). However, that the most recent vicar of Christ, Pope Clement V, might not offer the desired support for Henry is lodged in the last words of the epistle. Indeed, all would soon have reason to mistrust the pope's public approval of Henry's election and mission. Dante even allows Clement's formulation of the two *luminaria*, the Church as the sun, the empire as the moon, to stand unchallenged (he does challenge it in *Purgatorio* XVI and *Monarchia* III, iv). But as the concluding words of the epistle make clear, Dante is concerned with the limitations that the forces of the "greater light" might place upon those of the lesser. Where the light of the "spiritual ray" is not sufficient, there let the "lesser luminary" enlighten humankind ("ubi radius spiritualis non sufficit, ibi splendor minoris luminaris illustret"—V, 30). His use of Clement's words in this way probably reflects some intimation that the pope might lack enthusiasm for the emperor whom he had done so much, even if in furtherance of his own schemes, to sponsor.

The next epistle, addressed to "scelestissimis Florentinis" (the outrageously criminal Florentines), reveals that the emperor has fallen on difficult times. The scoundrels of Florence are so designated because they transgress laws both human and divine ("divina iura et humana transgredientes"—VI, 5) in their opposition to the new emperor. The elated optimism heard in Epistle V is replaced by the voice of a Hebrew prophet calling down the wrath of God upon his backsliding people: "Et si presaga mens mea non fallitur" (And if my prescient mind is not mistaken—VI, 17), most of the citizens of this new Troy will be killed or captured by the forces of the emperor, with some survivors coming to know the pain of exile. The language of this assault will resound again, in nearly precisely the same terms, in *Paradiso* XXVII and XXX, in passages linking the disobedient cupidity of Henry's opponents and the saintly emperor ("hic divus et triumphator Henricus" [this divine, triumphant Henry]—VI, 25). (*Cupidity* is the central word to express the arrogance of Florentine motives in this epistle—VI, 5 and 22.) In *Paradiso* XXX Dante will explain that Henry came before Italy was ready: only the word *triumphator* need be relegated to the dustbin of history, and Dante's "presaga mens" is seen, not as failing, but as having been premature in its vision. Henry is dead, long live the emperor!

The last of the three political epistles, written later in the spring of 1311, is addressed to the emperor himself. It spares no hyperbole either in praising Henry or in denigrating his Florentine opponents. Reading Virgil's fourth Eclogue as a political rather than a christological prophecy (as Dante does also in *Monarchia* I, xi, 1), Dante has Henry restoring the empire and bringing back the "virgin," Astraea, or justice (VII, 6). This is not to say that Henry is not also seen as taking on the role of the Redeemer. In the only reference we have to Dante's actual encounter with the emperor, he says (VII, 9–10) that he prostrated himself before him, touching his feet with his hands and kissing the earth before him, while within himself he heard his spirit speak the words "Ecce Agnus Dei, ecce qui tollit peccata mundi" (Behold the Lamb of God, behold the One who carries away the sins of the world—John 1:29). Abruptly, the praise turns to question (VII, 11): Why does the emperor delay in taking Florence? Dante's eagerness to spur Henry on allows him even to quote (VII, 16), among a plethora of biblical and classical texts, Curio's encouragement of Caesar to march on Rome, so roundly condemned in *Inferno* XXVIII, 96–99.[179] (Even if the words work, Dante apparently asks us to forget their context.) He advises his emperor/savior that cutting off the heads of the hydra of rebellion (VII, 20) but keeping out of Tuscany is a vain exercise. The problem that needs to be addressed is villainous Florence—in the rhetorical torrent that concludes the epistle (VII, 23–30), a vixen, a viper at its mother's breast, the sick sheep that infects the others in the flock, incestuous Mirra, mad Amata, the giant Goliath. Henry, the new David (VII, 29), must kill Goliath and restore the exiled Hebrews to their homeland. This was Dante's dream. It is not difficult to imagine his disappointment when Henry failed in his eventual siege of Florence and when he died in August 1313. On the other hand, we can reflect on the consequences that might have followed the emperor's success. Might not Dante have been called on to serve in a political capacity in conquered Florence? His public utterances in support of the emperor might well have had the effect of bringing him to power in the imperial city—might even have had this as a conscious purpose. And it is at least possible that Dante would then not have written *Paradiso*.

The three political epistles are joined by three other letters

(VIII–X), which Dante wrote in the spring of 1311 on behalf of Gherardesca, the wife of his host at Poppi, in the Casentino, Guido di Battifolle, to Margherita of Brabant, Henry's wife (who died in December of 1311). This set of six letters marks the beginning and the end of Dante's hopes in Henry. It is important to remember how quickly the emperor burst upon the scene: death of "Alberto tedesco" in 1308; coronation of Henry on the Feast of the Epiphany on 6 January 1309; arrival in Italy in October 1310; coronation with the iron crown in Milan, Epiphany 1311. But in 1311, barely two years after he had been crowned in Aquisgrana, began the rapid decline in the fortunes of the young king (born around 1275). First Milan and then other cities that had done obeisance rebelled; the pope began to reveal greater hesitations about the man he had helped to the throne; Henry's own actions against other cities brought him new enemies. In October of 1311 he was in Genoa; in March of 1312, at Pisa. Like many before (and after), he found himself overwhelmed by the complexities of Italian politics and made error after strategic error. Nonetheless, he did manage to have himself crowned emperor at Rome on 29 June 1312, not, however, at Saint Peter's, but in the ruined Lateran. When he finally followed Dante's advice and moved against Florence, it was a case of too little too late. He had to break off his siege of the city after a month, in October 1312. From Pisa, one of his last bastions, he chose to move south in order to attack the forces of Robert of Anjou, a campaign that was perhaps already doomed when, while attacking Siena on his way south, he grew feverish and died, at Buonconvento, 24 August 1313.

The next passage in *Purgatorio* that reflects Dante's political concerns is placed in the mouth of a Lombard courtier named Marco (his actual identity has caused considerable discussion[180]). Marco, discoursing on the human soul's propensity to love, turns his attention to politics. Where we might have expected him, expatiating on the natural weakness and malleability of human will, to mention the role the Church plays in keeping us on the straight path, he turns instead to the king, as performing exactly this role (*Purg.* XVI, 94–129). Because of the failure of the popes to guide, and because they have confounded the two forms of power, sacred and secular, there is need for a king (*rege*, v. 95). Rome used to have "due soli" (two suns — v. 107), but now (in 1300) the one has extinguished the other (a reference to Boniface's bull *Unam Sanctam?*). Although the passage does not refer to Henry by name, it reproduces exactly the sentiments that an imperialist thinker like Dante held. As we have seen, however, Henry's political and military problems made it difficult for Dante to give him a focal role in the political passages of the *Comedy.* From 1311 on, as Dante wrote the last two-thirds of *Purgatorio,* his hopes were always fixed on Henry; political reality is probably the main reason that we hear as little of him as we do, especially given the enormously enthusiastic hopes for him expressed in the political epistles. In this formulation, Dante is wildly enthusiastic about Henry's mission, even irrationally so, but cagey enough not to commit to it too publicly, lest the negative signs that he reads all too clearly turn out to be leading to an adverse conclusion, thereby undercutting his authority as political seer.

Readers might expect that the Statius episode, involving the interaction of three epic poets, would dwell on the question of empire, but that is not the case. For Statius, the fourth Eclogue is about Christ, not politics. The whole scene (*Purg.* XX–XXII) is without serious interest in the Roman Empire, for all the interest in it evinced in the writings of Statius and Virgil — and Dante. It is only in the Earthly Paradise (in *Monarchia,* we remember, the symbol of the active life, the "giardin de lo 'mperio," in the words of Dante's denunciation of "Alberto tedesco" [*Purg.* VI, 105]), that contemporary political reality will again intrude into the poem, and then not until the very end of canto XXXII, when we see the French king (the giant of the pageant) draw the papacy (the harlot) off through the wood, thus representing the recent events of the so-called Babylonian Captivity (Clement's election in 1305 and the actual removal of the papacy to Avignon in 1309). And these resonate into the next canto, where Beatrice comments on the scene and promises that an heir of the (imperial) eagle, a "cinquecento diece e cinque" (five hundred ten and five), will slay the harlot and the giant. Not only is this prophecy itself offered in such a way that it has become a knot of extraordinary difficulty for interpreters of Dante,[181] but it is conjoined with another enigma, the prophecy of the *veltro* in *Inferno* I.[182] To many it now seems that this second prophecy is surely imperial in nature, as perhaps the first one is as well (although this interpretation is more difficult to support, given Dante's less positive view at the time he composed *Inferno* of the possibility for a *renovatio imperii*). The words "non sarà tutto tempo sanza reda / l'aguglia" (not for all time shall the eagle be without an heir—*Purg.* XXXIII, 37-38) seem, beyond reasonable doubt, to allude to a temporal leader, and almost certainly an emperor. The most economical understanding is that Dante here, under the form of a prophecy that can always be taken back, should events so require (and so they did), refers to Henry. If he wrote these lines in 1312, he could not have been greatly optimistic about Henry's future as emperor. But under cover of the "enigma forte" (v. 50), he can take his chances. As we shall see, even after Henry's death Dante continued to believe that the empire would again make its shaping presence felt by those who live this life that is a race to death ("del viver ch'è un correre a la morte"—v. 54). The mentions of a *rex* by Marco in *Purgatorio* XVI and Beatrice in XXXIII both, in this view, refer to Henry.

Paradiso, some Dantists like to say, has left the shore of political life far behind as it presents the city of God. Though it is true that much of the last cantica is untouched by political concerns, it is more just to acknowledge that it is nonetheless surprisingly involved with them. And if the first five cantos allow us to believe that in the book of the heavens we will read only of heavenly things, the sixth puts us back on earth with Justinian's canto-long speech. This formal arrangement highlights the singularity of the canto, for it is the only one in the poem spoken in a single voice. What is perhaps as singular, given the expectations with which we come to *Paradiso,* is that its first 111 lines are entirely devoted to the principle of empire. Beginning, like the *Aeneid,* like the *Comedy,* and like the speech of Ulysses in *Inferno* XXVI, in medias res, Justinian's "epic" narrative describes the flight of the Roman eagle. (Its "hero," Aeneas, the hero of Virgil's epic, is mentioned in periphrasis in v. 3). In God's cosmic scheme, the sacred destiny of Rome is to rule the world. Justinian, the Christian emperor, is divinely inspired to set Roman law straight in his *Institutes.* He fulfills precisely the role, we may surmise, that Marco Lombardo has in mind for the king he envisions, who will, since no one else does, make Justinian's code of Roman law a reality once more in the fourteenth century.[183] Justinian is the model that Henry is seen as fulfilling; however, Henry is dead. The end of Justinian's speech is not, as was Beatrice's in *Purgatorio* XXXIII, a prophecy of a world event of greatest consequence, but a violent denunciation of both Ghibellines and Guelphs. We can speculate that, had Henry been alive when Dante wrote these lines, they would have had a different conclusion. For once again the empire, as it was in *Inferno,* is sacred but not in a position to accomplish its goals. Charles Martel has an opportunity to voice his concern (VIII, 49–84) for the lack of proper leaders, and Cunizza, after a passage (IX, 25–33) that well may reflect Dante's awareness of Albertino Mussato's *Ecerinis,*[184] goes on to refer to the Paduans' opposition to Henry and then to the imperial vicar, Cangrande, who defeated them at Vicenza in 1314 (IX, 46–48), but until we reach the middle of the last cantica, we find little more of significant political interest.

The fifteenth canto of the *Paradiso* introduces Dante's great-great-grandfather, Cacciaguida, and along with him a return to concerns with politics. The first obvious and textually specific citation of the *Aeneid* in *Paradiso* occurs in XV, 25–27, presenting Cacciaguida as Anchises to Dante's Aeneas.[185] The reference to the epic of Rome and its patrilinear succession leads, first, to Cacciaguida's description of an idealized past in Florence (XV–XVI).[186] Then Dante's ancestor turns to the present time of trouble and foretells the woes that attend his issue: exile and the enmity of the Black Guelphs, of Pope Boniface, and of his own fellow White Guelph exiles (XVII, 46–69). The result is that Dante will become a "parte per te stesso" (a party of yourself alone—XVII, 69). The events referred to were reflected also in Dante's first two epistles, the first, written in the spring of 1304 to Cardinal Niccolò da Prato, concerning the last effort at conciliation among the Florentine exiles before the failure of Niccolò's intervention and the disastrous battle at La Lastra (20 July 1304); the second, written probably later that year to Oberto and Guido, counts of Romena, revealing the bitter and powerless condition (II, 8) of this man who had become a "party of one." The second part of Cacciaguida's prophecy, more hopeful (XVII, 70–99), predicts better exilic days for Dante once he is welcomed in Verona, in actual fact no earlier than 1303 (and, if so, by Bartolomeo della Scala, who died early in March of 1304). The major concern of the passage is to praise the magnanimity of Cangrande della Scala, who came to power only after the death of his brother Alboino in 1311, and who was Dante's host during the middle years of the decade, from 1312–18, in Petrocchi's estimation.[187] Dantists frequently suggest that this canto was written as a grateful farewell to Cangrande, as Dante went off to Ravenna, his last refuge (1318–21). Yet it also reveals the tenacity of Dante's imperial hopes: even if Clement V will deceive Henry (named in v. 82), the imperial cause will find a champion in Cangrande. Of him Cacciaguida foretells "cose incredibili" (incredible deeds—vv. 92–93), but Dante does not share them with us. This suppressed political prophecy has a connection to those we have already heard concerning the Veltro and the DXV, as though to suggest that, even if he is currently uncertain what exactly will happen, Dante seems to believe that Cangrande, the imperial vicar, will serve a new emperor so well that the forces of the empire will be deployed, finally, in victory.

Cacciaguida's final gesture is to name eight other warriors who defended the faith (XVII, 37–48) against the forces of the East. That the members of the group are nine in number and include four of the Nine Worthies in Jacques de Longuyon's *Les voeux du paon,* may point to that work, or its tradition, as a source.[188] Here the secular leaders devoting their courage and strength to their religion reveal a higher dimension to political activity. The same may be said with respect to the next heaven, once we move from Mars to Jupiter, for now we see rulers in the eye of the Eagle who are less celebrated for their political accomplishments than for their personal justness: David, Hezekiah, Constantine, William the Good, and (surprisingly) Ripheus (XX, 43–72), the last no more than a bit player in the *Aeneid.* They offer an answer of sorts to the dilemma posed by the state of European political decline, in the year 1300, sketched in the acrostic verses that spell out "LUE," or "plague," in XIX, 115–141.[189]

It is in *Paradiso* XXVII that we again hear of the emperor. St. Peter, declaiming against the corruption of the contemporary papacy, suddenly predicts that Providence, which defended Rome against her enemies (Hannibal's forces) in the person of

Scipio, will do so again (vv. 61–63). This promise of a prophecy, clearly imperial in its drift, is made good at the end of the canto, when Beatrice delivers the third and final "world prophecy" in the poem, one that seems specifically applicable (as opposed to those by Cacciaguida and St. Peter, the first of which is not reported [XVII, 92–93] and the second of which is a widely applicable promise, lacking in particulars [XXVII, 61–63]). The final lines (144–48) of canto XXVII constitute a genuine prophecy of a major event to come: a "storm" that will turn around the errant ships of the "human family" (v. 141) and set them straight on course so that good fruit shall follow the blossoming of the flower. The fifteenth-century commentator John of Serravalle has the virtue of understanding that this prophecy is in line with the program of the first two, Veltro and DXV. He rather disappointingly, however, reads all three as tokens of a reform within the Church. It is probably better to see that the "fleet" (*classe*) that Dante has in mind is the City of Man, as Augustine would have insisted, the Rome to which Peter referred in his prophetic utterance earlier in the canto. The word *classe,* apparently used here for the first time in Italian, is the Roman term for "fleet," and indeed was the name for the harbor at Ravenna when that city was the capital of the empire. The "fleet" that Dante here has in mind would surely seem to be associated with the imperial destination of the historical voyage of the "human family." Such an interpretation is bolstered by the final imperial presence in the poem, that of Henry VII in *Paradiso* XXX, 133–38. That the emperor should be the first (and only still-living) presence in the Empyrean, with the crown-surmounted throne that is Dante's final tribute to him, reveals again this poet's fixation on the imperial idea. Henry had come to set Italy straight ("drizzare Italia") before she was ready. The phrasing draws us back to the prophecy in *Paradiso* XXVII, 147, where "la classe correrà diretta" (the fleet shall set its course straight). Thus, even at the end of this visionary poem, the empire is a part of the vision. Dante has still not given over his political engagement, so essential an element in his view of God's purpose.

The Poetry of the *Comedy*

This poem is so rich in meanings, so involved with moral, political, cosmological, and theological concerns, so complex in its challenge to the reader's ability to interpret its difficult passages, that we tend to forget its most distinguishing characteristic: its poetry. In recent years two of its readers, Tibor Wlassics and Teodolinda Barolini,[190] have made concerted efforts to remind Dantists that the marks of the poetic nature of the text are everywhere, whether we choose to observe them or not. And they deserve our attention, in that they absorbed so much of the author's.

Dante's invention of *terza rima* was, as Erich Auerbach observed, a brilliant solution for a narrative poem, for it both "looses and binds," at once bringing the verse to momentary conclusion and propelling it forward.[191] The use of rhyme, which would seem so barbarous to John Milton (see the prefatory note to *Paradise Lost,* where he seems to have Dante in mind as well as the 113th Psalm, a text so central to the explication of the *Comedy,* now employed by Milton to indicate the regained freedom of blank verse), was a given in the Italian poetry of this age. Dante would not have dreamed of imitating the Latin epics in this respect (he even has Virgil refer to his own verse as "rima" [*Inf.* XIII, 48], thereby eliding the difference that would mean so much to Milton). When he invokes the aid of the Muses, as he does several times, he seems to be calling on what he and other authors are able to learn about composing from the study of the trivium, the first three of the seven liberal arts—grammar, rhetoric, and dialectic. God may have granted him the substance of this vision, but it is a man that makes it into a poem. The experience has been vouchsafed him—or so he claims—but its recounting is completely within his competence. To put it another way (and to make reference to one of Dante's favorite devices), God is not the author of the hundreds of similetic comparisons that we find in this text.

Similes, whether developed and balanced, in imitation of the Latin poets (Virgil perhaps foremost among them), or more limited and briefer, in the simple comparison, occur some four hundred times in the work.[192] Metaphor, less frequent and less studied, is also prominent.[193] Addresses to the reader, a distinguishing trait of the poem, serve to put the reader into the text or at least alongside it, making marks in its margins.[194] There are at least nineteen of these, seven in each of the first two cantiche, at least five in *Paradiso*.[195] Invocations, perhaps the most insistent way a poet has to remind his audience of his special status, occur, as we have seen, nine times in the work. All these techniques for establishing the distance of the poem from prose keep the reader involved as a sort of partner in the enterprise. It is hard to imagine another poet who has done this part of the job so successfully; and indeed no single poem in the history of the West has received so much attention from its earliest days to the present.

One of Dante's most successful "games" with his reader involves his characteristic movement back and forth between being an "easy" poet and a difficult one, thus combining the two traits that distinguished two traditions of Provençal poetry, divided between *trobar leu* and *trobar clus*.[196] Among his many successful ways of reassuring the reader of this challenging poem is his occasional habit of employing a figure of speech that *seems* to be difficult and challenging but is actually extremely easy to decode. For instance, *Inferno* V, 61-62: "colei che s'ancise amorosa / e ruppe fede al cener di Sicheo" (she who broke faith with the ashes of Sichaeus and slew herself for love). No reader who has written on the passage has ever got it wrong; the reference is to Dido; no other need apply. Periphrasis is one of the most effective of tropes in making a reader labor, and it can be dazzlingly difficult.[197] One need only remember some of Dante's more baffling excursions into this rhetorical figure, referred to in the epistle to Cangrande as *circumlocutio* (*Ep.* XIII, 66). An example follows (*Par.* XXVII, 136–38): "Così si fa la pelle bianca nera / nel primo aspetto de la bella figlia / di quel ch'apporta mane e lascia sera" (Thus does the white skin of her original visage turn to black in the fair daughter of him who brings morning and leaves behind him evening—a translation that will not be accepted by all). This passage has caused nearly total mystification.[198] That first example of periphrasis, by contrast, is never debated. By using a "learned" trope but making it easy, Dante encourages his readers. It is a powerfully effective way of involving us.

The question of Dante's style has been magisterially treated by Ignazio Baldelli.[199] Based on Contini's view of Dante's *plurilinguismo,* that astounding range of all stylistic possibility that we find in the *Comedy,* Baldelli's discussion demonstrates, with patience and skill, the range of styles that we find in the poem, from the most plebeian local vernacular utterance to the loftiest Latin expression.[200] As Dante moves easily between the poles of difficult and easy, so he moves readily among the demands of various stylistic registers. At the same time, there is, within the poem itself, an insistence that, by definition, it is written in the low, or comic, style. Virgil is high, Dante, low.[201] Once again, Dante has things the way he wants them. He is a poet who demonstrates his stylistic variety, while insisting, for his own polemical and programmatic purpose, that his poem is— merely by virtue of being written in the vernacular—"comic."

Ours is not to argue, but only to understand the reason for his claim, even as we understand that the *Comedy* includes a stylistic range that had perhaps not ever been seen before.

Whatever explanation one may offer for the enduring popularity of the *Commedia*, it seems clear beyond any need of demonstration that the adulation bestowed on Dante's masterwork is, perhaps even more than his admirers themselves admit, based on the extraordinary effect of its poetry itself. This is not to deny the greatness of its author's vision, encompassing the known universe and the essential concerns of humankind, but rather to insist that the execution was everything. It is a poem that strikes readers as being both true and beautiful. On the other hand, even those who either do not particularly admire its brand of truth or undermine it in order to make Dante more like themselves are swept along by the greatness of his words, of the apparently unmediated contact with a higher order of comprehension and expression.

We would perhaps not admire the poem were it to have purveyed ideas that seem trivial. Yet we observe that *Monarchia*, which expresses essentially the same basic view of politics that we find in the poem, has had nothing like the exalted afterlife that the poem has had and continues to enjoy. The ideas that produced the Latin treatise, and the arguments that sustain them, are limited to Dante's time and place. They may be noteworthy, but they are not commanding. (The same ideas, expressed in the poem, seem much more potent.) The Dominican friar from Rimini Guido Vernani made a vicious attack around 1327 on the ideas and arguments of the treatise.[202] Even though it is easy to believe that Dante escapes the onslaught unscathed, one should read Guido's text before making any such judgment. Guido makes any number of telling criticisms. And the fact of the matter is that *Monarchia* is far more interesting because Dante wrote it than for anything it demonstrates. As a treatise on the political future of Europe it is remarkably without practical consequence; as a defense of the imperial principle it is convincing if one happens to share the author's views. It probably never did and never will change the views of anyone else.

MONARCHIA

Dante's overtly political writings (with the exception of *Vita nuova,* there is a "political" aspect to all the more important texts in his oeuvre, even *De vulgari Eloquentia*) are, after his first significant excursion in *Convivio* IV, largely confined to his epistolary responses to the descent of Henry VII into Italy (Epistles V–VII) or to the period after Henry's death in August of 1313 (Epistle XI, *Monarchia*). With the exception of the epistle to Cangrande, these four letters are the longest Dante wrote; barring none, they are the most passionately wrought. The first three of them have already been discussed in relation to the political concerns of the *Comedy.* The last serves here as prelude to discussion of *Monarchia.*

Epistle XI, addressed to the Italian cardinals attending the conclave at Carpentras (which began in May 1314) after the death of Pope Clement V on 20 April 1314, is attested by Giovanni Villani's *Cronica* IX, 136.[203] It was thus almost certainly written before 24 July 1314, when some of Clement's former supporters effectively closed the conclave down for two years. (When it was reconvened in Lyons in 1316, Jacques Duèse was chosen, to Dante's disgust, as the new pope—he would reign as John XXII until 1334.) It serves as a useful introduction to a reading of *Monarchia,* for it presents similar concerns, themes, and techniques. Drawing significantly on the Bible, as he will in *Monarchia,* Dante begins with the opening of Jeremiah's Lamentations, a text that has already resounded in *Vita nuova* (XXVIII, XXX) at the death of Beatrice. Now the city that sits solitary in her grief is Jerusalem, as the type not of Florence but of Rome, widowed by the Babylonian Captivity of Mother Church. These themes were fairly extensively visited in the final cantos of *Purgatorio*, with their ugly portraits of Clement and Philip the Fair, who were living at the time, both of whom are castigated under pseudonyms in the epistle (XI, 8). Dante's urgent concern that the College of Cardinals produce an Italian pope is of considerable significance, both in itself and as a backdrop to *Monarchia*, which tends to be read as being considerably more antipapal than it in fact is. Were Dante the representative of a new lay political vision that some of his interpreters have insisted he is, we would not have heard this impassioned plea for the restoration of the papacy to Italy, for in that case he would have been more likely to consider his homeland well rid of it.

It is difficult for us to imagine that a private citizen writing to the Italian cardinals in conclave could receive a serious hearing. Indeed, we have no record that Dante did actually send the epistle across the Alps. But the document itself either reports or imagines that some in his intended audience responded (the second hypothesis may be the more reasonable one). The terms in which Dante sets these remarks are remarkable. Fortified by the examples of David and Paul, he has made bold to address these new Pharisees (XI, 10). Someone (one of the cardinals, we are perhaps asked to believe) has accused Dante of being another Uzzah, daring to stretch out his hand to steady the tottering Ark of the Covenant, drawn by the oxen. Dante does not agree that he has merited the wrath of God, yet he does not entirely reject the charge of being the new Uzzah.[204] Instead, accepting the role of Uzzah (which he has so resolutely, if only intrinsically, disavowed in *Purg.* X, 55–57), Dante does not present himself as an Uzzah who tries to steady the ark, but as an Uzzah who tries to correct the course of the oxen, the cardinals of Italy. His "presumption" is thus not ungodly, but precisely what is required. One can only smile, yet with recognition that this is serious play indeed.

Dante's "monarchy," like his vulgare illustre, exists only as an ideal.[205] It refers to no precise past or existing temporal state, but to the divinely sanctioned polity of all Europe that should be the essential ordering force in the world of human affairs. (One must be careful in drawing such analogies but can hardly avoid thinking of the current debate concerning the political organization of Europe.)

The manuscript tradition, carefully documented by Ricci, is problematic. It is fairly late (no manuscripts earlier than the end of the fourteenth century) and filled with incorrect readings, exhibiting some twenty-one codices in all. *Monarchia* was translated into Italian by Marsilio Ficino (1467) and first published in Latin in Basel (1559). Despite the fragility of the tradition of the text's transmission and the considerable editorial labor that resulted, awareness of the work early on is readily evident. Boccaccio (*Trattatello* I, 195-96; II, 133-34) says that it was much used to defend imperial authority when Lodovico of Bavaria descended into Italy in 1328. And it drew the wrath of the Dominican Guido Vernani in 1327 and was publicly burned in 1329. Its polemical nature guaranteed that it would be much studied and often destroyed or else circulated clandestinely. Its *Nachleben* is perhaps the most agitated of that of any of Dante's minor works. Placed on the Index in 1554, it remained there until 1881.

The dating of the work has been fiercely and widely disputed in the twentieth century. The major schools of thought (and here I simplify a complex argument) have it written around 1308, between *Convivio* and *Comedy* (Bruno Nardi), during Henry VII's unsuccessful campaigns in Italy (1312-13: Michele Maccarrone, Gustavo Vinay), or after Henry's death and the composition of the early cantos of *Paradiso* (Pier Giorgio Ricci, Prue Shaw). The last opinion is now accepted by most students of the problem, both—and more importantly—because internal evidence supports it and because Dante himself says, at *Monarchia* I, xii, 6, "sicut in *Paradiso Comoedie* iam dixi" (as I have already said in the *Paradiso* of the *Comedy*—see *Par.* V, 19-24). The phrase, as has been demonstrated beyond any reasonable doubt, is present in all but three of the manuscripts, and has been erased in two of these, thus making it all but impossible to believe that it was inserted by a scribal hand.[206] In any case, it is now clear that arguments for a date preceding that of the early cantos of *Paradiso* are likely to have been put forward by scholars who had other agendas to advance. The philological evidence is profoundly convincing. But that still leaves us with a date as early as 1314 (Mazzoni) or as late as 1320 (Padoan). If we follow Petrocchi's dating for *Paradiso* (1316-21), 1316-17 (Mazzoni's *terminus post quem*) seems a most convincing possibility.[207]

The first of *Monarchia*'s three books begins with the first of the work's many universalizing statements: All human beings endowed by God with the love of truth (*amorem veritatis*) want to pass on what they have received, from those who preceded them, to their posterity (I, i, 1). Dante, speaking in the first-person singular, proposes to show his worth when he sets out to "intemptatas ab aliis ostendere veritates" (reveal truths that have not been attempted by others—I, i, 3). Among such hidden and useful truths is a knowledge of "temporalis Monarchie," that is, the model for rulership in this world (I, i, 5). Dante assumes this arduous task not so much on his own power as in the light of God (I, i, 6). While not as striking as his insistence on divine inspiration as source for his treatise on vernacular eloquence (*De vulgari Eloquentia* I, i, 1), the work's beginning, like its conclusion, inscribes political discourse under the sign of God. The term *temporalis Monarchia* is now restated as Imperium. The definition that follows is crucial to his argument: "unicus principatus et super omnes in tempore vel in hiis et super hiis que tempore mensurantur" (is a single sovereign authority set over all others in time—that is to say, over all authorities that operate in those things and over those things which are measured in time—I, ii, 2). Dante here both extends and limits his argument, universalizing the concept of empire but confining it to the secular realm. It is a clever maneuver, an attempt to reassure clerical critics, at once by separating the monarchy from the eternal world and by insisting on the ideal and total nature of such rulership. Brief reflection leads to the conviction that we have never known such rulership in fact, for even in Rome's greatest days of glory, she did not rule all the world. Thus Dante's monarchy, like his vulgare illustre, is a construct, an ideal. As was the case in *De vulgari Eloquentia*, however, he will pursue this ideal with many a practical concern, as is immediately apparent in the three main points of inquiry that, he says, have roiled the question, each of which will fill one book of the treatise (I, ii, 3):

1. Is monarchy necessary to the well-being of the world?
2. Did the Roman people take on the office of the monarch by right?
3. Does the monarch's authority derive immediately from God or from some (mediating) minister or vicar of His?

Unlike *Convivio* and *De vulgari Eloquentia*, *Monarchia* begins with an explicit outline of its eventual content. And we receive exactly what we here are promised, an indication of the careful planning of the argument of the work.

The subject of the text having been defined, Dante turns to his method in it (I, ii, 4). "Since every truth that is not a first principle must be demonstrated with reference to the truth of some first principle," that *principium* must now be found. And because the subject of *Monarchia* is politics, it is clear that the purpose of the work "non ad speculationem per prius, sed ad operationem ordinatur" (is not directed primarily toward theoretical understanding but toward action—I, ii, 6). And since this principle is (Aristotle's) final cause, the eventual goal of human society is the first principle that must be discovered (I, ii, 8). Since God and nature do nothing in vain (I, iii, 3), since humans (unlike angels) have possible intellects, that is, intellects that reflect their human potentiality, these must eventually be actualized. As Averroës says in his commentary on Aristotle's *De anima,* that actualization must take the form of intellectual speculation that has (a secondary) practical result (I, iii, 6–10). And just as the individual is perfected through contemplation, so the human race has its true happiness in *pax universalis* (I, iv, 2), as Scripture attests, and that is the first principle we seek (I, iv, 5). Dante's insistence on the authority of Averroës with regard to the nature of the possible, or potential, intellect has led to a number of discussions in the past half-century.[208] Nardi, who sees all of *Monarchia* as Averroistic, therefore argues for an early date, between the dates of *Convivio* and the *Comedy.* The extent of Dante's rejection of Averroës, however, in *Purg.* XXV, 63–66, is perhaps at times overstated. What Dante says emphatically in that passage is not that the *intelletto possibile* does not exist, but that Averroës errs when he claims that it exists "disgiunto da l'anima." Dante's view, both in *Monarchia* and *Comedy,* would seem rather to reflect that of Albertus Magnus, who (unlike Thomas Aquinas, as Vasoli points out) finds accommodation in Christian terms for the concept, binding it into his complex view of the rational soul.

Having established his central concerns, Dante returns to the first of the three questions about monarchy that he has delineated: Is it necessary for the well-being of the world? Resorting to the Scholastic form of argumentation, he develops his first principle, pax universalis, by conjoining to it Aristotle's authoritative dictum that holds it necessary, when a plurality of things are ordered toward a common goal, that one of these must guide or direct and the others be guided or directed (I, v, 3), as Dante had already said, translating the same passage in Aristotle, at *Convivio* IV, iv, 5. Moving up the chain of human relationships, from the individual to the household, a small community, a city, and finally a kingdom, he says that in all of these there must be a single governor. In the kingdom there must be a king (I, v, 4–8). The examples he has adduced for the smaller entities, however, do not all support his argument. The intellectual faculty, the pater familias, the man who is chosen to govern the small community, all these are indeed individual entities. But his example for the city is *unum regimen*. The probable examples of Aristotle's Athens in the *Politics* or of Dante's own Florence, both cities governed by more than a single ruler, serve to undercut the argument. And since Dante will so insist on the individuality of the sovereign, he would probably have done better simply to have leaped from the small community to the kingdom.

As he proceeds, his argument becomes still more evidently syllogistic (he himself first uses this term at I, vi, 3). He spends the rest of the first book offering ten further "demonstrations" that the monarchy is necessary for the well-being of mankind, each treated in a separate chapter (I, vi–xv). As a coda to these eleven "proofs," Dante now, in conclusion, adds the evidence of history: Christ chose to be made flesh during the reign of Augustus—as Paul said, "plenitudo temporis" (in the fullness of time). From this zenith of human happiness, Christ's coming to the world in the kingship of Augustus (I, xvi, 2), we have descended to our present misery. Humankind fails in its use of higher (speculative) and lower (practical) intellect, and its affective nature does not nurture the love breathed into us by the Holy Spirit (Psalm 132:1): "Ecce quam bonum et quam iocundum, habitare fratres in unum" (Behold how good and how

pleasant it is for brethren to dwell together in unity—I, xvi, 5).
That is the aim, currently unfulfilled, of our race.

The second book turns from Aristotle's authority toward that
of Virgil, mainly because of its topic, now firmly anchored in
history. Lucan is here, too, as are Livy and Orosius. And the subject is no longer the philosophical abstraction monarchy, but the
Roman imperium as it existed in time and space. Again Dante
must distinguish a first principle. This time it is that "illud quod
Deus in hominum societate vult, illud pro vero atque sincero iure
habendum sit" (what God wills in human society must be considered true and pure right—II, ii, 6). Dante progresses from the
abstract formulation of philosophical principles to concrete historical consideration of the one previous true monarchy, Rome.

The book begins with the three opening verses of the second
Psalm. Where the ending of the last book had reflected Psalm
132:1, offering a hopeful if fragile vision of humankind united in
brotherhood, thus mirroring both the Augustan age of Christ's
birth and Dante's hopes for a new "fullness of time" in a restored
monarchy, the first three verses of Psalm 2 bring us back to the
dreadful current history of our race, with which the first book
ended (I, xvi, 5). Against this picture of the diseased intellects
and wills of both subjects and rulers, the third verse calls for
an exodus: "Dirumpamus vincula eorum, et proiciamus a nobis
iugum ipsorum" (Let us burst their chains and cast their yoke
from us—II, i, 1). Dante begins with a confession (II, i, 2). Once
he had believed, astonished at how they had succeeded so easily,
that the Romans held sway only through force of arms (*armorum . . . violentia*). As soon as he understood that Rome's hegemony was the work of Providence (is he referring to *Convivio* IV,
iv?), his amazement turned to scorn for those who opposed the
monarchy. And he again recites the first three verses of Psalm 2,
reading them now as a Caesarian hymn (II, i, 4). Dante's confession has raised various forms of speculation about the dating of

his "conversion" to the idea that the imperium was legitimate. It seems clear that his Ghibelline swerve is documented first in *Convivio* IV, that he was Guelph in his essential political views until sometime after 1305. We cannot be sure about this, but it seems a reasonable understanding.

David's call for freedom from tyranny is now in Dante's mouth, but he turns its words against kings and princes who side with the hierocrats' cause, which is opposed to true monarchy. It is a strong and daring statement (II, i, 5). Demonstrating the justness of Roman imperium will both convince those kings and princes who arrogate power to themselves that they have no right to do so, and instruct their subjects that such as they are in fact free of their governors' yoke (II, i, 6). The true answer to the question will be found "non solum lumine rationis humane, sed etiam radio divine auctoritatis" (not only by the light of human reason but also by the radiance of divine authority—II, i, 7).

To begin with, he must induce the first principle (II, ii, 1) from an investigation of the question of whether Rome assumed the dignity of empire by right (*ius*) and not by force (*vis*). Just as he did with regard to the first issue studied, the necessity of empire (I, ii–iv), he must find a first principle adequate to this task. Considerations of art and nature lead to the hypothesis that, as we have seen, governs this second book of the work: "What God wills in human society must be considered true and pure right" (II, ii, 6). Now, since God's will is invisible, evidence of its election can be found only in those things that it has done in this world, which is as the wax to its stamping seal (II, ii, 8). This image, used to similar effect in *Purgatorio* (X, 43–45; XVIII, 37–39; XXXIII, 79–81) and *Paradiso* (I, 40–42; VIII, 127–29; XIII, 73–75), allows for a second kind of demonstration, one rooted in our ability to examine the evidence of history, not in logical procedures alone.

Dante first, however, turns back to the syllogism, supported by the testimony of Livy and Virgil: "It is appropriate that the noblest race should rule over all the others; the Roman people was the noblest; therefore, it was appropriate that they should rule over all the others" (II, iii, 2). This syllogism is developed at length on the basis of the evidence supplied by authority, first in defense of Rome's nobility, reflected in the nobility of Aeneas, whether by birth or by marriage (II, iii, 6-17). The second "proof" is that God frequently intervened miraculously in support of Rome (II, iv); the third, that Rome was a model of civic probity (II, v). It is in this chapter, the longest in the work, that, in a paradox that still is largely unnoticed as such, Dante justifies imperium on the basis of the virtues exhibited, not by emperors, but by their predecessors, nine heroes of the Roman republic: Cincinnatus, Fabricius, Camillus, Brutus, Mucius Scaevola, the three Decii, and Cato. Dante's republican interests and sympathies had first been apparent in *Convivio* IV (v, 12-17), where all these names are heard, along with those of Torquatus, of the Drusi, and of Regulus. His sympathies are apparent in the *Comedy* as well.[209] It should also be noted that Julius Caesar, the first monarch, plays so small a role in the treatise on monarchy as to be virtually absent. He is mentioned only at II, v, 17, and then only as the captor of Cato and other (virtuous) republicans. Thus the Dante of *Monarchia* is even less accommodating to the founding emperor than is the author of the *Comedy,* where Julius is often maligned, as he was by Lucan, but at least sometimes praised,[210] and where he is named in *Paradiso* VI, written perhaps at nearly the same time as *Monarchia,* as the first emperor. Of the early emperors in Dante's striking list in *Paradiso* VI, only Augustus (I, xxi, 1; II, viii, 14; II, x, 8) and Tiberius (II, xi, 6) are referred to in terms that resemble those used for them there, while Julius and Titus, for very different reasons, one must assume, are omitted.

The central chapter of Dante's middle book, a privileged

space, if we attend to a numerical program in the numbers of chapters in the three books of *Monarchia* (16 + 11 + 16),[211] turns to a deeper reason for Roman ascendancy, now perceived as embedded in the very purpose of a providentially inspired nature. Again combining syllogistic reasoning with the authority of great poetry, Aristotle (II, vi, 5-7) with Virgil (II, vi, 9-11), Dante satisfies himself that Rome was ordained by nature to rule the world. And this concern leads inevitably to the question of how God's will may be found revealed in the workings of history. We come to know it by reason and by faith (II, vii, 2). When that will is hidden from us, when it is not perceptible either in nature or in Scripture, it sometimes can be understood by special grace (II, vii, 7). This itself may occur either in direct revelation or else "quandoque revelatione disceptatione quadam mediante" (sometimes being revealed through some kind of putting-to-the-test—II, vii, 7). This seeming digression has carried Dante's argument exactly where he has wanted it to proceed, for the latter form of "proof" will be his central evidence in his examination of the signs of Rome's political sovereignty. The two forms of "test" to which he alludes are the *duellum,* or combat between two champions, and the footrace, a contest among several (II, vii, 9). The following two chapters consider these two forms of contest. He first resorts to metaphor: the Roman people who "cunctis athletizantibus pro imperio mundi prevaluit" (won the race to rule the world against all competition) did so by divine decree (II, viii, 1). Others who tried were never so successful, not the Assyrians under Ninus (and Semiramis), not the Egyptians under Vesages, not the Persians under Cyrus and then Xerxes, not the Macedonians under Alexander—who came the closest (II, viii, 3-10). Then Virgil, Lucan, Boethius, and St. Luke are all cited in proof that Rome won its race and therefore did so by divine judgment, and thus by right (II, viii, 11-15). Dante next turns to *duellum,* a term that he employs in an extended sense to include combatants who are more than two in number (but are joined in one of two groups). This sort of trial by combat is resorted to, he says, only when all other means of resolution escape human judgment (II, ix, 1) and when the decision is sought "solo zelo iustitie" (only out of zealous love of justice—II, ix, 2). This rather optimistic view of the motivations of conflicting forces is clearly necessary to his purpose. Without it, it would have been difficult for him to assert that, if God is present in such conflicts, only justice can triumph, so that what is acquired by duellum is acquired by right (II, ix, 6). Though Dante is clearly aware that not all contend for such lofty reasons (II, ix, 9), his account of Roman history (II, ix, 12–18) presents the Romans as having fulfilled his two conditions (that there be no other means of resolution of the conflict and that both sides seek justice from it), and therefore as having come to imperium justly (II, ix, 19–21), the triumphant conclusion of this part of his argument in the second book.

The last two chapters of that book reveal a change in tactic. Dante will now make the case for Roman hegemony from within the principles of the Christian faith (II, x, 1). In a real sense, we have entered the essentially theological part of the work.[212] The tenth chapter begins with a huge outburst against hierocrats in the Church, whose moral integrity as prelates is impugned, to speak mildly (II, x, 1–3). His following argument is potentially still more disturbing: If Rome's empire was not based on right, Christ would have consented to injustice in choosing to be born under its aegis, and this proposition is manifestly false (II, x, 4). Further, if the empire was not based on right, then Adam's sin was not punished and expiated in Christ—a similarly unwarranted conclusion (II, xi, 1). Both these deliberately provocative arguments are rounded off by a bitter thrust at the clear target of these barbs: "Desinant igitur Imperium exprobrare romanum qui se filios Ecclesie fingunt, cum videant sponsum Chris-

tum illud sic in utroque termino sue militie comprobasse" (So
let those who pass themselves off as sons of the Church stop attacking the Roman Empire, seeing that Christ the bridegroom
sanctioned it in this way at the beginning and at the end of his
earthly campaign—II, xi, 7). That God chose to make himself
flesh and to inflict pain on that flesh under the rule of Rome is
the last and warmest moment in Dante's passionate appeal to the
justness of the temporal monarchy in its only previous genuine
earthly manifestation. This message, so close in sentiment and
in tone to what Dante expresses in the Heaven of Mercury in
Paradiso, comes to its conclusion—as, on other occasions as well,
Dante enjoyed concluding parts of his texts (*Paradiso* XXX, for
instance, ends with Beatrice's denunciations of Clement V and
Boniface VIII)—with a swipe at the enemy, Constantine presented as Judas, if his pious intentions in the Donation are nonetheless allowed him (II, xi, 8).

The final book of *Monarchia,* concerned with what in modern discussions would be referred to as the separation of church
and state, is clearly the point toward which Dante has been
aiming from the outset. This is the ultimate question, involving the eventual earthly and heavenly destination of humankind.
The Monarchist must face down the negations of the Hierocrat.
Everything has prepared for this, most notably the final chapters
of the second book. And now the newness of his project is apparent, especially when we look back to *Convivio* IV. If we consider the broadly similar conception of the Roman Empire there
advanced, we also realize what is missing: any consideration of
the papacy. That lacuna is finally, and conspicuously, filled by
the sixteen chapters in which Dante spells out the independent
roles of the "two suns," empire and Church. It is no accident, as
Richard Kay has pointed out,[213] that the third book lacks even
one citation of a classical source. Dante's urgent polemic in favor

of imperialist claims against those of the hierocrats, making use, as he chooses among them, of the major arguments of the day,[214] may still seem troubling today, as it did in its own time. This attack on the papacy's claims for temporal authority has left, and continues to leave, some readers perplexed. Does Dante leave any authority to the papacy at all? The third book is so insistent, even strident, in its argument that some readers find the penultimate sentence of the work, where the pope's authority is finally lent some credence, problematic, out of keeping with the rest of Dante's argument. It is perhaps useful to begin a study of the third book with its ending (III, xvi, 17–18): "The truth concerning this last should not be taken so literally as to mean that the Roman prince is not in some sense subject to the Roman pontiff, since this earthly happiness is in some sense ordered toward immortal happiness. Let Caesar therefore show that reverence toward Peter which a firstborn son should show his father, so that, illumined by the light of paternal grace, he may the more effectively light up the world, over which he has been placed by Him alone who is ruler over all things spiritual and temporal."

To have ended *Monarchia* without such a statement, which limits the eventual powers enjoyed by the emperor, might have seemed to put Dante among those Ghibellines, like Farinata and Ottaviano degli Ubaldini (*Inf.* X), whose political identities were so fervent that they omitted God and his Church from any significant role in their political considerations. Some have seen this ending as simply a polite imposture; others as being added later by Dante at another stage in his thought (an argument, like that for a rifacimento of the *Vita nuova,* for which neither philological nor manuscript evidence exists); still others as being a perfunctory gesture of propitiation toward a papacy that he only tolerates; and still others as a heartfelt but puzzling last-minute swerve from his otherwise clear intention. It is probably better to conclude that Dante's effort is to harmonize the two supreme powers, with the result that we perceive "a Dante who opposes, then, papal power in temporal things, but not a relationship founded on the principle of the superiority of the spiritual purpose of humankind over its temporal goals."[215] Indeed, we have Dante's clear interest, expressed roughly at this time or at most a few years earlier (1314), in having an Italian pope succeed Clement V. And we should attend to the fact that he never in his work even seemed to doubt the scriptural authority accorded the papacy by Jesus' words to Peter, which runs the length of the *Comedy* (from *Inf.* II, 22–24, a passage that has unconvincingly been put to the task of demonstrating that Dante was still not "imperialist" in his broader political views,[216] to *Paradiso* XXVII, 22–27, St. Peter's cry against bad popes, a passage that underlines Dante's continuing hopes for a good one.) Dante, in other words, was both a monarchist and a thoroughly "orthodox" believer in the Petrine papacy, a man who is most serious about the doctrine of the two "suns" (not a single sun and a cesspool of corruption that should be abandoned). In short, there is not a line in anything that Dante ever wrote that exhibits the slightest doubt about the institution of the papacy, no matter what Guido Vernani or any other hierocrat might have thought, no matter what some more recent readers of *Monarchia* might choose to believe.

The ending of *Monarchia* is thus not forced or false, but represents the traditional judgment of any child of True Church. The empire is independent of the Church in establishing its authority to govern on this earth. The emperor and his subjects all have, ultimately, a higher goal. And the direction of their spiritual lives is, ipso facto, the province of the pope. It is precisely for that reason that the pages of the *Comedy* so often cry out against papal malfeasance and that, at the very center of *Purgatorio*, temporal leaders are seen as the only hope for moral (and not merely political) guidance in a language that anticipates the later theory of separate imperial and papal authorities (*Purg.* XVI, 94–114). Far from being an embarrassment, Dante's last gesture reaffirms what he has always believed and always said, publicly at least from the time of the writing of *Inf.* II, where we find the first mention of the papacy in his work.[217] For him, to say that the emperor derives his authority directly from God was not to suggest that the pope did not. Because his elevation of the emperor is so forceful, so striking, so deliberately confrontational, some of his readers have let themselves be carried beyond the point authorized by his various texts regarding the question.

The third book opens with righteous Dante escaping from the lions' mouths, a new Daniel, safe among his harmful enemies, carrying God's word, which sanctions His empire. Once God found justice in Daniel's heart ("coram eo iustitia inventa est in me" [Dan. 6:22]), King Darius punished the prophet's enemies and confirmed his own and Daniel's rulership in the name of the Living God (Dan. 6:26). Dante, who sees himself in exactly such an executive role as the servant of God and empire, hopes for exactly such protection as he deals with the third question broached by *Monarchia:* Does the emperor's authority derive directly from God or from some minister or vicar of His? Dante is fully aware of the controversial nature of his thesis, fully aware that the last book of *Monarchia* is what will draw the most violent reaction from his opponents. In his opening flourish he takes pains to provide himself with glorious precursors and divine favor: Daniel (imprisoned by the contrivance of rival politicians by Darius), Solomon, Aristotle, Paul, Isaiah, the power of God, and the Holy Spirit speaking through David (III, i, 1–4). In the texts of Daniel and David, Dante discovers the word that is central to his own self-definition: justice (*iustitia* in Dan. 6:22; *iustus* in Ps. 111:7 [112:6]). From the beginning of his discussion (III, i, 5) it is clear that Dante has no will or desire to debate the absolute spiritual authority of the pope, "quem Petri successorem intelligo, qui vere claviger est regni celorum" (by which I mean Peter's successor, who assuredly holds the keys to the kingdom of heaven). He will, however, champion the emperor's independent temporal authority. And he will spare no effort in doing so.

The deductive principle of this third book is found in the following: that which is counter to the intent of nature (*intentio naturae*) is counter to the will of God, a principle that is "proven" by "the law of contradiction" (cf. *Inf.* XXVII, 120; *Par.* VI, 21): if this were not true, then God would will what He does not will (III, ii, 7)—an impossible construct. Dante divides the opponents of imperial authority into three groups (III, iii, 6–17). The first are portrayed as overzealous in their defense of papal authority and rights, the second as motivated by greed (*cupiditas*), the third as comprising "decretalists." It is only the first of these that he considers worthy of debate, and it is to them that he turns for most of the rest of the third book (iv–xii), opposing those who, perhaps from excessive zeal, make the authority of the emperor dependent on the pope as a builder's work must follow the plans of the architect (III, iv, 1). Their arguments are at this point placed into one of three categories: those based on Scripture (III, iv–ix), those based on the historical relations between pope and emperor (III, x–xi), and those based on reason alone (III, xii).

The six scriptural texts cited by the hierocrats, discussed in each of six consecutive chapters, are Gen. 1:16 ("duo magna luminaria"—that is, the sun and the moon); Gen. 29:34–35 (Levi and Judah as fathers of spiritual and temporal powers, respectively); 1 Kings 10:1; 15:23–28; 16:13 (Samuel's appointment and removal of Saul); Matt. 2:1–13 (the gifts of the Magi to Jesus); Matt. 16:19 (Christ's words to Peter regarding the latter's dominion); Luke 22:38 (Peter's words to Christ about the "two swords," a discussion that includes a perhaps unexpected elaboration of Peter's various "unthoughtful" utterances in the Gospels [III, ix, 9-16] as proof that Peter's words are to be taken with circumspection—even the first pope, it seems, was fallible.) Dante's main historical discussion concerns, not surprisingly, the Donation of Constantine.[218] Had Dante but known what Lorenzo Valla would discover in 1440, that the Donation of Constantine was in fact a forgery, one can only imagine the triumphant tone that would have informed the entire *Monarchia*. Forced to accept the authenticity of the document, he must resort to debating the conclusions of those who base their arguments on it. Neither was the donor competent to relinquish the rights of empire (*Imperii dignitatem* [5-12]), nor was the recipient empowered to accept them (13-17). Christ, and not Peter, is represented as the "rock" upon which the Church is built ("Ipse est petra super quam hedificata est Ecclesia" [7]); empire is similarly constructed upon a single foundation: human right (*ius humanum*). No emperor has the authority to abrogate the universal monarchy, and thus the central tenet of the *donatio* and of its supporters is simply invalid.

Turning his attention to the recipient, Dante adds a second argument, superfluous, given the force and compass of the first, but now attacking the claims of the hierocrats directly. The Church, he insists, was not authorized to receive such a gift, on the basis of Christ's words proscribing the Apostle's acceptance of gold and silver (Matt. 10:9-10). Similarly, the argument that popes had called on emperors to serve them proves nothing, for "usurpatio enim iuris non facit ius" (the usurpation of a right does not establish a right—xi, 3). And if it did, Dante continues, one could as easily "prove" that the Church owes its authority to the emperor, because an emperor (Otto I) once restored a deposed pope (Leo VIII) and deposed another (Benedict V—xi, 3). One can imagine Dante's satisfaction with the final detail, which is allowed to stand, without embellishment, as his last word at this stage of his argument.

Now he turns to the last of the three categories of defensive arguments used by those who, out of excessive zeal, allege the pope's authority over the empire. (We remember that he has excluded from consideration as unworthy of response those who oppose the emperor's authority out of greed, as well as the decretalists [III, iii, 8–9]—who may not have enjoyed the company Dante places them in.) To their misuse of scriptural texts and of examples drawn from history he now adds their failed argument based on reason, exemplified in faulty syllogism (xii, 3–5), alone, and so he completes his triad of proofs, based on Scripture, history, and reason. Having finished with the negation of his opponents' arguments, he turns to the overriding positive statement made in *Monarchia:* the authority of the emperor derives directly from God.

The case for this proposition is made first negatively (the Church has no authority over empire) and then by syllogism (xiii, 2–4) supported by biblical evidence (xiii, 5–9); it continues with a second negative argument (if the Church had such authority, it would derive from a source; yet clearly none exists— xiv, 1–7), and then a third (a thing cannot have as one of its powers something that opposes its very nature—xv, 1–10). And now Dante can finally advance his positive proof (xvi, 2). Human beings are uniquely of a nature both corruptible (flesh) and incorruptible (soul) and thus uniquely have two ultimate goals (3–6). These are figured by the Earthly Paradise (happiness [*beatitudo*] in this life) and the Heavenly Paradise (happiness in life eternal),[219] the first attained by studying philosophy (using reason), the second by spiritual teaching that transcends reason (7–9). Thus humankind has need of two guides, the emperor and the pope (10). It is Dante's point that the emperor, who is necessary for our moral guidance in this world, is chosen without intermediary, by God alone (11–12), so that the "electors" who choose the emperor should rather be called "proclaimers of Divine Providence" (*denuntiatores divine providentie*—13), from which source alone the monarch derives his authority (15).

Having reached his goal, Dante summarizes the arguments of *Monarchia:* the monarch is necessary to the world's well-being; the Romans took unto themselves the empire as their right; the authority of the emperor derives from God alone (16). And here Dante adds the necessary disclaimer that has so concerned some of his readers, and with which we began, when he admits that the prince is in some respect (*in aliquo*) subject to the pontiff, since earthly happiness is in some way (*quodammodo*) ordered to lead toward immortal happiness (17). This is less a retraction than a necessary concluding gesture. Dante, after all, was not a Protestant.

LATE LATIN WORKS

The looming presence of the accomplishment represented by the *Paradiso,* a work in which the subject of theology, hitherto almost necessarily written about in Latin, is triumphantly addressed in the vernacular, has tended to deflect attention from the extent of Dante's engagement with Latin in the last years of his life. The epistle to Cangrande, the *Questio de aqua et terra,* and the two Latin eclogues all were written after 1316, as was, most probably, *Monarchia.* Thus, even if we include the unfinished *De vulgari Eloquentia* and the dozen earlier epistles, the majority of Dante's work in Latin was written after he turned fifty. This is not to compare his bilingual career with that of Boccaccio, who spent many of the last twenty-five years of his life writing in Latin, urged on by the words and the example of Petrarch, but only to insist upon the increasing importance of Latin to Dante when he put himself forward as a writer of a certain erudition. On the other hand, the works have little that bind them one to another and give no evidence of a "program" for these Latin writings. Whether Dante would have composed still more pieces in Latin cannot be ascertained on the basis of these efforts. Nonetheless, that so much of his last work is in Latin does say something about his desire to engage a learned audience, perhaps those he may have felt that he had alienated by his allegiance to vernacular.

The difference between Dante's Latin of the second decade of the century and Boccaccio's, some three decades later, is palpable. There is little in Dante's that can be described as "prehumanist," at least not when we consider his prose. Rather, we see in that prose the traces of what is most "medieval" in him, whether the Scholastic argumentation found in *Monarchia*, the tradition of the *accessus* in the epistle, or the tradition of Scholastic debate that is joined in the *Questio*. All Dante's Latin prose looks more like the past than it does like the future. The eclogues, on the other hand, while formally in the tradition of the medieval poetic debate — together with the poems of Giovanni del Virgilio, they create a sort of high-sounding tenzone between friendly antagonists — are, generically, at least on Dante's part, an attempt to resuscitate the Virgilian eclogue in Italian. If Albertino Mussato had taken on a similar challenge with respect to Senecan tragedy in his *Ecerinis* (for which he received the laurel wreath in Padua in 1315), Dante's sole adventure into the heady realm of revivifying a classical genre in the Latin of a new age rides forth upon the pages of his two eclogues.

The thirteenth and last of Dante's epistles that have come down to us, the letter to Cangrande, has caused the most heated discussion, whether its authenticity, first doubted only in 1819,[220] is in question or, if it is considered Dantean, its applicability to the interpretation of the *Comedy*. Both debates continue into our own day.[221] The two most recent editions strongly support authenticity.[222]

A subsidiary issue involves the dating of the work. Among those who have little or no doubt about the authenticity of the document, there is dispute over whether Dante wrote it soon after completing the first canto of *Paradiso* (Mazzoni), around 1317, or only after he had finished composing the last cantica (Padoan).[223] Both these arguments have strong points in their favor, but it is not clear whether either is ultimately convincing. Thus a date between 1317 (composed before Dante left Verona) and 1320 (written in Ravenna) is as close as one can currently come to a reasonable estimate.

The text as we find it is divided into thirty-three paragraphs, a fact that has attracted a certain notice, given that number's Dantean currency.[224] Yet we cannot be sure that Dante, if he was indeed the author of the epistle, divided it in precisely this way, or that, if he did, he "counted" his paragraphs. Furthermore, the manuscript tradition is a belated one. There are nine extant manuscripts, the earliest three of which, all from the fifteenth century, contain only the first four paragraphs of dedication to Cangrande; the six containing the entire epistle all date from the sixteenth century.

The epistle is in five parts: a dedication to Cangrande (1–4); an accessus to the poem as a whole and to this part, *Paradiso* (5–16); commentary on the literal sense of the *prologus,* or, in fact, half of it, the first eighteen verses of *Paradiso* I (17–31); final gesture toward Cangrande, hoping for his further support (32);[225] brief sketch of the "executive portion" (*pars executiva*) of *Paradiso:* I, 37–XXXIII, 145 (33). Whoever wrote it, it is a remarkable document. Efforts have been made to show that its larger interpretive strategy, adapted from the fourfold exegesis of the Bible (7–8)—not to mention a number of its other particular judgments—does not coincide with Dante's practice in the *Comedy.*

Sustainers of the authenticity of his authorship have been able to provide plausible responses to all such objections. The result is that, although the question cannot be considered resolved, the preponderance of evidence, from the citations by early commentators to the congruence of Dante's ideas and style in the epistle with what we find in his other writings, strongly favors authenticity. To put this another way, in order to negate the canonical status of the epistle, confirmed in the early fifteenth century by Filippo Villani, and only first questioned in 1819 (by Scolari), those who contest the authenticity of its authorship by Dante would need to have discovered far more convincing evidence of the intervention of another author than they in fact have. That they have been unable to do so, despite all the effort expended, is itself perhaps a sufficient argument in favor of authenticity. The burden of proof still lies on those who would deny Dante's paternity.

In addition to what it suggests about an exegetical procedure for reading the *Comedy,* the epistle, once its author assumes the role of *lector* of the poem (paragraph 4), treats of matters that reveal an interest in theological and philosophical concerns that is entirely consonant with Dante's usual interests. As soon as the epistle reaches its "executive part" (the phrase that is used, at 17 and 33, to distinguish the prologue [vv. 1–36] of the first canto of *Paradiso* from the narrative), Dante turns from the epistolary mode, in which he flatters Cangrande as magnanimous patron, to the exegetical mode. He will expound the sense both of the work's last cantica and of its entirety. He discusses the allegorical meaning (7), subject (8), form (9), and title (10) of the entire work. This last offers him the occasion to expound upon the difference between tragedy and comedy. The next series of remarks clarifies the specific application of these definitions to *Paradiso* (11–16), the last specifying that the philosophical aim of the work is ethical, and not merely speculative, since, as Aristotle says in his *Metaphysics,* the final end of speculation is action. Dante then proceeds to examine the literal sense of the prologue of *Paradiso,* but really only the first eighteen of its thirty-six verses (17–31). Finally, he again takes up the epistolary style, with an appeal to Cangrande for support (32–33), and concludes with a reference to the same biblical verse with which he ended *Vita nuova:* "qui est benedictus in saecula" (Romans 1:26, 2 Corinthians 11:31).[226] There is nothing here that most Dante scholars consider foreign to Dante's mode of thought and expression. On the contrary, what is here seems to some dantisti precisely and singularly in accord with his procedures and no one else's. The most unfortunate aspect of the recent controversy (it is less than two hundred years old, not so very long in the history of Dante studies) is that it has kept students from drawing a full measure of excitement from being able to read the opening verses of *Paradiso* with the very words of their author as a gloss, to think of the global plan for the *Commedia* as it was presented by Dante himself.

The *Questio de aqua et terra* was first published in 1508 by Giovanni Benedetto Moncetti at Venice.[227] In the last two centuries some have believed either that Moncetti himself had written it and supplied Dante's name as author, or that he had simply discovered, and then attributed to Dante, the work of an earlier writer. These arguments have now been effectively dismissed.[228] The final sections of the treatise, written in the form of a traditional *prise de position* with regard to a debated issue, establish precise dates and places. Spurred by a debate he had previously heard in Mantua (2), on Sunday, 20 January 1320, in the little church of Sant' Elena in Verona, Dante put forward his thesis (87–88). Present were all the clergy of Verona except those who were either inhospitable or envious (87).

The question to be resolved is developed from a commonly accepted medieval cosmological structure. The center of the Earth is the center of the universe. Around it and beneath the lunar sphere circle four elemental layers: earth, water, air, fire. The question is this: How can we account for the fact that the lowest element, earth, seems, at least in our northern hemisphere, to stand above water? In Mantua Dante had heard some defend the other view, namely that water stood above the land. Now he attends to the final and efficient causes (in this at first surprising order) of the land's higher status. Arguing on the side of the angels (or at least of the mountains, hills, and beaches), Dante demonstrates the physical superiority of some of this globe's landmass. It is, of course, not the physical facts that guide Dante's enthusiastic involvement in the debate, but the spiritual reasons that explain them. Since all things generated and corruptible require a mixture of elements for their production,[229] so *Natura universalis,* that higher and creating nature, handmaid of God, ordained that land, the lowest element, should rise up, in some places, above the waters (47–48). This is the high point in Dante's argument, in every sense. The metaphysical problem having been posed—the explanation of the final cause—he only now turns to the lesser question, bound up entirely in the physical nature of things, in order to resolve the lesser problem, the efficient cause of the phenomenon. How does our Earth take on its "humpbacked" appearance, thicker (because of the added landmass) in its northern hemisphere than in the southern one? The stars, more numerous over our half of the globe, drew the land up toward them and above the water. They are the efficient cause of the rising of the landmass that we see about us. The rest of the treatise is devoted to the destruction of the five best arguments of Dante's adversaries (79–85), which he has delineated earlier (7–16).

That the *Questio* is indeed from the hand of Dante has been sustained by its most competent editors—Moore, Biagi, Pa-

doan, and Mazzoni—on the basis of lexical, stylistic, and ideo-
logical similarities with others of Dante's works. Other scholars
have shown that the nature of the *cursus* found in it also links it
with others of Dante's Latin works.[230] The last major effort to
deny Dante's paternity of the work was made by Nardi.[231] To all
intents and purposes, this is a debate no longer. Further, Mazzoni had some time ago produced no less a witness than Pietro
Alighieri, who twice in the third redaction of his *Commenta-
rium* paraphrases fairly long passages of the text and in one of
these clearly ascribes the work to his father: "Dantes auctor iste,
disputando semel scilicet an terra esset alcior aqua vel econtra,
sic arguebat" (Thus once reasoned Dante, the author, disputing
whether the land rose above the water, or the opposite).[232] Such
compelling evidence makes the task for those who would deny
the authenticity of the *Questio* difficult at best.

Like the letter to Cangrande and the *Questio*, Dante's two
Latin eclogues have also been suspected of being inauthentic.[233]
First printed in 1719, they continue to be considered genuine
by most students of the problem.[234] Eight manuscripts are extant, the most notable being the earliest, Laurenziano 29.8, the
so-called *Zibaldone Laurenziano*, a manuscript from the hand
of Giovanni Boccaccio. This exchange of poetic correspondence
between the Bolognese Giovanni del Virgilio and Dante is datable on the basis of internal evidence to the period between the
early days of 1319 and the last months of 1320. Boccaccio, in a
note in the text of Giovanni del Virgilio's eclogue to Albertino
Mussato (1327), says that Dante's second eclogue was written a
year after Giovanni's and that Dante died before sending it on,
so that Giovanni only received it from one of Dante's sons. And
thus we find ourselves confronting a perhaps unlikely companion to the late cantos of the *Comedy*, a Latin debate concerning
the relative worth of *gramatica*[235] and the vernacular, a revisi-

tation of the question examined in *De vulgari Eloquentia* some fifteen years earlier.

The exchange was initiated by the Bolognese professor of letters in a verse epistle of fifty-one hexameters. Praising Dante for his poem about the three realms of the otherworld, Giovanni also chides him for preparing his poem for a vulgar audience by his choice of vernacular verse (*carmine . . . laico*—I, 15) and thus casting his pearls before swine (I, 21). If Dante will turn his poetic attention, in Latin, to the great political and military feats of the recent past and present (I, 26–29), he will gain universal fame in the Latin-reading world of Europe and Giovanni will present him to the *studium* at Bologna, his temples wreathed in laurel (I, 37–38). Giovanni concludes by hoping that the swan, Dante, will deign to answer the request of this mere goose (I, 50–51). And so he would do, if not in terms that would greatly please his interlocutor.

Giovanni had hoped that Dante would turn from low vernacular to lofty Latin, from a poem about the otherworld to one about the political reality of this one. Behind his urging stands a major figure, Albertino Mussato.[236] His *Ecerinis*, a Latin tragedy in imitation of Seneca, castigating Ezzelino da Romano (who had been damned by Dante in *Inf.* XII), led to his laureation in Padua in 1315. The details all fit. Giovanni's suggestion, as far as Dante is concerned, is that he become a second Mussato. Dante's response indicates that he understood the challenge perfectly. He now turns it back on his provoker, by seeming to accede to at least one aspect of Giovanni's invitation by composing a Latin poem. Dante's first eclogue is, in fact, the first postclassical eclogue written in Europe. He has left to Mussato, we may choose to understand, the lofty style of Senecan tragedy and resorted to the lowest spoke in the "wheel of Virgil,"[237] so to speak. Thus his choice of a genre reflects both his desire to emulate Mussato's practice and Giovanni's program for poetic excellence and, more centrally, to reject these. Just as the *Comedy* is in the (definitionally "low"—as Giovanni has insisted) vernacular, so his first Latin poem is resolutely—even if it is in Latin—in the low style.[238] Further, there is a second generic identity to the poetic correspondence, once Dante enters into it. It becomes, even if it is composed in Latin verses, a tenzone and therefore in this respect is also identified with the low style. It is important to remember that it was Dante, not Giovanni (who offered a verse epistle, not an eclogue), who chose to emulate the classical genre, thus already going a step beyond his Latin-flaunting challenger.

"In black letters upon a white background I saw sounds (*modulamina:* modulations) milked for me from a muse's breast": so begins Dante's confident retort to Giovanni del Virgilio, opening, like Giovanni's verses, with a compliment before engaging in oppositional discourse. True to his Virgilian model, Dante's eclogue records a conversation between two shepherds. Dante is known as Tityrus, while Melibeus, the other character in the work, is generally identified as Dino Perini, a notary and fellow exile from Florence, also living in Ravenna. While they rest under an oak, having fed their she-goats, Melibeus wants Tityrus to reveal the content of the song he has been sent by Mopsus (Giovanni—it is evident that the bucolic setting and the names of the "shepherds" are drawn from Virgil's *Eclogues*). Tityrus, who for a time modestly resists the entreaties of Melibeus, finally admits that Mopsus calls him to the laurel (II, 33). When Melibeus asks if it is his wish to continue to live unlaureated (II, 34–35), Tityrus indicates that he does indeed long for the laurel—not the prize offered at Bologna, but rather the one he hopes to receive in his native Florence (II, 41–44). Melibeus (in what turns out to have been accurate judgment) warns that time may outpace this hope. Ever the optimist, Tityrus-Dante observes that this time will come once he has finished

Paradiso, as he has completed the cantiche that describe the two *infera regna* (II, 48–50)—if Mopsus is willing. When Melibeus requests clarification of the possible negative views of Mopsus, Tityrus responds: "Don't you understand that Mopsus disapproves of the use of comic diction?" (*comica . . . verba*—II, 52), whether because women speak in such terms or because the Muses do not care for the comic mode (II, 53–54). His first formulation may, as several commentators suggest, reflect Epistle XIII, 31: "locutio vulgaris in qua et muliercule comunicant" (vernacular speech, in which even the most ordinary women make themselves understood); the two combine to clarify the issue that lies between Giovanni and Dante: the use of the vernacular for serious versifying. On the heels of this provocation Tityrus reads the poem of Mopsus to Melibeus, as proof of his claim that Mopsus deprecates the *Comedy.* After he listens to the poem, Melibeus wonders what Tityrus plans to do to overcome such opposition. He will, he says, send Mopsus ten cups of milk drawn from the udders of his favorite sheep (II, 58–64). The allusion, it seems to most who have studied it, is to the *Paradiso.* In *Paradiso* XXV, 7, Dante says that he will return from his heavenly journey "con altra voce omai, con altro vello" (with another voice and another fleece). The reference, as some have suggested,[239] is indirect but clear, a presentation of the *Paradiso* as the golden fleece that Jason brought back from Colchis—and is not coincidental, given that poem's similar concerns with Dante's potential return to Florence for his laureation after finishing *Paradiso* (in the first verse of Dante's second eclogue, which begins, "Velleribus Colchis"). This "sheep" is known to Melibeus (II, 58) and thus cannot represent Latin poetry, as some interpreters have proposed, for Melibeus is portrayed as having no Latin (II, 11–33). And thus the most reasonable interpretation of Dante's *oves gratissima* (II, 58) is that it represents the *Paradiso.* The second part of Dante's metaphor, the *decem . . . vascula* that Tityrus will send to Mopsus are, therefore, to be construed not as ten Latin eclogues (as Virgil's ten *Eclogues* may invite us to propose), but as ten cantos of *Paradiso,* perhaps the first ten. Whatever our resolution of this little riddle, it is clear that Dante's program in his first eclogue is to deny the invitation to compose a major new Latin work, by composing a minor one in defense of his vernacular—a tactic that he had employed before, in *De vulgari Eloquentia.*

One reaction of Giovanni del Virgilio to Dante's eclogue was to bind himself to closer imitation of Virgilian bucolics. (When, in 1327, he sent an eclogue to Mussato, he would finally achieve the dialogic structure that is such a leading feature of the classical genre—but not yet. In this poem, his answer to Dante's, the tone and names are imitated from Virgil's *Eclogues,* but not the form.) Written, according to Cecchini, between September 1319 and early April 1320, Giovanni's response to Dante is composed in ninety-seven hexameters. Tityrus-Dante has become a second Virgil (III, 33). Lamenting his exile, Mopsus (Giovanni has now assumed the name lent him by Dante in his first responsive eclogue) invites Tityrus, while he waits for Florence's response, to come to his "grottoes" in Bologna where, in the midst of an admiring company, they will sing together. He seems aware that his lengthy invitation (III, 47–87) is not likely to move Tityrus to leave Ravenna. In a sudden moment of exasperation, Mopsus threatens, if Tityrus will not come to him, to travel to Padua (III, 88–89). The meaning is clear. If you, Tityrus, will not have me as your champion, I shall become the champion of Mussato. In conclusion, he thinks of sending Tityrus ten pails of milk from his cow—except that it might seem presumptuous to send milk to a shepherd (III, 90–96).

Giovanni's second verse epistle shows that he has essentially given up hope of inserting himself into Dante's great career. And it is in recognition of that spirit of resignation that Dante composed his response. It, too, has ninety-seven hexameters. It is clear that this is no accident. Dante pays particular notice to Giovanni's poorly chosen number (IV, 41–43), citing the first line of his second Latin provocation verbatim and then going on to suggest that, had his rival sung three more verses, he would have enchanted the listening shepherds. Here the poet who is shortly to finish his great one-hundred-part vernacular master-work chides the Latinizing poetaster for his numerically un-gainly effort. As Sarolli was the first to point out, Dante's ref-erence to the number one hundred in his phrase "one hundred verses" (*centum carminibus*) occurs in verse 43 of his eclogue; if we turn to the same place in Giovanni's poem, we find the same number present in the description of the hundred times a vine wraps itself around an elm tree (*per centum vincula nexu*—III, 43).[240] There are no mere numerical coincidences here. Rather, we find a wonderfully wry riposte from the "poet of one hun-dred" to the "poet of ninety-seven." Advised by Alphesibeus (the Certaldese medical man Feduccio de' Milotti, according to the glossator—Boccaccio himself?—in Boccaccio's manuscript) not to accede to Mopsus' invitation by leaving Ravenna for Bologna, Tityrus-Dante responds that Mopsus does not know how pleasing the pastures of Ravenna are, but that he would nevertheless honor his friend's request except that he fears Poly-phemus (IV, 73–75). Whether Polyphemus is meant to stand for Fulcieri da Calboli, elected captain of the people in Bologna late in 1320 or early in 1321, or King Robert of Naples (referred to in I, 29), or perhaps another of Dante's several powerful political enemies, it is clear that Dante wants no part of the political life or the career of political poet proposed in Giovanni's first episto-lary poem.[241] No, he will stay where he is, at the court of Guido

Novello of Ravenna, who is described, under the name Iollas, in the final three verses of the eclogue (IV, 95–97), as overhearing the conversations of Tityrus and Alphesibeus and reciting them to Dante, who now sends them on to Mopsus. His last word, "poymus" (I make into song), is familiar from *De vulgari Eloquentia* II, iv, 2: "poesi[s] . . . nichil aliud est quam fictio rethorica musicaque poita" (poeticizing is nothing other than something invented that is given poetic expression in accord with the rules of rhetoric and music).[242] Dante's last word in this penultimate poetic work that probably only barely precedes the completion of the *Comedy* is a fitting one, a present-tense insistence on the centrality of his poetic making as his distinguishing mark. It is a good word with which to end.

Dante's extraordinary gifts as poet—and these are the most salient aspects of what he has left behind—enable him to reach everyone who loves to watch or hear language do everything it can do. In this he is like Homer and Shakespeare. And, like them, he enjoys some of this power even when he is translated. He has the further ability to enter the hearts of nearly everyone; he would probably be surprised at the vast number of those who share neither his politics nor his religion and yet consider his poem one of the few absolute monuments of human achievement. All of us read our own Dante and admire what we read. How would Dante react, if he came back to experience it, to all this fuss over him? It seems reasonable to believe that, first of all, he would be pleased with the extraordinary amount of attention his work continues to attract. The poet who, with unbelievable boldness, in *Inferno* IV, made himself one of the six major poets between antiquity and his own day (Homer, Virgil, Horace, Ovid, Lucan, . . . Dante), now looks modest, in the world's estimation; he has eclipsed, for most readers, all but Homer. But then, do we not imagine hearing him complain insistently about how badly we contrive to read him? Expounding his work in public, whether in the classroom or in written texts, is a terrifying task. It becomes nearly impossible if we imagine him sitting there, eyes wide in disbelief, or reading over our shoulder, equally amazed, perhaps even disgusted, as we write our scribbles in the margins of his texts.

NOTES

1. In our time, Giorgio Petrocchi is the leading authority not only on the text of the *Commedia* but on the life of Dante. Although some question certain of his conclusions, the discussion and debate are not likely to come to closure anytime soon. See Petrocchi, *Vita di Dante* (Bari: Laterza, 1983); "Biografia: Attività politica e letteraria," *ED* VI, pp. 1–53; *Itinerari danteschi*, Premessa a cura di Carlo Ossola (Milan: Franco Angeli, 1994 [Bari: Laterza, 1969]). See also Gianfranco Folena, "La tradizione delle opere di Dante Alighieri," in *Atti del Congresso internazionale di studi danteschi*, vol. 1 (Florence: Sansoni, 1965), pp. 1–78. For a revisionist view of some of the data behind Petrocchi's *itinerarium mentis* of Dante, see Giorgio Padoan, *Il lungo cammino del "Poema sacro": Studi danteschi* (Florence: Olschki, 1993).

2. For one observation of this phenomenon, see Petrocchi, *Itinerari*, pp. 230–31.

3. For basic information and bibliography related to these four writers, see the apposite entries in *ED*. For the extensive bibliography of work dedicated to the various aspects of Dante's life, see *ED* VI, pp. 550–60. Still valuable is Paget Toynbee's Appendix, "Bibliographical Note of the Earliest Biographies and Biographical Notices of Dante," in his *Dante Alighieri: His Life and Works*, ed. C. S. Singleton (New York: Harper & Row, 1965 [1910]), pp. 276–82. Toynbee's essays on Dante's life, gathered in this collection, remain extremely useful.

4. Giorgio Petrocchi, *La Commedia secondo l'antica vulgata*, 2nd ed. (Florence: Le Lettere, 1994 [1966–67]). See the review of Federico Sanguineti, "Per l'edizione critica della *Comedìa* di Dante," *Rivista di letteratura italiana* 12 (1994): 277–92.

5. *La Commedìa: Nuovo testo critico secondo i più antichi manoscritti fiorentini*, ed. Antonio Lanza (Anzio: De Rubeis, 1995; 2nd ed., 1996 [1997]).

6. The most recent revisionary study of the stemma is that of Federico Sanguineti, "Prolegomeni all'edizione critica della *Commedia*," in *Sotto il segno di Dante: Scritti in onore di Francesco Mazzoni*, ed. Leonella Coglie-

vina and Domenico De Robertis (Florence: Le Lettere, 1998), pp. 261–82. Sanguineti is currently preparing a new critical edition.

7. Giorgio Petrocchi, "Itinerari nella *Commedia*," *Studi danteschi* 41 (1964): 55–73.

8. But for a challenging response see Giorgio Padoan, *Il lungo cammino.*

9. The three editions of the *Rime* that are currently fundamental to any study of Dante's lyrics are those of Gianfranco Contini, *Rime* (Turin: Einaudi, 1995 [1939]); Michele Barbi and Francesco Maggini, *Rime della "Vita Nuova" e della giovinezza* (Florence: Le Monnier, 1956); and Kenelm Foster and Patrick Boyde, *Dante's Lyric Poetry*, 2 vols. (Oxford: Clarendon, 1967).

10. For the question of the *Rime*, of their variety and of the inadmissible idea that the poems gathered by later editors into them constitute a "canzoniere," see two comprehensive overviews of Dante's lyric production found in *Le "Rime" di Dante*, ed. Michelangelo Picone (= *Letture classensi* 24 [1995]): Giovanni Cappello, "Per un ordinamento delle *Rime* di Dante," pp. 11–51; and M. Picone, "Dante rimatore," pp. 171–88. See also Guglielmo Gorni, *Il Dante perduto* (Turin: Einaudi, 1994).

11. For a recent appreciation of Dante's "experimentalism," see Zygmunt G. Barański, "Dante fra 'sperimentalismo' e 'enciclopedismo,'" in *L'enciclopedismo medievale*, ed. M. Picone (Ravenna: Longo, 1994), pp. 373–94.

12. The modern discussion of *Il Fiore* is dominated by the work of Gianfranco Contini, editor of the standard text: *"Il Fiore" e "Il Detto d'Amore" attribuibili a Dante Alighieri*, ed. G. Contini (Milan: Mondadori, 1984). For Contini's and others' contributions in the debate over the paternity of the text, see his annotated bibliography, pp. xxiii–xliv. Contini's essential views are shared by Luigi Vanossi, *Dante e il "Roman de la Rose": Saggio sul "Fiore"* (Florence: Olschki, 1979). Perhaps the most vehement and persistent opponent of Dantean authorship has been Remo Fasani, whose four contributions between 1967 and 1975 are listed and (critically) described in Contini's bibliography. Among the contributions of those who remain unconvinced are: E. Jeffrey Richards, *Dante and the "Roman de la Rose"* (Tübingen: Niemayer, 1981); Joseph Barber, "A Statistical Analysis of the *Fiore*," *Lectura Dantis [virginiana]* 6 (1990): 100–122; Remo Fasani, *Le parole che si chiamano: I metodi dell'officina dantesca* (Ravenna: Longo, 1994), pp. 245–79. A journal issue is devoted to the text of *Il Fiore* and several essays on the work: *Lettura del "Fiore,"* ed. Z. G. Barański, P. Boyde, and L. Pertile, *Letture classensi* 22 (1993): 13–302. Pertile's observations on the possible erotic meaning of the author's sobriquet, Durante,

would cast some doubt on Dantean paternity (pp. 149-153). An important survey of the situation and of the work itself is found in the many and varied contributions in *The "Fiore" in Context: Dante, France, Tuscany,* ed Z. G. Barański and Patrick Boyde (Notre Dame, Ind.: University of Notre Dame Press, 1997). As if the whole question were not vexed enough, yet another point of view is offered by Mauro Cursietti, "Ancora per il *Fiore:* Indizi cavalcantiani," *La parola del testo* 1 (1997): 199-218. Yet it is the latest contribution to the debate that may at last have found the "Durante" who wrote the *Fiore:* Guillaume Durand (Guilielmus Duranti), born ca. 1230-37 in southern France, died 1296, author of the *Speculum iudiciale* and the *Rationale divinorum officiorum.* See Maurizio Palma Di Cesnola, "La battaglia del *Fiore:* omaggio a Remo Fasani," *Studi e problemi di critica testuale* 59 (1999): 5-42.

13. Petrocchi, *Vita di Dante,* p. 23.

14. For a supposed dependence on *Rose* (v. 5921) of *Inf.* XIV, 94, see Leo-nella Coglievina, " 'In mezzo mar siede un paese guasto' . . . *(Inf.* XIV, 94-102)," (Florence: Società Dantesca Italiana, 1981), pp. 1-10.

15. But see Francesco Mazzoni, "Il canto V dell'*Inferno,*" in *Inferno (Letture degli anni 1973-76)* (Rome: Bonacci, 1977), pp. 118, 139, for a possible echo of *Rose* in *Inf.* V.

16. See Paul Oppenheimer, *The Birth of the Modern Mind: Self, Consciousness, and the Invention of the Sonnet* (New York: Oxford University Press, 1989), p. 22.

17. For consideration of Dante's continuing hostile engagement with the poetic career of Guittone see Teodolinda Barolini, *Dante's Poets* (Princeton, N.J.: Princeton University Press, 1984), esp. pp. 94-110.

18. E.g., Mario Marti, "Guittone d'Arezzo e i guittoniani," *ED* III, pp. 334-36, with bibliography. For Guittone's continuing importance for Dante, see Guglielmo Gorni, "Guittone e Dante," pp. 309-35; Roberto Antonelli, *"Subsistant igitur ignorantie sectatores,"* pp. 337-49; and Francesco Mazzoni, "Tematiche politiche fra Guittone e Dante," pp. 351-83, all collected in *Guittone d'Arezzo nel settimo centenario della morte: Atti del Convegno internazionale di Arezzo, 22-24 aprile 1994,* ed. M. Picone (Florence: Cesati, 1995).

19. For the continuing, if until now unsuccessful, attempt to deny the authen-ticity of the *tenzone,* which began with Domenico Guerri's debate with Michele Barbi in the early 1930's, and which Guerri's student, Antonio Lanza, reopened in the early 1970's, his opposition to authenticity now supported by his own student, see Mauro Cursietti, *La falsa tenzone di Dante con Forese Donati* (Anzio: De Rubeis, 1995). The position of Guerri,

Lanza, and Cursietti is supported by Ruggero Stefanini, " 'Tenzone' sì e 'tenzone' no," in *Lectura Dantis [virginiana]*, 18-19 (1996): 111-24. And for the most recent overview of the current debate, with necessary bibliography and polemical insistence on inauthenticity, see Antonio Lanza, "A norma di filologia: ancora a proposito della cosiddetta 'Tenzone tra Dante e Forese,' " *L'Alighieri*, 10 (1997): 43-54. A strong rebuttal is found in Fabian Alfie, "For Want of a Nail: the Guerri-Lanza-Cursietti Argument Regarding the *Tenzone*," *Dante Studies* 116 (1998): 141-59. For a study that continues to maintain the authenticity of the tenzone see Bernhard König, "Formen und Funktionen grober Komik bei Dante (zu *Inferno* XXI-XXIII)," *Deutsches Dante-Jahrbuch* 70 (1995): 7-27. See also Antonio Stäuble, "La tenzone di Dante con Forese Donati," in *Le "Rime" di Dante*, ed. M. Picone (= *Letture classensi* 24 [1995]): 151-70.

20. For a review of the several points of contact between Cecco and Dante, as well as some basic bibliography, see the entry "Angiolieri, Cecco," by Mario Marti (*ED* I, pp. 276-77). For a recent study of Cecco's responses to Dante in *L'Acerba* see Gabriele Frasca, " 'I' voglio qui che 'l quare covi il quia': Cecco d'Ascoli 'avversario' di Dante," in *Dante e la scienza*, ed. Patrick Boyde and Vittorio Russo (Ravenna: Longo, 1995), pp. 243-63.

21. For the eventual falling out of Guido and Dante, see Enrico Malato, *Dante e Guido Cavalcanti: Il dissidio per la "Vita nuova" e il "disdegno" di Guido* (Rome: Salerno, 1997).

22. See, in favor of the authentic authorship by Cino of the late verses in complaint against Dante, Luca Carlo Rossi, "Una ricomposta tenzone (autentica?) fra Cino da Pistoia e Bosone da Gubbio," *Italia medioevale e umanistica* 31 (1988): 45-79.

23. The current standard edition remains that of Domenico De Robertis: *Vita Nuova* (Milan: Ricciardi, 1980). For some of the essential bibliography see that edition, pp. 20-24. Without eventual prejudice, the text referred to in this essay is that established by Barbi, first in 1907, finally in 1932 in the Edizione Nazionale, which is reprinted by De Robertis. There is a new edition by Guglielmo Gorni (Turin: Einaudi, 1996) that offers quite different results in some particulars and with respect to the divisions into chapters as these were established by Barbi. Gorni's bibliography of editions and studies of the work is the most useful available, pp. 353-79. Also to be taken into account is the edition of Dino S. Cervigni and Edward Vasta (Notre Dame, Ind.: University of Notre Dame Press, 1995).

24. For the notion of the work as deliberately mystifying, see E. H. Strauch, "Dante's *Vita Nuova* as Riddle," *Symposium* 21 (1976): 324-30.

25. For bibliography on and discussion of this problem see the entry "Boezio"

by F. Tateo, *ED* I, pp. 654–58. See also Domenico De Robertis, *Il libro della "Vita Nuova"* (Florence: Sansoni, 1970), pp. 18–19, 67–68, for the possible resonance of the scene of Lady Philosophy's appearance at the foot of Boethius' bed in chap. 12. However, Gorni's edition, ad loc., does not refer to the possible Boethian provenance of the scene.

26. For the original suggestion of the influence of Provençal collections see Pio Rajna, "Lo schema della *Vita nuova*," in *La biblioteca delle scuole italiane* (1890).

27. A major study of the prose of the work remains that of Alfredo Schiaffini, *Tradizione e poesia nella prosa d'arte italiana dalla latinità medievale al Boccaccio* (Rome: Edizioni di Storia e Letteratura, 1969 [1934]), pp. 89–112.

28. For the Greek roots of this tradition, see Joseph A. Mazzeo, "Dante and the Phaedrus Tradition of Poetic Inspiration," in *Structure and Thought in the "Paradiso"* (Ithaca, N.Y.: Cornell University Press, 1958), pp. 1–24.

29. For one example of Boccaccio's carnal reading of Beatrice, see *Decameron* IV, Introduction, 33.

30. See Mario Marti, "Guinizzelli, Guido," *ED* III, pp. 330–33. And for Dante's responses to his various poetic predecessors and companions, see Marti, *Con Dante fra i poeti del suo tempo* (Lecce: Milella, 1966); Teodolinda Barolini, *Dante's Poets*. For a monograph dedicated to the Bolognese poet, see Vincenzo Moleta, *Guinizelli in Dante* (Rome: Edizioni di Storia e Letteratura, 1980).

31. For the problematic friendship between Dante and his "first friend," see Mario Marti, "Cavalcanti, Guido," *ED* I, pp. 891–96, with bibliography through 1969 devoted to various of the questions that surround the relationship between the two poets. For some more recent bibliography, see Michele Dell'Aquila, *Al millesmo del vero* (Fasano: Schena, 1989), pp. 93–95.

32. See Nancy Vickers, "Widowed Words: Dante, Petrarch, and Metaphors of Mourning," in *Discourses of Authority in Medieval and Renaissance Literature*, ed. Kevin Brownlee and Walter Stephens (Hanover, N.H.: University Press of New England, 1989), pp. 97–108.

33. Ronald L. Martinez, "Mourning Beatrice: The Rhetoric of Threnody in the *Vita nuova*," *Modern Language Notes* 113 (1998): 1–29.

34. For the contributions of Pietrobono, Barbi, Nardi, and others, see Mario Marti, "Vita e morte della presunta doppia redazione della *Vita nuova*," in *Studi in onore di Alfredo Schiaffini* (Rome: Edizioni dell'Ateneo, 1965), 657–69.

35. See Maria Corti, *La felicità mentale* (Turin: Einaudi, 1983), pp. 146–55.

36. Even Corti must admit as much, ibid., p. 154.
37. For this aspect of Dante's authorial strategy in the libello, see Olivia Holmes, "The *Vita nuova* in the Context of Vatican MS Chigiano L. VIII.305 and Dante's 'Johannian' Strategy of Authorship," *Exemplaria* 8 (1996): 193–229.
38. See, again, G. Padoan, *Il lungo cammino*, pp. 5–23.
39. See Kenelm Foster and Patrick Boyde, *Dante's Lyric Poetry*, in a similar vein with regard to the verse collected in *VN* (vol. 2, p. 274). They discuss Dante's choice of words fit to be included in the "illustrious vernacular" (*DvE* II, vii): "Confining his examples to nouns, Dante describes these 'most noble' words as *virilia, urbana, pexa*, and *yrsuta*. From a study of his practice in his earlier poems we can see that by the emotive metaphorical terms *virilia, urbana*, Dante meant nouns that were already current in the elevated lyric or that shared the same characteristics as those nouns. Broadly speaking, a noun would be acceptable if it was abstract and drawn from a severely limited field (in the 676 lines of verse in *VN*, there are only 229 nouns, and 150 of them are abstract)."
40. See Mark Musa, *Dante's "Vita Nuova": A Translation and an Essay*, 2nd ed. (Bloomington: Indiana University Press, 1972), pp. 106–34.
41. See Nicolò Mineo, *Profetismo e apocalittica in Dante* (Catania: Università di Catania, 1968), p. 104, who registers eight, but limits his category to "visions," thus omitting actual appearances of Beatrice to Dante; Dino Cervigni, *Dante's Poetry of Dreams* (Florence: Olschki, 1986), pp. 39–62, who seems to believe there are eleven sightings of Beatrice by Dante. See also, on the three different kinds of "seeing" in *VN*, Ignazio Baldelli, "Visione, immaginazione e fantasia nella *Vita Nuova*," in *I sogni nel medioevo*, ed. Tullio Gregory (Rome: Edizioni dell'Ateneo, 1985), pp. 1–10.
42. For the number of Beatrice's appearances to Dante and the carefully controlled vocabulary that describes the various kinds of vision with which Dante beholds her, see Robert Hollander, "*Vita Nuova*: Dante's Perceptions of Beatrice," *Dante Studies* 92 (1974): 1–18. And see Ignazio Baldelli, "Visione, immaginazione e fantasia nella *Vita Nuova*," in *I sogni nel medioevo: Seminario internazionale, Roma, 2–4 ottobre 1983*, ed. Tullio Gregory (Rome: Edizioni dell'Ateneo, 1985), pp. 1–10.
43. Quodvultdeus, *PL* XL, p. 667.
44. For the numerical structure of the poems of the work, see C. S. Singleton, *An Essay on the "Vita Nuova"* (Baltimore, Md.: Johns Hopkins University Press, 1977 [1949]), p. 79. Musa's system is found in the first edition of his translation (Indianapolis: Indiana University Press, 1962), pp. vii–

xxii. An early attempt to account for Dante's structuring of the poems is found in the translation of Charles Eliot Norton (Boston: Houghton, Mifflin, 1867). And see Kenneth McKenzie, "The Symmetrical Structure for Dante's *Vita Nuova,*" *PMLA* 18 (1903): 341–55.

45. See Paolo Amaducci, *La fonte della Divina commedia scoperta e descritta da Paolo Amaducci,* 2 vols. (Rovigo: Tipografia Sociale, 1911). Amaducci spent a quarter of a century trying to convince the world that Dante's text was structured by his reading of Peter Damian's exegesis of the forty-two *mansiones* of the Israelites in the desert found in Num. 33. For his bibliography see Enzo Esposito, "Amaducci, Paolo," *ED* I, pp. 193–94.

46. Hart's mathematical and geometrical studies of the *Commedia* are rich and challenging. See his most recent, which picks up strands from his several earlier pieces and serves to summarize his long campaign to bring this sort of analysis to bear on Dante: Thomas Hart, " 'Per misurar lo cerchio' (*Par.* XXXIII, 134) and Archimedes' *De mensura circuli:* Some Thoughts on Approximations to the Value of π" in *Dante e la scienza,* ed. P. Boyde and V. Russo (Ravenna: Longo, 1995), pp. 265–335. See also, for much different, numerological studies of Dante, two by Manfred Hardt: *Die Zahl in der "Divina Commedia"* (Frankfurt: Athenäum, 1973); and "I numeri nella poetica di Dante," *Studi danteschi* 61 (1989): 1–27. And see two others by G. R. Sarolli, "numero," *ED* IV, pp. 87–96; and *Analitica della "Divina Commedia"* (Bari: Adriatica, 1974).

47. For a list of the Latin phrases in *VN,* see *Vita nova,* Gorni, ed., p. 390.

48. In our time no one has demonstrated more fully and clearly than Domenico De Robertis the extent of Dante's biblical referentiality in the libello. See *Il libro della "Vita Nuova,"* passim.

49. See Erwin Panofsky, *Gothic Architecture and Scholasticism* (Cleveland, Ohio: World, 1957), p. 39.

50. Leo Spitzer, "A Note on the Poetic and the Empirical 'I' in Medieval Authors," *Traditio* 4 (1946): 414–22; C. S. Singleton, *An Essay,* p. 25; Rocco Montano, *La storia della poesia di Dante,* vol. 1 (Naples: Quaderni di Delta, 1962), pp. 367–76; Gianfranco Contini, *Un'idea di Dante* (Turin: Einaudi, 1976 [1958]), pp. 33–62.

51. C. S. Singleton, *Dante Studies 1* (Cambridge: Harvard University Press, 1954), p. 62.

52. For a discussion of this problem, see Ignazio Baldelli, "Realtà personale e corporale di Beatrice," *Giornale storico della letteratura italiana* 169 (1992): 161–82. For a reading from a more contemporary point of view, see Robert P. Harrison, *The Body of Beatrice* (Baltimore, Md.: Johns Hopkins University Press, 1988).

53. For a study that suggests how deeply the example of Francis affected the portrayal of saintly women before Dante (and thus perhaps Dante's sense of Beatrice) see Vittore Branca, "Poetica del rinnovamento e tradizione agiografica nella *Vita Nuova*," *Biblioteca dell'Archivium Romanicum* 86 (1966): 123–48 [= *Studi in onore di Italo Siciliano* (Florence: Olschki 1966)].

54. For the view that the essential signifying mode of *VN* is figural, see Robert Hollander, "Dante *Theologus-Poeta*," *Dante Studies* 94 (1976): 100–102.

55. Francesco Mazzoni, "Il 'trascendentale' dimenticato," in *Omaggio a Beatrice (1290-1990)*, ed. Rudy Abardo (Florence: Le Lettere, 1997), pp. 93–132. For a "middle ground" with regard to the theological disposition of *VN*, which is seen as rehearsing a Christian drama but in the secular costume of literary artifice, see Giorgio Barberi Squarotti, "Artificio e escatologia della *Vita Nuova*, in *L'artificio dell'eternità* (Verona: Fiorini, 1972), pp. 35–105. And for a monograph studying *VN* as a complex whole and emphasizing its biblical antecedents, see Sergio Cristaldi, *La "Vita Nuova" e la restituzione del narrare* (Soveria Mannelli: Rubbettino, 1994).

56. For a recent Italian response to the problem that is, on the other hand, in central accord with the "American" approach, see Stefano Giovannuzzi, "Beatrice, o della poesia," in *Paragone* 44 n.s. (1993): 56–78.

57. Perhaps the first wave of contemporary Italian "typological" readers includes Silvio Pasquazi, *All'eterno dal tempo* (Florence: Le Monnier, 1966); *D'Egitto in Ierusalemme* (Rome: Bulzoni, 1985); Angelo Jacomuzzi, *L'imago al cerchio* (Milan: Silva, 1968), esp. pp. 29–152, and *Il palinsesto della retorica* (Florence: Olschki, 1972), esp. pp. 117–78; and Giuseppe Giacalone's commentary to the *Commedia* (Rome: Signorelli, 1968).

58. Emilio Bigi, "Genesi di un concetto storiografico: *Dolce stil novo*," *Giornale storico della letteratura italiana* 132 (1955): 369–70, makes the point that it was only in 1880, when, spurred by De Sanctis, Adolfo Bartoli took up the term, that it "becomes accepted as an indisputable matter of fact and is officially validated with the label proposed by them without need for further proof and almost in passing" (p. 369). Others in disagreement with the "standard" view include Guido Favati, *Inchiesta sul Dolce Stil Nuovo* (Florence: Le Monnier, 1975); G. Contini, *Un'idea di Dante*, pp. 52–56; J. A. Scott, "*Paradiso* XXX," in *Dante Commentaries*, ed. David Nolan (Dublin: Irish Academic Press; and Totowa, N.J.: Rowman and Littlefield, 1977), p. 178, n. 6, insisting that the dolce stil novo "has nothing to do with a school of poets or *stilnovisti* invented by nineteenth-century historians of literature." For the most recent global treatment of

the subject, see Emilio Pasquini, "Il *dolce stil novo*," in *Storia della letteratura italiana*, dir. Enrico Malato, vol. 1 (Rome: Salerno, 1995), pp. 649–721.

59. Robert Hollander, "Dante and Cino da Pistoia," *Dante Studies* 110 (1992): 201–31; "Dante's *dolce stil novo* and the *Comedy*," in *Dante: Mito e poesia. Atti del 2° Seminario Internazionale Dantesco*, ed. M. Picone and T. Crivelli (Florence: Cesati, 1999), pp. 263–81. For a discussion along more traditional lines, see Emilio Pasquini, "Il mito dell'amore: Dante fra i due Guidi," ibid., pp. 283–95.

60. Maria Corti, *Percorsi dell'invenzione* (Turin: Einaudi, 1993), p. 93; also Barolini, *Dante's Poets*, p. 86.

61. For a recent discussion of this phase of Dante's work in lyric see Angelo Jacomuzzi, "Sulle *Rime* di Dante: Dalle rime per la 'pargoletta' alle 'petrose,' " in *Le forme e la storia* 6 (1994): 15–30.

62. Luciano Rossi, " 'Così nel mio parlar voglio esser aspro' (CIII)," in *Le "Rime" di Dante*, ed. M. Picone (= *Letture classensi* 24 [1995]), pp. 69–89, argues, against the traditional dating of the petrose, for a date roughly contemporaneous with the composition of *De vulgari Eloquentia*, around 1304–5.

63. For a lengthy, detailed, and controversial reading of the petrose, see Robert Durling and Ronald Martinez, *Time and the Crystal: Studies in Dante's "Rime Petrose"* (Berkeley: University of California Press, 1990). The authors insist that the four lyrics are positioned in relation to Neoplatonic cosmology and are to be understood as harmonizing the conflicts that they present. While it is one thing to say that the petrose are an essential stylistic step toward the *Comedy*, it is a far more challenging assertion that these violently erotic poems somehow rise to "crystallization," the freedom from time and its discontents and resolution into creative clarity and peace.

64. For its role among a series of palinodes for the severe ending of "Così nel mio parlar" (CIII), see Emilio Pasquini, "La terzultima palinodia dantesca," *Atti della Accademia delle scienze di Bologna* 72 (1983–84): 73–82. And, for the most recent interpretation, see Guglielmo Gorni, "La canzone 'montanina,' " in *Le "Rime" di Dante*, ed. M. Picone (= *Letture classensi* 24 [1995]), pp. 129–50.

65. Michelangelo Picone, in "Dante rimatore," p. 171, is of the opinion that the canzone was finished before the *Commedia* was begun.

66. For encyclopedism in Dante see Giuseppe Mazzotta, *Dante's Vision and the Circle of Knowledge* (Princeton, N.J.: Princeton University Press, 1993).

67. The most important recent editions are those by Giovanni Busnelli

and Giuseppe Vandelli, introduction by Michele Barbi (Florence: Le Monnier), 1934–37, 2nd ed. "con appendice di aggiornamento a cura di A. E. Quaglio" (Florence: Le Monnier, 1964), 2 vols.; Maria Simonelli (Bologna: Pàtron, 1966); Dante Alighieri, *Opere minori*, vol. 1, part 2, ed. C. Vasoli and D. De Robertis (Milan: Ricciardi, 1988); Franca Ageno Brambilla (Florence: Le Lettere, 1995), 3 vols. For the essential bibliography, see the Introduction to Vasoli's edition, pp. xciv–c.

68. For an argument in favor of these possible dates, see Michele Barbi, introduction to the Busnelli-Vandelli edition, pp. xvi–xix.

69. E. R. Curtius, *European Literature and the Latin Middle Ages*, trans. Willard R. Trask (New York: Harper & Row, 1963 [1948]), p. 222.

70. Vasoli, Introduction, *Opere minore*, p. lxxx.

71. Ulrich Leo, "The Unfinished *Convivio* and Dante's Rereading of the *Aeneid*," *Mediaeval Studies* 13 (1951): 41–64 (quotation on p. 49).

72. E.g., in his remarks at II, vi, 1; III, xii, 1; IV, ii, 4; vi, 1; ix, 1; xvi, 2; xx, 4; xxvi, 5; xxx, 1.

73. See Bruno Nardi's views of Dante's less than ardent reliance on Thomas, as discussed by Cesare Vasoli in *Otto saggi per Dante* (Florence: Le Lettere, 1995), pp. 117–32. Most recently see Marc Cogan, *The Design in the Wax: The Structure of the "Divine Comedy" and Its Meaning* (Notre Dame, Ind.: University of Notre Dame Press, 1999), pp. xxiii–xxiv: "Despite Nardi's efforts to convince us that Albert the Great was Dante's preferred philosophical source, it is Aquinas whom Dante chooses as the principal spokesman for theology in the *Paradiso*, not Albert or any other theologian."

74. The English translations of the *Convivio* are my own but reflect those of Richard H. Lansing, *Dante's "Il Convivio"* (New York: Garland, 1990).

75. For the immense problem of Dante's philosophical and theological "sources," and for his resultant syncretistic "Thomism," including strands of Averroistic, Neoplatonic, and other philosophical approaches, there is perhaps no better review and discussion of the findings of its principle investigators—Etienne Gilson, in *Dante et la philosophie* (Paris: Vrin, 1953 [1939]) and Bruno Nardi, in *Saggi di filosofia dantesca* (Florence: La Nuova Italia, 1967 [1930], *Dante e la cultura medievale* (Bari: Laterza, 1949 [1942]), *Nel mondo di Dante* (Rome: Edizioni di "Storia e Letteratura," 1944), *Dal "Convivio" alla "Commedia"* (Rome: Istituto storico italiano per il Medio Evo, 1960), and still others—than that offered by Cesare Vasoli, "Filosofia e teologia in Dante," in *Otto saggi*, pp. 13–40. For a balanced view of Dante's sense of St. Thomas's prime authority, matched, however,

by his welcoming of many other (and at times divergent) authorities, see Kenelm Foster's entry "Tommaso d'Aquino," *ED* V, pp. 626–49.

76. See *La felicità mentale*, pp. 142–44.

77. For the question of the relative dating of the two works, see Vasoli's note to *Convivio* I, v, 10, with discussion of the positions of Rajna, Barbi, Mengaldo, Nardi, Corti, and Alessio (for whom see also G. C. Alessio, "A Few Remarks on the *Vulgare Illustre*," *Dante Studies* 113 [1995]: 57–67) and reference to the differing hypothesis of Ileana Pagani, *La teoria linguistica di Dante* (Naples: Liguori, 1982). See also Simone Marchesi, "La rilettura del *De officiis* e i due tempi della composizione del *Convivio*" (forthcoming in *GSLI*), for indirect support of Corti's thesis that *DvE* was written after Dante had concluded the third treatise of *Convivio*.

78. The current standard edition is Dante Alighieri, *Opere minori*, vol. 2, *De vulgari Eloquentia*, ed. P. V. Mengaldo (Milan: Ricciardi, 1979). For the essential bibliography, see pp. 22–25. See also Mengaldo's original edition: Dante Alighieri, *De vulgari eloquentia*, ed. P. V. Mengaldo, vol. 1, *Introduzione e testo* (Padua: Antenore, 1968).

79. See P. V. Mengaldo's entry "De vulgari Eloquentia," *ED* II, pp. 405–6.

80. *De vulgari Eloquentia* II, iv, 1 and 6; viii, 8; xiii, 1.

81. See Mengaldo, *ED* II, p. 403.

82. E.g., I, ii, 1; iv, 4; vii, 8; II, ii, 8.

83. But for an exception, see Z. G. Barański, "La linguistica scritturale di Dante" in *"Sole nuovo, luce nuova": Saggi sul rinnovamento culturale in Dante* (Turin: Scriptorium, 1996), pp. 79–128. And see the previous English version, "Dante's Biblical Linguistics," *Lectura Dantis [virginiana]*, 5 (1989): 105–43 (reference on p. 128).

84. But, for its centrality, see Barański, "Dante's Biblical Linguistics," pp. 118–21.

85. For a consideration of Dante's knowledge of and fairly hostile attitudes toward the French vernacular see P. V. Mengaldo, "oïl," *ED* IV, p. 131a.

86. For a countering view, see the numerous studies of M. Picone that argue for clandestine knowledge and use of Old French and Provençal sources underlying Dante's poetic production. See his *"Vita nuova" e tradizione romanza* (Padua: Liviana, 1979); "I trovatori di Dante: Bertran de Born," *Studi e problemi di critica testuale* 19 (1979): 171–94; "Giraut de Bornelh nella prospettiva di Dante," *Vox romanica* 39 (1980): 64–85; "La poesia romanza della *Salus:* Bertran de Born nella *Vita nuova*," *Forum italicum* 15 (1981): 3–10; "Dante e la tradizione arturiana," *Romanische Forschungen* 94 (1982): 1–18; "*Paradiso* IX: Dante, Folchetto e la diaspora

trobadorica," *Medioevo romanzo* 8 (1981–83): 47–89; "Baratteria e stile comico in Dante," in *Studi americani su Dante*, ed. G. C. Alessio and Robert Hollander (Milan: Franco Angeli, 1989), pp. 63–86; "Presenze romanzesche nella *Vita nuova*," *Vox Romanica* 55 (1996): 1–15.

87. On the political resonances of this passage, see J. A. Scott, "An Uncharted Phase in Dante's Political Thought," in *Essays in Honour of John Humphreys Whitfield*, ed. H. C. Davis and others (London: St. George's Press, 1975), pp. 41–52.

88. Dante presents a slight variant of it in *VN* II, 4–6.

89. For discussion, see the essay of Albert Russell Ascoli, "*Neminem ante nos:* Historicity and Authority in the *De vulgari eloquentia*," *Annali d'italianistica* 8 (1991): 186–231.

90. For a cogent review of the problem, see Mengaldo's note to this passage (II, iv, 2), pp. 161–63.

91. As Mengaldo points out, Dante's definition of the high style (II, iv, 7) follows closely the pseudo-Ciceronian *Rhetorica ad Herennium* IV, viii, 11.

92. See also Mengaldo's original edition, *De vulgari eloquentia*, pp. xcix–cii.

93. See Maria Simonelli, "Convivio," *ED* II, p. 193.

94. On the subject of the character of the "digressions," see C. Vasoli, "L'immagine 'enciclopedica' del mondo nel *Convivio*," in *Otto saggi*, pp. 83–102.

95. The difficulty presented by the twin problems of dating and of interpreting this canzone can be appreciated if one considers closely four (of the many available) treatments of these stubborn questions: Giorgio Petrocchi, "Donna gentile," *ED* II, pp. 574–77; Mario Pazzaglia, "Voi che 'ntendendo il terzo ciel movete," *ED* V, pp. 1116–19; Foster and Boyde, *Dante's Lyric Poetry*, vol. 2, pp. 341–62; Cesare Vasoli, *Convivio*, pp. lii–lxi. English translations of the poems cited in this section are heavily indebted to those of Foster and Boyde.

96. Foster and Boyde, in *Dante's Lyric Poetry*, vol. 2, p. 167, amplify this point, as do a number of other discussants.

97. See C. T. Davis, "scuola: La scuola al tempo di Dante," *ED* V, pp. 106–9.

98. Vincenzo Pernicone, "Amor che ne la mente mi ragiona," *ED* I, pp. 217–19.

99. D. De Robertis, *Convivio*, p. xci.

100. For Dante's division of the canzone into two larger parts, following the proemial stanza, see *Conv.* IV.iii.1.

101. For the debate over prime matter and the status of Averroës among Christian thinkers, see Bruno Nardi, *Dante e la cultura medievale* (Bari: Laterza, 1949), pp. 248–59. For a review of the entire problem, with ample bibli-

ographies, see the entries "Averroè" and "averroismo" by Cesare Vasoli in *ED* I, pp. 473–81.

102. For a treatment of the problems represented by attempts to reconcile the literal and allegorical dimensions of the first two canzoni, see Vittorio Russo, " 'Voi ch' intendendo' e 'Amor che ne la mente': La diffrazione dei significati secondo l'auto-commento del *Convivio*," in *L'autocommento: Atti del XVIII convegno interuniversitario (Bressanone, 1990)*, ed. G. Peron (Padua: Esedra, 1994), pp. 11–19.

103. For the most recent work on the nature of Dante's response to Guittone, see the contributions of Guglielmo Gorni, Roberto Antonelli, and Francesco Mazzoni in *Guittone d'Arezzo*. See also Teodolinda Barolini, "Guittone's *Ora parrà*, Dante's *Doglia mi reca*, and the *Commedia*'s Anatomy of Desire," in *Seminario dantesco internazionale: Atti del primo convegno tenutosi al Chauncey Conference Center, Princeton, 21–23 ottobre 1994*, ed. Z. G. Barański (Florence: Le Lettere, 1997), pp. 3–23.

104. See Peter Dronke, *Dante's Second Love: The Originality and the Contexts of the "Convivio"* (Exeter: Society for Italian Studies, 1997), p. 35.

105. Ulrich Leo, "The Unfinished *Convivio*," p. 64.

106. For *Convivio* IV, iii, 14–18, as the first tracing of the *Commedia*, see Maria Simonelli, *ED* II, p. 201; Vasoli, *Convivio*, pp. lxiii–lxiv.

107. Leo's theory in "The unfinished *Convivio*" is convincing in the main, but one should be aware that citations of Latin texts more or less conforming to his description do in fact occur earlier than *Conv.* IV, xxv: e.g., III, xi, 16 (*Aen.* II, 281–83; *Theb.* V, 608–11); IV, iv, 11 (*Aen.* I, 278–79); IV, xi, 3 (*Phars.* III, 118–21); IV, xiii, 12 (*Phars.* V, 527–31); IV, xv, 8 (*Metam.* I, 78–83). Simone Marchesi has examined the presence of a similar phenomenon with respect to a text of Cicero and found that, beginning at *Conv.* IV, viii, Dante's citations of *De officiis* show evidence of his having been influenced by a recent close rereading: see n. 77.

108. For the view that, from the vantage point of the *Commedia*, Dante subjected the entire project of *Convivio* to a harsh and revisionist glance, see Antonio Gagliardi, *La tragedia intellettuale di Dante: Il "Convivio"* (Catanzaro: Pullano, 1994). Gagliardi's work, as its title implies, is close in spirit to Luigi Valli's chapter "Ulisse e la tragedia intellettuale di Dante," in *La struttura morale dell'universo dantesco* (Rome: Ausonia, 1935), pp. 26–40. In the eyes of both Valli and Gagliardi, Dante's Ulyssean *Convivio* is a cause of some concern to the later poet. See also Robert Hollander, *Allegory in Dante's "Commedia"* (Princeton, N.J.: Princeton University Press, 1969), pp. 115–16. For a still stronger view, that all of Dante's major work derives from a gnostic religious viewpoint, see Antonio Lanza, *Dante e*

la gnosi: Esoterismo del "Convivio" (Rome: Edizioni Mediterranee, 1990). Recent supporters of the view that there is no radical disjuncture between the two works include, in addition to Peter Dronke in *Dante's Second Love,* J. A. Scott, "The Unfinished *Convivio* as Pathway to the *Comedy,*" *Dante Studies* 113 (1995): 31-56; Mario Trovato, "The True *Donna gentile* as Opposed to the Apocalyptic Whore," *Dante Studies* 112 (1994): 177-227 (in which the Donna represents the Church Militant); Giuliana Carugati, "Retorica amorosa e verità in Dante: Il *De causis* e l'idea della donna nel *Convivio,*" *Dante Studies* 112 (1994): 161-75 (in which both ladies are versions of the Truth). Carugati's demonstrations of the extent of Dante's dependence on the Neoplatonizing work of Proclus in *Convivio* II and III unintentionally lends support to those who argue that, from the vantage point of the *Comedy,* the deference to Lady Philosophy in *Convivio* is cause for more than a little concern.

109. For a discussion of this revisionist behavior, see Albert Russell Ascoli, "The Vowels of Authority (Dante's *Convivio* IV.vi.3-4)," in *Discourses of Authority in Medieval and Renaissance Literature,* ed. Kevin Brownlee and Walter Stephens (Hanover, N.H.: University Press of New England, 1989), pp. 42-43, and p. 261, n. 47.

110. See John Freccero, "Casella's Song," in *Dante Studies* 91 (1973): 73-80; Robert Hollander, "Cato's Rebuke and Dante's *scoglio,*" *Italica* 52 (1975): 348-63.

111. E.g., Daniel J. Ransom, "A Palinode in the *Paradiso,*" *Dante Studies* 95 (1977): 81-94; Maria Corti, *Percorsi dell'invenzione* (Turin: Einaudi, 1993), p. 155.

112. For discussions of the implicit further correction of *Convivio* here, see Hollander, "Cato's Rebuke," pp. 351-53; Rachel Jacoff, "The Post-Palinodic Smile," *Dante Studies* 98 (1980): 111-22; Barolini, *Dante's Poets,* pp. 71-75.

113. This is the position recently advanced by Lino Pertile, "Il nodo di Bonagiunta, le penne di Dante e il Dolce Stil Novo," *Lettere italiane* 46 (1994): 52-61. For support of Pertile's views, see Guglielmo Gorni, "Appunti sulla tradizione del *Convivio,*" *Studi di filologia italiana* 55 (1997): 11n.

114. See Peter Dronke, *Verse with Prose from Petronius to Dante: The Art and Scope of the Mixed Form* (Cambridge: Harvard University Press, 1994); for Dante see the discussion on pp. 106-14.

115. See Petrocchi, *Itinerari,* summarizing his argument on pp. 9-10 (and all of chapter 5); an attempt to establish a very different set of dates is found in Padoan, *Il lungo cammino,* summarized on pp. 121-23: *Inferno* 1306-15; *Purgatorio* 1315-16; *Paradiso* 1316-21. For Petrocchi the several events

referred to in the poem that have not yet occurred (most clamorously, the death of Clement V in 1314, referred to in *Inf.* XIX) are the result of Dante's revisions of the first two *cantiche* undertaken in 1313–15. In Petrocchi's view, *Inferno* was released entire only in 1314 (or very early in 1315), *Purgatorio* late in 1315. The first references to texts in the poem are found in 1316 (to *Purg.* II, 81) and 1317 (to *Inf.* III, 94–96). Padoan's thesis for the dating of Dante's schedule of work attacks Petrocchi's hypothesis (concerning a period of revision of the first two *cantiche* before their publication). The discussion and debate will continue, especially if more evidence comes to light. For now it seems fair to say that Petrocchi's hypotheses depend on the least speculation and may serve as the guiding principles in current discussions. For early attacks on them, see Gianfranco Folena, *La tradizione delle opere;* Colin Hardie, "The Date of the *Comedy* and the *Argomento barberiniano,*" *Dante Studies* 86 (1968): 1–16. Petrocchi is supported by Bruno Basile and Ezio Raimondi, "*Commedia:* 2. Composizione," *ED* II, pp. 81–82. For what seems to be a conclusive argument concerning a related issue see Charles T. Davis, "The Malispini Question," in *Dante's Italy and Other Essays* (Philadelphia: University of Pennsylvania Press, 1984 [1970]), pp. 94–136.

116. In a paper written in 1999, Stefano Giannini, a graduate student at Johns Hopkins University, examined all the references to events occurring after 1300 in *Inferno.* His provisional results are as follows: twenty-two references to events occurring between 1300 and 1304; four references to events occurring between 1306 and 1309 (all between cantos XXVI and XXIX); this sole reference to an event occurring as late as 1314. These results would certainly seem to support those who maintain that the passage is a later interpolation and that *Inferno* was essentially completed during the first decade of the fourteenth century.

117. Of essential current importance are the following: Giorgio Petrocchi, *La Commedia secondo l'antica vulgata,* vol. 1, pp. 57–91; Marcella Roddewig, *Dante Alighieri, Die göttliche Komödie: Vergleichende Bestandsaufnahme der "Commedia"-Handschriften* (Stuttgart: Hiersemann, 1984); Antonio Lanza, *La Commedìa: Nuovo testo critico secondo i più antichi manoscritti fiorentini,* pp. cxiii–cxviii; Federico Sanguineti, *Prolegomeni all'edizione critica,* pp. 261–82. In the year 2000 the results of a census of the manuscripts undertaken by the Società Dantesca Italiana under the guidance of its president, Francesco Mazzoni, are scheduled to be presented in electronic form at the Third International Dante Seminar.

118. See John Ahern, "Hermeneutics and Manuscript Production in *Paradiso* XXXIII," *PMLA* 97 (1982): 800–809.

119. Bruno Basile, "Viaggio," *ED* V, pp. 995–99, offers a helpful review of the question.

120. Emmanuel Poulle, "Profacio," *ED* IV, p. 693, sketches out, with bibliographical indications, the central position of his study of the problem: Dante took his star charts from the *Almanach* of Prophacius Judaeus (ca. 1236–1304). The astronomical data found in the poem correspond only to the stars' positions between 25 March and 2 April 1301. If Poulle is right, Dante set the action of his poem between those dates, if not in that year. As for 1301, it is inconceivable that the reader is supposed to believe that the date within the poem is other than 1300. However, if Dante was using Profacius' work, the star charts for 1300 fail to include data for the Sun and for Venus; Dante found March dates for them only in the charts for 1301. Since it took seven hundred years for someone to catch him out, we can surmise that, rather than calculate the missing data himself, he simply appropriated the charts for 1301 for his use.

121. Robert Hollander, "The Invocations of the *Commedia*," in *Studies in Dante* (Ravenna: Longo, 1980), pp. 31–38: *Inf.* II, 7; XXXII, 10–12; *Purg.* I, 7–12; XXIX, 37–42; *Par.* I, 13–21; XVIII, 83–88; XXII, 112–23; XXX, 97–99; XXXIII, 67–75. That there are nine invocations in a work that takes so much of its inspiration from Beatrice should not be a surprise. For the first (and perhaps only previous) acceptable listing of the invocations in the poem see Fabio Fabbri, "Le invocazioni nella *Divina Commedia*," *Giornale dantesco* 18 (1910): 186–92.

122. Robert Hollander, "Dante *Theologus-Poeta*," pp. 91–136, responding to, among others, J. A. Scott, "Dante's Allegory," *Romance Philology* 26 (1973): 571–91; Franco Ferrucci, "Comedía," *Yearbook of Italian Studies* 1 (1971): 29–52.

123. Hollander, "Dante *Theologus-Poeta*," p. 112. While the point is well taken (and has been made subsequently by a number of American Dantists), it must be pointed out that Hollander, nodding, confuses the wings of the Griffin with those of the gospel beasts.

124. Parts of the arguments presented in this, the third, and the fifth sections of this study have been published. See Robert Hollander, "Dante: A Party of One," in *First Things* 92 (April 1999): 30–35; see also the "lectures" on these three subjects in the Princeton Dante Project, http://www.princeton.edu/dante.

125. Introductory studies of Dante's allegory exist, accompanied by extensive bibliographies on the subject. Readers of Italian can find an overview of the subject in the article "allegoria" by Jean Pépin, *ED* I, pp. 151–65; for those who read French, see Pépin's somewhat fuller treatment, *Dante et*

la tradition de l'allégorie (Montreal: Institut d'études médiévales, 1970);
for the most recent brief treatment in English, consult Ronald Martinez's entry "allegory" in the *Dante Encyclopedia*, ed. Richard H. Lansing
(New York: Garland, 2000). Important monographic contributions include Johan Chydenius, *The Typological Problem in Dante* (Helsingfors:
Societas scientiarum fennica, 1958); A. C. Charity, *Events and Their
Afterlife* (Cambridge: Cambridge University Press, 1966); Giuseppe Mazzotta, *Dante, Poet of the Desert: History and Allegory in the Divine Comedy*
(Princeton, N.J.: Princeton University Press, 1979). For a more recent
treatment of the subject, see Otfried Lieberknecht, *Allegorese und Phil-
ologie* (Stuttgart: Steiner, 1999). Those interested in this writer's view of
the subject can consult a book and an article written some time ago: *Allegory in Dante's "Commedia"* (Princeton, N.J.: Princeton University Press,
1969); "Dante *Theologus-Poeta*," *Dante Studies* 94 (1976): 91–136. The
classic work on the general subject is Henri de Lubac, *Exégèse médiévale:
Les quatre sens de l'Ecriture* (Paris: Aubier, 1959–64). A brief review of
the history of biblical exegesis in English is found in Robert M. Grant,
A Short History of the Interpretation of the Bible (New York: Macmillan,
1963).
126. For a differing approach to the problem of "fictiveness" in medieval literature, see Peter Dronke, *Fabula: Explorations into the Uses of Myth in
Medieval Platonism* (Leiden: Brill, 1974).
127. For general discussion, see E. R. Curtius, *European Literature*, pp. 452–55;
for discussion with particular reference to Dante, see Hollander, *Allegory*,
pp. 256–58.
128. Maria Simonelli, "L'Inquisizione e Dante: Alcune osservazioni," *Dante
Studies*, 97 (1979): 129–49. That the writer accepts the authenticity of the
epistle to Cangrande, which says in so many words that he chose to write
in the mode of theological allegory, makes it difficult to accept her notion
that he would not have employed the "allegory of the theologians" in the
poem for fear of the Inquisition.
129. E.g., Teodolinda Barolini, "For the Record: The Epistle to Cangrande
and Various 'American Dantisti,'" *Lectura Dantis [virginiana]* 6 (1990):
142; Robert Hollander, "*Purgatorio* II: The New Song and the Old,"
Lectura Dantis [virginiana] 6 (1990): 33, 43.
130. An important study of this subject remains Erich Auerbach's essay
"Figura," in *Scenes from the Drama of European Literature*, trans. Ralph
Manheim (New York: Meridian Books, 1959 [1938]), pp. 11–76.
131. Cited by Hollander, "The Tragedy of Divination in *Inferno* XX," in
Studies in Dante, p. 142.

132. For studies of such adaptations see Earl Miner, ed., *Literary Uses of Typology* (Princeton, N.J.: Princeton University Press, 1977).

133. For Nardi's telling objections to Petrocchi's denial that Dante would have put Celestine, who was canonized in 1313, in hell, see "Dante e Celestino V," in *Dal "Convivio" alla "Commedia"* (Rome: Istituto storico italiano per il medio evo, 1992 [1960]), pp. 315–30. Petrocchi's essay of the same title, first published in *Studi romani* in 1955, can be found in *Itinerari*, pp. 41–59. See also Maria Simonelli, *"Inferno" III*, in *Lectura Dantis Americana* (Philadelphia: University of Pennsylvania Press, 1993), pp. 41–58, for a more recent argument that strongly favors the identification of Celestino.

134. See T. K. Swing, *The Fragile Leaves of the Sibyl: Dante's Master Plan* (Westminster, Md.: Newman, 1962), p. 299, and Hollander, *Allegory*, pp. 112–13.

135. For the second correspondence see Ezio Raimondi, "Rito e storia nel I canto del *Purgatorio*," in *Metafora e storia* (Turin: Einaudi, 1970 [1962]), pp. 81–83; for both see Hollander, *Allegory*, pp. 124–29.

136. The question of the "ontological" status of Virgil in Dante's poem remains the cause of some debate, even though since Auerbach—who insisted that in Dante's poem Virgil is not an allegorical representation of *any* quality but rather the historical Virgil himself—many contemporary Dantists no longer attempt to understand Virgil as representing some sort of allegorical formulation. See Erich Auerbach, "Figura," in *Scenes from the Drama of European Literature*, trans. Ralph Manheim (New York: Meridian, 1959), pp. 67–71. For a clear statement of an opposing view, see G. A. Scartazzini, "Il significato allegorico di Virgilio," in his *Scritti danteschi*, ed. M. Picone and J. Bartuschat (Locarno: Armando Dadò, 1997 [1899]), part of the entry "Virgilio" in Scartazzini's *Enciclopedia dantesca*. According to Scartazzini, Virgil represents the empire and thus, as the secular authority in the poem, philosophy, while Beatrice represents theology. His schema, based on *Monarchia* III, xv, 30, Dante's statement of the two overarching aims of human life (earthly and then heavenly bliss), is so firmly set in his mind that he must deny that St. Bernard is the third guide in the poem, an assertion that seems nothing less than untenable.

137. Frank Ordiway, "In the Earth's Shadow: The Theological Virtues Marred," *Dante Studies* 100 (1982): 77–92.

138. Richard Lansing, "Narrative Design in Dante's Earthly Paradise," *Dante Studies* 112 (1994): 101–13.

139. Lino Pertile, "Poesia e scienza nell'ultima immagine del *Paradiso*," in

Dante e la scienza, ed. Patrick Boyde and Vittorio Russo (Ravenna: Longo, 1995), pp. 133–48.

140. But see Hollander, *Allegory,* pp. 308–20, for a "decorative" presence of the seven capital vices even in *Inferno.*

141. The bibliography here is vast. For some essential contributions, see Giovanni Busnelli, *L'Etica nicomachea e l'ordinamanto morale dell'"Inferno" di Dante* (Bologna: Zanichelli, 1907); W. H. V. Reade, *The Moral System of Dante's "Inferno"* (Oxford: Clarendon, 1909); for a revisionary treatment of the subject, see Cogan, *The Design in the Wax.*

142. See *Inferno,* trans. Robert Hollander and Jean Hollander, with notes by Robert Hollander (New York: Doubleday Anchor, 2000), notes to canto XI.

143. Francesco Mazzoni, *Canto XI dell' "Inferno,"* Lectura Dantis neapolitana, dir. Pompeo Giannantonio (Naples: Loffredo, 1985), p. 14.

144. Ibid., pp. 10–14.

145. Ibid., pp. 25–45.

146. See Alfred A. Triolo, "Malice and Mad Bestiality," in *Lectura Dantis: "Inferno,"* ed. Allen Mandelbaum, Anthony Oldcorn, Charles Ross (Berkeley: University of California Press, 1998), pp. 150–64. Triolo's initial work on the subject dates to 1968 (see his bibliographical note).

147. E. R. Curtius, *European Literature,* p. 358.

148. See Paget Toynbee, "Virgilio," in *A Dictionary of Proper Names and Notable Matters in the Works of Dante,* ed. C. S. Singleton (Oxford: Clarendon Press, 1968 [1898]), for a convenient listing of all Virgil's appearances as character in the poem.

149. See Gian Carlo Alessio and Claudia Villa, "Per *Inferno* I, 67–87," in *Dante e la "bella scola" della poesia: Autorità e sfida poetica,* ed. A. A. Iannucci (Ravenna: Longo, 1993 [1984]), pp. 41–64.

150. For articles summarizing an approach that observes a certain distance in Dante's treatment of Virgil as author (and as character in the poem), see Christopher J. Ryan, "Virgil's Wisdom in the *Divine Comedy," Classica et Mediaevalia* 11 (1982): 1–38; and Robert Hollander, "Dante's Virgil: A Light That Failed," *Lectura Dantis [virginiana]* 4 (1989): 3–9. This position has only recently begun to be accepted by some Italian dantisti; e.g., Stefano Prandi, "I gesti di Virgilio," *Giornale storico della letteratura italiana* 172 (1995): 56–75. For a representative sampling of the "American" view, see the essays in *The Poetry of Allusion: Virgil and Ovid in Dante's "Commedia,"* ed. Rachel Jacoff and Jeffrey T. Schnapp (Palo Alto, Calif.: Stanford University Press, 1991).

151. On Dante's reading in his Latin past, see Edward Moore, *Studies in*

Dante. First Series: Scripture and Classical Authors in Dante (Oxford: Clarendon, 1969 [1896]), pp. 166–97, 344–48. For recent essays by various scholars on Dante's classical sources, see *Dante e la "bella scola" della poesia: Autorità e sfida poetica*, ed. A. A. Iannucci (Ravenna: Longo, 1993); and *The Poetry of Allusion*. Monographs on the subject include Felicina Groppi, *Dante traduttore*, 2nd ed. (Rome: "Orbis Catholicus" Herder, 1962); Robert Hollander, *Il Virgilio dantesco* (Ravenna: Longo, 1983); Paola Rigo, *Memoria classica e memoria biblica in Dante* (Florence: Olschki, 1994); Massimiliano Chiamenti, *Dante Alighieri traduttore* (Florence: Le Lettere, 1995). For the role of Virgil as a character in the *Comedy*, see Domenico Consoli, "Virgilio," *ED* V, pp. 1030–44, and *Significato del Virgilio dantesco* (Florence: Le Monnier, 1967). Still indispensable for the entire question of Dante's investment in the Roman roots of the "Italy" he longed to believe in is Charles T. Davis, *Dante and the Idea of Rome* (Oxford: Oxford University Press, 1957). For the most recent (if provisional) "census" of Virgilian text in the *Commedia*, see Robert Hollander, "Le opere di Virgilio nella *Commedia* di Dante," in *Dante e la "bella scola,"* pp. 247–343.

152. See Hollander, *Allegory*, pp. 81–92.

153. See Domenico Comparetti, *Vergil in the Middle Ages*, trans. E. F. M. Benecke (Hamden, Conn.: Archon Books, 1966 [1872]).

154. For an opposing view of this matter, see Henry A. Kelly, *Tragedy and Comedy from Dante to Pseudo-Dante* (Berkeley: University of California Press, 1989), e.g., pp. 35–36.

155. For an expression of the more traditional view of Dante's affection for Virgil, see A. A. Iannucci, "The Mountainquake of *Purgatorio* and Virgil's Story," *Lectura Dantis [virginiana]* 20–21 (1997): 48–58.

156. For the problem of the epic status of the *Comedy*, see Robert Hollander, "Dante and the Martial Epic," *Mediaevalia* 12 (1989): 62–91.

157. For a review of the problematic interpretations of this dream, see Dino Cervigni, *Dante's Poetry of Dreams*, pp. 117–52; Z. G. Barański, "Dante's Three Reflective Dreams," *Quaderni d'italianistica* 10 (1989): 213–36, studies the context of the three dreams in the second cantica.

158. See Robert Hollander, "A Note on Dante's Missing Musaeus (*Inferno* IV, 140–141)," *Quaderni d'italianistica* 5 (1984): 217–21.

159. For the "coincidence" of Dante's unique self-nomination in this passage with Virgil's unique self-nomination in *Georgics* IV, 563, see Hollander, *Il Virgilio dantesco*, pp. 132–34. Apparently the first commentator to cite the earlier passage in the *Georgics* (IV, 525–27, the lament of Orpheus for Eurydice as source of Dante's for Virgil), was Gabriele (1525–27): *Anno-*

tationi nel Dante fatte con M. Trifon Gabriele in Bassano, ed. Lino Pertile (Bologna: Commissione per i testi di lingua, 1993), p. 236. Gabriele also (p. 237) believes that Dante's self-nomination is based on Virgil's. Bernardino Daniello, Gabriele's student, followed the master in regard to the first particular only.

160. For the almost certain reference to the episode of his love for the donna gentile in *VN*, see the commentary of Umberto Bosco in his introduction to *Purg.* XXX, pp. 508–10.

161. Hollander, "The Invocations."

162. See Sergio Corsi, *Il "modus digressivus" nella "Divina Commedia"* (Potomac, Md.: Scripta humanistica, 1987).

163. See Robert Hollander, "*Paradiso* XXX," *Studi danteschi* 60 (1988 [= 1993]): 31–33.

164. For basic information and bibliography, see Raoul Manselli, *ED* I, pp. 601–5. See also Mario Aversano, *San Bernardo e Dante: Teologia e poesia della conversione* (Salerno: Edisud, 1990), esp. pp. 5–36. The most recent studies of Bernard's importance for Dante are found in the three contributions on the subject in "Dante e la tradizione mistica: San Bernardo di Clairvaux" in *Atti del Seminario dantesco internazionale 1*, pp. 147–278, by Steven Botterill, Francesco Mazzoni, and Lino Pertile. See also Giorgio Petrocchi, "Dante e san Bernardo," in *L'ultima dea* (Rome: Bonacci, 1977), pp. 137–55; S. Botterill, *Dante and the Mystical Tradition: Bernard of Clairvaux in the "Commedia"* (Cambridge: Cambridge University Press, 1994).

165. See Etienne Gilson, *Dante et la philosophie,* pp. 278–79. Gilson's view is supported by Manselli and others.

166. Auguste Valensin, *Le christianisme de Dante* (Paris: Aubier, 1954), pp. 132–35. Botterill also holds to this view.

167. See, again, Manselli, *ED,* I, pp. 601–5.

168. See Francesco Mazzoni, "San Bernardo e la visione poetica della *Divina Commedia,*" Lino Pertile, "La puttana e il gigante (*Purgatorio* XXXII, 148–60)," both in *Atti del Seminario dantesco internazionale 1,* esp. pp. 178–80, 192–230; 262–64. See also Pertile, *La puttana e il gigante: dal Cantico dei Cantici al Paradiso Terrestre di Dante* (Ravenna: Longo, 1998).

169. Two recent works in English offer an overview of the political situation of Dante and of his poem: Joan M. Ferrante, *The Political Vision of the "Divine Comedy"* (Princeton, N.J.: Princeton University Press, 1984); John A. Scott, *Dante's Political Purgatory* (Philadelphia: University of Pennsylvania Press, 1996).

170. This fact supports Petrocchi's dating of *Inferno,* since, once Henry VII

has been crowned and advances into Italy (1310), Dante's imperial concerns could move from the theoretical to the practical.

171. For a recent overview of the literary ambiance of Frederick II's court, see Roberto Antonelli, "La corte «italiana» di Federico II e la letteratura europea," in *Federico II e le nuove culture. Atti del XXXI Convegno storico internazionale, Todi, 9–12 ottobre 1994* (Spoleto: Centro italiano di studi sull'alto medioevo, 1995), pp. 319–45.

172. See Robert Hollander, "Dante's Harmonious Homosexuals (*Inferno* 16.7–90)," *Electronic Bulletin of the Dante Society of America* (June 1996), http://www.princeton.edu/~dante.

173. See Davide Conrieri, "Letture del canto XXI dell'*Inferno*," *Giornale storico della letteratura italiana* 158 (1981): 8–10, opposing such "autobiographical" readings.

174. Cited by Hollander, "The Tragedy of Divination in *Inferno* XX," in *Studies in Dante*, p. 142.

175. See William Stull and Robert Hollander, "The Lucanian Source of Dante's Ulysses," *Studi danteschi* 63 (1991 [= 1997]): 8–12.

176. For the question of Henry VII, see Ovidio Capitani, "Enrico VII," *ED* II, pp. 682–88.

177. Domenico Consoli, in "ricreare," *ED* IV, p. 919a, is among the few to read the literal sense of this verse as it probably should be understood: "Rudolph of Hapsburg having neglected to cure the condition of Italy, 'she will be set in order' only tardily and by the effort of another emperor (the present has the value of a future tense, as in *If* VI 99, XVI 54, *Pg* VIII 133, XIV 166)." Benvenuto da Imola said much the same thing: Italy will be reformed by Henry VII, as was touched on in *Purg.* VI and more fully in *Par.* XXX.

178. For a recent study of the three "political epistles," see Lino Pertile, "Dante Looks Forward and Back: Political Allegory in the Epistles," *Dante Studies* 115 (1997 [1999]): 1–17.

179. For a much different resolution of this problem, based on the notion that Dante is ironically recanting the *earlier* citation of the passage in Lucan in the epistle (an interpretation that relies on a radical revision of the dating of the composition of the *Comedy*), see Colin Hardie, "The Date of the *Comedy*," pp. 7–11. Hardie remained, until his death in 1998, one of the few still dedicated to the notion that Dante began the poem only after the death of Henry VII in August 1313. For his own listing of his other work in this vein, see the last note on p. 16 of his article.

180. In a paper read in Padua on 9 April 1983, the Paduan historian Giorgio Cracco pointed out that a Venetian living in Lombardy wrote an as yet

unpublished chronicle (ca. 1292) of the provinces of Venice. His text, in which he names himself simply as "Marco," contains a number of concerns and phrases that coincide with Dante's. See G. Cracco, "Tra Marco e Marco: Un cronista veneziano dietro al canto XVI del *Purgatorio?*" in *Viridarium floridum: Studi di storia veneta offerti dagli allievi a Paolo Sambin,* ed. M. C. Billanovich, G. Cracco, A. Rigon (Padua: Antenore, 1984), pp. 3–23.

181. For the history of the debate over the meaning of this prophecy (with bibliography through 1966), see Pietro Mazzamuto, "Cinquecento diece e cinque," *ED* II, pp. 10–14. In the intervening years debate has continued—and probably always will.

182. The first major prophecy in the poem has engendered about as much debate and controversy as any passage in the poem. For a clear-headed and full review (with bibliography through 1969), see C. T. Davis, "veltro," *ED* V, pp. 908–12. There seems no reason to believe that a solution acceptable to most is likely to be found soon; however, for a closely argued thesis that attempts to account for the shifting valences of the various prophecies as the poem progresses, see Maurizio Palma Di Cesnola, *Semiotica dantesca: Profetismo e diacronia* (Ravenna: Longo, 1995).

183. For the medieval understanding of the divinity found in kingship, see Ernst Kantorowicz, *The King's Two Bodies* (Princeton, N.J.: Princeton University Press, 1957). For a balanced critique of Kantorowicz's views of the treatment of kingship in Dante, see C. T. Davis, "Kantorowicz and Dante," in *Ernst Kantorowicz,* ed. R. L. Benson and J. Fried (Stuttgart: Steiner, 1997), pp. 240–64.

184. Guido Martellotti, "Mussato, Albertino," in *ED* III, p. 1067.

185. For a monographic consideration of this scene, see Jeffrey T. Schnapp, *The Transfiguration of History at the Center of Dante's "Paradiso"* (Princeton, N.J.: Princeton University Press, 1986).

186. See C. T. Davis, "Il buon Tempo Antico," in *Dante's Italy,* pp. 71–93.

187. For a review of the entire question of the date of Dante's arrival in Ravenna, see Eugenio Chiarini, "Ravenna," *ED* IV, pp. 861–64.

188. See Ferrante, *The Political Vision of the "Divine Comedy,"* p. 287. And see L. S. Seem, "Dante's Nine Worthies," *Forum Italicum,* forthcoming.

189. Lia Baldelli, "acrostico," *ED* I, p. 44, points out that Dante's deployment of this technique escaped the notice of the early commentators; it was only in 1903 that Francesco Flamini noticed the acrostic in these lines. (In 1898 Antonio Medin had noticed the presence of another, based in the word VOM [or UOM, "uomo," or "man"], at *Purg.* XII, 25–63.) Most now accept that these two acrostics were deliberately constructed by the

author. Spurred by these findings, others—e.g., J. P. T. Deroy, Philip Berk, Richard Kay, and Karla Taylor—have tried to establish more elaborate patterns. For a convincingly skeptical response to these ingenious efforts, see Teodolinda Barolini, *The Undivine "Comedy": Detheologizing Dante* (Princeton, N.J.: Princeton University Press, 1992), pp. 308–10.

190. See Tibor Wlassics, *Dante narratore: Saggi sullo stile della "Commedia"* (Florence: Olschki, 1975); Barolini, *The Undivine "Comedy"*.

191. Erich Auerbach, *Dante: Poet of the Secular World*, trans. Ralph Manheim (Chicago: University of Chicago Press, 1961 [1929]), p. 133.

192. See Antonino Pagliaro, "similitudine," *ED* V, pp. 253–59; Richard H. Lansing, *From Image to Idea: A Study of the Simile in Dante's "Commedia"* (Ravenna: Longo, 1977); Madison U. Sowell, "A Bibliography of the Dantean Simile to 1981," *Dante Studies* 101 (1983): 167–80.

193. See Francesco Tateo, "metafora," *ED* III, pp. 926–32; Ezio Raimondi, "Ontologia della metafora dantesca," *Letture classensi* 15 (1986): 99–109; Emilio Pasquini, "Le icone parentali nella *Commedia*," *Letture classensi* 25 (1996): 39–50.

194. See Hermann Gmelin, "Die Anrede an den Leser in der *Göttlichen Komödie*," *Deutsches Dante-Jahrbuch* 30 (1951): 130–40; Erich Auerbach, "Dante's Addresses to the Reader," *Romance Philology* 7 (1954): 268–78; Leo Spitzer, "The Address to the Reader in the *Commedia*," *Italica* 32 (1955): 143–66.

195. See Vittorio Russo, "Appello al lettore," *ED* I, 324–26: *Inf.* VIII, 94–96; IX, 61–63; XVI, 127–32; XX, 19–24; XXII, 118; XXV, 46–48; XXXIV, 22–27; *Purg.* VIII, 19–21; IX, 70–72; X, 106–11; XVII, 1–9; XXIX, 97–105; XXXI, 124–26; XXXIII, 136–38; *Par.* II, 1–18; V, 109–14; X, 7–27; XIII, 1–21; XXII, 106–11. Russo also points out that *Par.* IX, 10–12, might be considered an address to the reader, and that the passage at X, 7–27, should perhaps be considered two separate addresses. The total may thus be either twenty or twenty-one. Dante's tendency to balance his composition would strengthen the case for the last accounting, twenty-one in all, seven in each cantica. But it is far from clear that that is the case.

196. See Gianluigi Toja, "trobar clus," *ED* V, pp. 732–36.

197. See Francesco Tateo, "perifrasi," *ED* IV, pp. 419–20.

198. For a recent review and discussion see Lino Pertile, " 'Così si fa la pelle bianca nera': L'enigma di *Paradiso* XXVII, 136–138," *Lettere italiane* 43 (1991): 3–26. Pertile opposes perhaps the most persistent interpretation, one that identifies the «bella figlia» with Circe, *filia solis* in some classical formulations; he proposes instead that we understand her as the human

soul, as represented by the *sponsa* in the Song of Songs. But see Bodo Guthmüller, " 'Che par che Circe li avesse in pastura,' " in *Dante: Mito e poesia*, pp. 248–49, arguing, against Pertile, for a return to the Circean explanation. For the recent resuscitation of a continuing tradition, beginning with Iacopo della Lana's comment on the passage that identifies the *figlia del sole* with the Church, see Anna Maria Chiavacci Leonardi, *Paradiso, con il commento di A. M. C. L.* (Milan: Mondadori, 1997), p. 763. The context of Peter's denunciation of the papacy in the first part of the canto (vv. 22–60) certainly makes this interpretation attractive.

199. See Ignazio Baldelli, "Lingua e stile delle opere in volgare di Dante," *ED* VI, esp. pp. 93–111 (for the *Comedy*). For a study of Dante's earlier stylistic practice, see Patrick Boyde, *Dante's Style in His Lyric Poetry* (Cambridge: Cambridge University Press, 1971). See also P. V. Mengaldo, "stili, Dottrina degli," in *ED* V, pp. 435–38. See also *Dante and "Genre,"* special issue of the *Italianist*, supplement to no. 15, 1995, ed. Z. G. Barański. And see Arianna Punzi, *Appunti sulle rime della "Commedia"* (Rome: Bagatto, 1995), for a recent study of Dante's practice as *rimatore* in the *Comedy* (bibliography, pp. 12–13). For Dante's metrics, see Remo Fasani, *La metrica della "Divina Commedia" e altri saggi di metrica italiana* (Ravenna: Longo, 1992), esp. pp. 11–95; Guglielmo Gorni, *Metrica e analisi letteraria* (Bologna: Il Mulino, 1993), refers frequently to Dante's metrics. See also Patrick Boyde, "Note on Dante's Metric and Versification," in *Dante's Lyric Poetry*, ed. K. Foster and P. Boyde, vol. 1 (Oxford: Oxford University Press, 1967), pp. xliv–lv.

200. Contini's definition, repeated often in his work and by now a staple in discussions of Dante's "mixed" style, was perhaps first formulated in his essay on Petrarch (1951), reprinted in *Varianti e altra linguistica* (Turin: Einaudi, 1970), pp. 169–92. Most recently see Z. G. Barański, "I trionfi del volgare: Dante e il plurilinguismo," in *"Sole nuovo, luce nuova,"* pp. 41–77, an expanded version of his study "*Significar per verba:* Notes on Dante and Plurilingualism," *Italianist* 6 (1986): 5–18.

201. Perhaps no essay on the subject has treated it as well as Auerbach's "Sermo Humilis," in *Literary Language and Its Public in Late Latin Antiquity and in the Middle Ages*, trans. Ralph Manheim (Princeton, N.J.: Princeton University Press, 1965 [1941]), pp. 25–81.

202. See his *De reprobatione Monarchiae composita a Dante*, first printed in 1741, then again in 1746. The text can be consulted in a modern edition: Nevio Matteini, *Il più antico oppositore politico di Dante: Guido Vernani da Rimini. Testo critico del "De reprobatione Monarchiae"* (Padua: CEDAM, 1958). Anthony Cassell has done an English translation of *De reproba-*

tione to accompany his translation of *Monarchia,* which to date has not been published. For information about Guido, see Pier Giorgio Ricci, "Vernani, Guido," *ED* V, pp. 967–68.

203. See Arsenio Frugoni, "Dante tra due Conclavi: La lettera ai Cardinali italiani," *Letture classensi* 2 (1969): 69–91.

204. For Dante's playful casting of himself as Uzzah, see Robert Hollander, "Dante as Uzzah? (*Purgatorio* X, 57, and Epistle XI, 9–12)," in *Sotto il segno di Dante: Scritti in onore di Francesco Mazzoni,* ed. Leonella Coglievina and Domenico De Robertis (Florence: Le Lettere, 1998), pp. 143–51.

205. For the text of the work, see Dante, *Monarchia,* ed. Prue Shaw (Cambridge: Cambridge University Press, 1995). English translations are drawn from Shaw in that volume, in which a "select bibliography" is found on pp. 151–59. Still important is the edition of Pier Giorgio Ricci (Milan: Edizione Nazionale a cura della Società Dantesca Italiana, 1965). See also the new edition and translation by Richard Kay, *Dante's "Monarchia"* (Toronto: Pontifical Institute of Mediaeval Studies, 1998).

206. See Shaw's remarks, *Monarchia,* pp. xxxviii–xxxix, in which she aligns herself with Ricci, who in 1965 gave this argument a full exposition.

207. Dante Alighieri, *Monarchia, epistole politiche,* ed. F. Mazzoni (Turin: Edizioni RAI, 1966). See Mazzoni's "Saggio introduttivo," *Teoresi e pratica in Dante politico,* pp. ix–cxi, for the status of the questions surrounding the work up to 1965, with special attention devoted to the arguments of Nardi, Maccarone, and Vinay, pp. xcvii–c, and to the dating problem, pp. lxi–lxv, ciii–cvi. See also Italo Borzi, "Bruno Nardi e il pensiero politico di Dante," *L'Alighieri* 37 (1996): 37–59. For Padoan's dating (1320–21) see *Il lungo cammino,* p. 116. With regard to the possibility of 1314, see Maurizio Palma Di Cesnola, " 'Isti qui nunc': La *Monarchia* e l'elezione imperiale del 1314," *Studi e problemi di critica testuale* 57 (1998): 107–30. Palma's argument requires an earlier dating of the first cantos of *Paradiso* (ca. 1313–14) than many would accept.

208. For a careful discussion, see Cesare Vasoli, "intelletto possibile," *ED* III, pp. 469–72.

209. On the importance of the republic for Dante see C. T. Davis, *Dante's Italy and Other Essays* (Philadelphia: University of Pennsylvania Press, 1984), esp. "Roman Patriotism and Republican Propaganda: Ptolemy of Lucca and Pope Nicholas III" [1975], pp. 224–53; "Ptolemy of Lucca and the Roman Republic" [1974], pp. 254–89; see also Robert Hollander and Albert Rossi, "Dante's Republican Treasury," *Dante Studies* 104 (1986): 59–82.

210. See Stull and Hollander, "The Lucanian Source of Dante's Ulysses," pp.

33–43, for examination of Dante's varying attitudes toward Julius in the *Commedia.*

211. For discussion of her discovery, see Shaw, *Monarchia,* pp. xxxvi–xxxvii.

212. For these two chapters see Prue Shaw, "Some Proposed Emendations to the Text of Dante's *Monarchia," Italian Studies* 50 (1995): 1–8.

213. See Richard Kay, "The *Mentalité* of Dante's *Monarchia," Res publica litterarum* 9 (1986): 183–91.

214. For documentation, see Giovanna Puletti, "Temi biblici nella *Monarchia* e nella trattatistica politica del tempo," *Studi danteschi* 61 (1989 [= 1994]): 231–88.

215. P. G. Ricci, "Monarchia," *ED* III, p. 994a.

216. For convincing counterarguments, see Michele Barbi, *Problemi fondamentali per un nuovo commento della "Divina Commedia"* (Florence: Sansoni, 1956), pp. 107–8; Francesco Mazzoni, *Saggio di un nuovo commento alla "Divina Commedia"* (Florence: Sansoni, 1967), pp. 198–220.

217. For Dante's views of the papacy, see Ovidio Capitani, "Papato," *ED* IV, pp. 276–80.

218. See Giovanna Puletti, "La donazione di Costantino nei primi del '300 e la *Monarchia* di Dante," *Medioevo e rinascimento* 7 (1993): 113–35.

219. For the concordance between Dante's two forms of human happiness and the thoughts of St. Thomas concerning the *duplex hominis beatitudo,* see F. Mazzoni, *Monarchia,* p. xciv.

220. Filippo Scolari, *Note ad alcuni luoghi delli primi cinque canti della "Divina Commedia"* (Venice: Picotti, 1819), pp. 17–21.

221. In the debate at midcentury, Nardi attacked Mazzoni's arguments in favor of Dantean authorship; in the recent one Hollander attacks those of Brugnoli, Kelly, and Barański, all of whom question or oppose Dante's paternity. For a bibliography, see Robert Hollander, *Dante's Epistle to Cangrande* (Ann Arbor: University of Michigan Press, 1993), pp. 103–10. A much neglected and important contribution to the discussion is that of E. K. Rand, "The Latin Concordance of Dante and the Genuineness of Certain of His Latin Works," *Annual Report of the Dante Society* 29 (1910): 7–38.

222. See *Das Schreiben an Cangrande della Scala,* ed. and trans. Thomas Ricklin (Hamburg: Felix Meiner, 1993); and *Epistola a Cangrande,* ed. Enzo Cecchini (Florence: Giunti, 1995).

223. G. Padoan, *Il lungo cammino,* pp. 108–16.

224. For the most cited recent notice, see Curtius, *European Literature,* p. 222.

225. Those who argue that the final twenty-nine paragraphs of the epistle are from another hand than that of the dedicatory letter (paragraphs 1–4)

are hard put to account for the identical form of address of Cangrande found in paragraphs 1 and 32: *vestra Magnificentia*. If the author of the "executive portion" of the epistle was ignorant of the dedicatory portion, as some have argued, is it not an extraordinary coincidence that he uses the same phrase? Further, how could a second compositor be so awkward as to introduce a recipient of an epistle into a document which has heretofore been without any indication that it is in fact a letter, much less one sent to a particular individual?

226. In *VN* XLII, 3, the clause runs, "qui est per omnia secula benedictus"; in the epistle, "qui est benedictus in secula seculorum."

227. See Giorgio Padoan, "Moncetti, Giovanni Benedetto," *ED* III, pp. 1004–5.

228. For this and all other matters related to the *Questio*, see the magisterial edition of Francesco Mazzoni, in Dante Alighieri, *Opere minori*, vol. 2 (Milan: R. Ricciardi, 1979), pp. 691–880: *Introduzione*, pp. 693–737; *Nota al testo*, pp. 738–39; Latin text of the work with facing Italian translation, pp. 745–73; *Note*, pp. 774–880. Little of note has appeared since 1978, when Mazzoni finished his work, with its exhaustive bibliography. But see Silvio Pasquazi, "Sulla cosmogonia di Dante (*Inferno* XXXIV e *Questio de aqua et terra*)," in *D'Egitto in Ierusalemme* (Rome: Bulzoni, 1985), pp. 121–56. Certainly the most notable recent treatment of the question of authenticity available in English is found in John Freccero, "Satan's Fall and the *Quaestio de aqua et terra*," *Italica* 38 (1961): 99–115. In this review of Bruno Nardi's *La caduta di Lucifero e l'autenticità della "Quaestio de aqua et terra"* (Turin: SEI, 1959; Lectura Dantis romana, now in B. Nardi, *"Lecturae" e altri studi danteschi*, ed. Rudy Abardo [Florence: Le Lettere, 1990], pp. 227–65), Freccero counters Nardi's arguments. See also Manlio Pastore Stocchi, "Quaestio de aqua et terra," in *ED* IV, pp. 761–65.

229. For a strikingly similar statement, see Boccaccio, *Esposizioni*, esp. litt., *Inf.* IV, 55.

230. E. G. Parodi, "La *Quaestio de aqua et terra* e il *cursus*," *Bullettino della Società Dantesca Italiana* 24 (1917): 168–69; Paget Toynbee, "Dante and the *Cursus*: A New Argument in Favour of the Authenticity of the *Quaestio*," *Modern Language Review* 13 (1918): 420–30; P. V. Mengaldo, *Linguistica e retorica di Dante* (Pisa, Nistri-Lischi, 1978, pp. 273–75).

231. See "La caduta di Lucifero." His negative judgment was based essentially on supposed "contradictions" between the *Questio* and Dante's account of the development of the landmass in the northern hemisphere in *Inferno* XXXIV. Nardi's arguments have been strongly and effectively attacked by Mazzoni, Freccero, Padoan, Pastore Stocchi, and Pasquazi, who ar-

gues that there is no contradiction, since the *Questio,* dealing with the physical phenomena in themselves, accounts for the efficient cause (the stellar attraction of the landmass), while *Inferno* XXXIV deals only with the material cause (the origin of the northern landmass in the southern hemisphere). See "Sulla cosmogonia," p. 153.

232. Mazzoni, *Questio,* pp. 694, 839, 843. See also the first redaction of Pietro's commentary (1340) to *Purg.* II, 1–6, referring to "quaedam pallottola terrae" (a certain ball of clay) that is "nostra terra et aqua" (our land and water), language that may reflect his awareness of the language of his father's *disputatio* in Verona and the treatise that followed.

233. See Aldo Rossi, "Dante, Boccaccio e la laurea poetica," *Paragone* 150 (1962): 3–41; "Il carme di Giovanni del Virgilio a Dante," *Studi danteschi* 40 (1963): 133–278; and "Boccaccio autore della corrispondenza Dante-Giovanni del Virgilio," *Miscellanea storica della Valdelsa* 69 (1963): 130–72; "'Dossier' di un'attribuzione," *Paragone* 216 (1968): 61–125.

234. P. H. Wicksteed and E. G. Gardner, *Dante e Giovanni del Virgilio* (Westminster, England: A. Constable, 1902); Guido Martellotti, "Egloghe," *ED* II, pp. 644–46; and Dante Alighieri, *Opere minori,* vol. 2, ed. Enzo Cecchini (Milan: Ricciardi, 1979), pp. 645–89.

235. See P. V. Mengaldo, "gramatica," *ED* III, pp. 259–64.

236. See Guido Martellotti, "Mussato, Albertino," *ED* III, pp. 1066–68.

237. See P. V. Mengaldo, "stile, Dottrina degli," *ED* V, pp. 435–38.

238. For the view that the eclogues defend Dante's use of the low style, see Mauda Bregoli-Russo, "Le Egloghe di Dante: Un'analisi," *Italica* 62 (1985): 34–40.

239. See G. R. Sarolli, *Prolegomena,* p. 399; and Robert Hollander, *Allegory,* p. 224.

240. See G. R. Sarolli, *Analitica,* vol. 1, p. 21. And see the supporting discussion in Guy P. Raffa, "Dante's Mocking Pastoral Muse," *Dante Studies* 114 (1996): 276.

241. For close consideration of the significance of the Virgilian and Ovidian sources of Dante's Polyphemus, see Raffa, "Dante's Mocking Pastoral Muse," pp. 274–86.

242. For a discussion of the term *poiesis,* see Dante *De vulgari Eloquentia,* P. V. Mengaldo, ed., pp. 161–63.

Bibliographical Note

Since a relevant bibliography for the study of Dante includes many thousands of items, those who deal with the subjects that branch out from the works of this writer are condemned to immoderate labor and a sense that they are always missing something important. While even half a century ago it was possible to develop, in a single treatment, a fairly thorough compendium of the most significant items (e.g., Siro A. Chimenz, *Dante*, in *Letteratura italiana: I maggiori*, Milano, Marzorati, 1954, pp. 85–109), the situation today would require far more space. Fortunately, the extraordinary aid to study represented by the *Enciclopedia dantesca* (*ED*), 6 vols., directed by Umberto Bosco (Rome: Istituto della Enciclopedia Italiana, 1970–78), has given Dante studies their single most important bibliographical resource, leaving only the last quarter-century—which happens to be the most active period in the history of Dante studies— not covered. The bibliography in *ED* VI—whose length, at 120 double-column oversized pages, exceeds that of this entire study—contains about five thousand items and is of considerable use, breaking the material into convenient categories. (The bibliographical list of bibliographies alone runs six double-column pages.) The *ED*, of course, also contains important bibliographical indications in many of its entries.

The most complete collection of materials related to the study of Dante in the United States is housed at the John M. Olin Library at Cornell University, the catalogue of which, complete through 1920, is still an important resource: Theodore W. Koch, comp., *Catalogue of the Dante Collections Presented by Willard Fiske*, 2 vols. (Ithaca, N.Y.: Cornell University), 1898–1900; and Mary Fowler, comp., *Additions, 1898–1920* (Ithaca, N.Y.: Cornell University, 1921). Later publications that serve as supplements to the Cornell catalogue include Niccolò D. Evola, *Bibliografia dantesca, 1920–1930* (Florence: Olschki, 1932); "Dante" [for 1931–34], in his *Bibliografia degli studi sulla letteratura italiana* (Milan: "Vita e pensiero," 1938), pp. 292–333; and "Bibliografia dantesca, 1935–1939," *Aevum* 15 (1941). For the 1930s, see also Helene Wieruszowski, "Bibliografia dantesca" [for 1931–37], *Giornale dantesco* 39 (1936 [1938]), and "Bibliografia dantesca" [for 1938–39], *Giornale dantesco* 41 (1938 [1940]). For the following decade see Aldo Vallone, *Gli studi danteschi dal 1940 al 1949* (Florence: Olschki, 1950). The next two decades are covered in Enzo Esposito, *Bibliografia analitica degli scritti su Dante dal 1950 al 1970* (Florence: Olschki, 1990); and see also *Dalla bibliografia alla storiografia: La critica dantesca nel mondo dal 1965–1990,* ed. Enzo Esposito (Ravenna: Longo, 1995). For a still fuller analytical bibliography (more than three thousand items), consult Leonella Coglievina, ed., "Bibliografia Dantesca, 1972–1977," *Studi danteschi* 60 (1988 [1992]): 35–314; the next installment in that periodical is scheduled to cover the years 1978–84.

Current bibliography is available in a number of periodicals, particularly the following: *L'Alighieri* and *Rassegna della letteratura italiana* (Italy); *Dante Studies* (United States); *Deutsches Dante-Jahrbuch* (Germany); *MLA International Bibliography* (United States); *The Year's Work in Modern Language Studies* (United Kingdom).

In the past dozen years, Dante studies, perhaps more than any other postclassical area of literature, has moved into the computer age. There is a growing bibliography available on-line, developed from the American bibliography overseen by Christopher Kleinhenz for the Dante Society of America. The on-line version (http://www.princeton.edu/~dante), developed by Richard H. Lansing, includes an increasing number of Italian items. Fifty-nine commentaries to the *Commedia* are now available through the Dartmouth Dante Project (opened 1988), still best reached via Telnet (telnet library.dartmouth.edu; at the prompt type "connect dante"), but soon to be available on the World Wide Web as well. The new Princeton Dante Project was opened to public use in 1999 (http://www.princeton.edu/dante); a multimedia text of the *Commedia,* overseen by Robert Hollander, also functions as an entry point to most of the many Dante sites on the Web; perhaps most notably, the Dante site established and maintained by Otfried Lieberknecht in Berlin (http://members.aol.com/lieberk/welc_fr.html) is the source for an enormous amount of information about the quantities of material already available in electronic form. Any number of other projects are in preparation. A major site is scheduled to open in September 2000 under the auspices of the Società Dantesca Italiana (www.danteonline.it).

In short, those seeking bibliographical help in their study of Dante are well served by the labors of many who have helped to make the record available. Their work makes an otherwise impossible task thinkable; it does not make it less daunting.

INDEX

Charles of Valois, 71
Chaucer, Geoffrey, 1, 92
Chiamenti, M., 200 (n151)
Chiarini, E., 203 (n187)
chiasmus, 31
Chiavacci Leonardi, A. M., 205 (n198)
Chydenius, J., 197 (n125)
Cicero, 13, 110, 111, 193 (n107)
Cino da Pistoia, 11, 12, 63–65, 67, 70–71
circumlocutio (periphrasis), 146
classe, 143
Clement V, Pope, 4, 44, 45, 92, 134, 142, 148, 149, 160, 162, 195 (n115)
Cogan, M., 113, 190 (n73), 199 (n141)
Coglievina, L., 9, 183 (n14)
comedy, 55, 69, 146
Commedia, 90–148; allegory, 97–104; Beatrice in, 121–27; Bernard in, 127–29; dates of composition, 91–92; dating of events in, 93; invocations in, 94–95; moral order of afterworld, 109; moral situation of reader, 104–9; poetry of, 144–48; politics in, 129–44; truth and poetry, 94–96; Virgil in, 114–21
Comparetti, D., 200 (n153)
concepire, concetto, 59, 95
Conrieri, D., 202 (n173)
consolare, 22–23
Consoli, D., 200 (n151), 202 (n177)
Constantine, 160, 165
Contini, G., 8, 146, 182 (n12), 187 (n50), 188 (n58), 205 (n200)
Convivio: I, 45–54, 56, 57, 58, 59, 61, 66, 78, 83, 105; II, 13, 25, 47,

68, 74–79, 85, 86, 89, 90, 97, 98, 99, 125; III, 47, 68, 79–84, 85; IV, 2, 6, 23, 47, 49, 52, 56, 67, 70, 75, 81–90, 130, 132, 148, 154, 155, 157, 160, 192 (n100), 193 (n106)
correction or perfection of intellect, 127
correction or perfection of will, 127
Corsi, S., 201 (n162)
Corti, M., 23, 40, 54, 185 (n35), 186 (n36), 189 (n60), 191 (n77), 194 (n111)
Cracco, G., 202 (n180)
Cristaldi, S., 188 (n55)
Croce, B., 104, 124
Cunizza da Romano, 140
Curio, 132, 136
Cursietti, M., 183 (n12), 183 (n19)
cursus, 173
Curtius, E. R., 114, 190 (n69), 197 (n127), 199 (n147), 207 (n224)
Cyrus, 158

Daniello, Bernardino, 201 (n159)
Dante Alighieri: autobiographical nature of works, 2; first lyrics of, 7–12; as Ghibelline, 130; later lyrics of, 40–45; prior of Florence, 4; visit to France (?), 8. *See also* under individual titles
Dante da Maiano, 9, 11, 36
Darius I (of Persia), 163
David, 122, 136, 149, 156, 163
Davis, C. T., 192 (n. 97), 195 (n. 115), 200 (n151), 203 (n182), 203 (n183), 203 (n186), 206 (n209)
Dell'Aquila, M., 185 (n31)
De Robertis, D., 78, 185 (n25), 187 (n48), 192 (n99)
Deroy, J. P. T., 204 (n189)

Thomas Aquinas. *See* Aquinas,
Thomas
Tiberius, 157
Titus, 157
Toja, G., 204 (n196)
Toynbee, P., 181 (n3), 199 (n148),
208 (n230)
tragedy, 69, 72
Trinity, the, 16, 22, 27, 38–39, 127
Triolo, A., 113, 199 (n146)
Trissino, Gian Giorgio, 55
trobar clus, 145
trobar leu, 145
Trovato, M., 194 (n108)
type and antitype, 101

Uzzah, 149

Valensin, A., 201 (n166)
Valla, Lorenzo, 165
Valli, L., 193 (n108)
Vanossi, L., 182 (n12)
Vasoli, C., 46, 153, 190 (n70), 190
(n73), 190 (n75), 191 (n77), 192
(n94), 192 (n95), 193 (n101), 193
(n106), 206 (n208)
Vernani, Guido, 147, 150, 162
Vesages, 158
Vickers, N., 185 (n32)
vidas, 14
Villa, C., 199 (n149)
Villani, Filippo, 2, 102, 130, 170
Villani, Giovanni, 2, 47, 148
viltà, 23, 77

Vinay, G., 150, 206 (n207)
Vita nuova, 12–40; I, 51; II, 192
(n88); III, 9, 12; V, 46; XIX, 78;
XXIII, 126; XXV, 58, 59, 63, 67,
68; XXVI, 80; XXVIII, 149;
XXX, 149; XXXI, 126; XXXIV,
126; XXXV, 75; XXXVI, 75;
XXXVII, 75; XXXVIII, 75,
76–77; XLII, 46, 79
Violence, 109
Violetta, 10, 29
Virgil, 87, 158; as allegory of Reason, 103, 115; and authority as
writer, 117–20; as "comic" poet,
120; in Dante, 114–21; as guide,
115–17; as "tragic" poet, 119–20;
Aen. I, 117; II, 119, 142; III, 119;
VI, 70, 119, 141; X, 119; XII,
120; *Egl.* IV, 116, 119, 123, 135,
138
virtues, seven, 109
vis, 156
voluntas nocendi, 111

"wheel of Virgil," 174
Whitman, Walt, 58
Wicksteed, P. H., 209 (n234)
"widowed verse," 22
Wlassics, T., 144, 204 (n190)

Xerxes, 158

ydioma triparium, 61